Got a hot date? Put him to the test. Don't get caught in a relationship with a man who wants to take advantage of you, control you, or reduce your self-esteem to rubble. Before you invest an ounce of energy in a loser, learn to recognize the telltale signs of:

The Rescuer
He'll loan you money, fix your car, and make your decisions. He's a knight looking for a damsel in distress. Escape—before he slays your pet dragon.

The Brainwasher
He'll tell you what to wear, what to eat, what to think. Your man is flexibility-challenged. Get deprogrammed.

The Show-off
If he's doing more strutting than a rooster on Viagra, this guy's a turkey. Cook his goose.

The Pleaser
The pedestal he's put you on is giving you vertigo. He's so thoughtful, caring, and considerate you're ready to scream. It's time to please yourself—with someone else.

The Burdened

He's carrying too much ~~~~~~~~~~~~~~~~~ ast and he's on a one-way trip ~~~~~~~~~~~~~ and resentment. Pack war~~~~~~~~~~~~~~~~~~~ out.

Gary S. Aumiller, Ph. ~~~~~~~ nationally known lecturer, police consultant, and the ~~~~~or of *Keeping It Simple: Sorting Out What Really Matters in Your Life*.

Daniel A. Goldfarb, Ph.D., runs a private mental-health center and serves as webmaster to several psychology self-help sites on the Internet. Both authors have served as presidents of the Society of Police and Criminal Psychology. In their collective careers, they have helped more than 4,000 patients solve problems and make better decisions.

ALSO BY DR. GARY S. AUMILLER

Keeping It Simple:
Sorting Out What Really Matters in Your Life

RED FLAGS!

How to Know When You're Dating a Loser

Gary S. Aumiller, Ph.D., and
Daniel A. Goldfarb, Ph.D.

A PLUME BOOK

PLUME
Published by the Penguin Group
Penguin Putnam Inc., 375 Hudson Street, New York, New York 10014, U.S.A.
Penguin Books Ltd, 27 Wrights Lane, London W8 5TZ, England
Penguin Books Australia Ltd, Ringwood, Victoria, Australia
Penguin Books Canada Ltd, 10 Alcorn Avenue, Toronto, Ontario, Canada M4V 3B2
Penguin Books (N.Z.) Ltd, 182–190 Wairau Road, Auckland 10, New Zealand

Penguin Books Ltd, Registered Offices: Harmondsworth, Middlesex, England

First published by Plume, a member of Penguin Putnam Inc.

First Printing, September, 1999
10   9

 REGISTERED TRADEMARK—MARCA REGISTRADA

LIBRARY OF CONGRESS CATALOGING-IN-PUBLICATION DATA

Aumiller, Gary S.
    Red flags : how to know when you're dating a loser / Gary S. Aumiller and Daniel A.
Goldfarb.
        p.   cm.
    ISBN 0-452-28117-2
    1. Dating (Social customs)—United States—Psychological aspects. 2. Man–
woman relationships—United States. 3. Men—United States—Psychology.
I. Goldfarb, Daniel A.   II. Title.
HQ801.Aa82564   1999
646.7'7—dc21   99-13699
                                                                                     CIP

Printed in the United States of America
Set in Garamond Light
Designed by Eve L. Kirch

To Rebecca Anderson *for her beauty, style, character, and love that has brought such joy and inspiration to my life.*
—G.A.

To Lisa, Judith, and Max Goldfarb; *with such a loving and devoted family no man could be a Loser.*
—D.G.

Acknowledgments

We would like to thank:

. . . our women friends and patients, especially Kristine and Regina, who helped us define and refine the application of Red Flags into a dating lifestyle.

. . . Shiobhan Donohue for her comments and editorial advice on our initial book proposal.

. . . Lisa Taxman-Goldfarb for her voice of reason when we were off-track.

. . . Rebecca Anderson for the countless hours of editing, proofreading, suggestions, and encouragement that transformed our psycho-babble into a book.

. . . our agent, Arielle Eckstut, for her vision, hard work, and patience with our dumb questions throughout the project.

. . . and, our editor, Deb Brody, for her wonderful direction, insight, and graciousness as she truly handled her work with pure class.

Contents

What Is a Red Flag?

*The Early Warning Detection
System for Losers*

It was probably something sweet—a turned smile, a joke told with glorious manner, maybe a moment of compassion for your asphalt-branded knee, or perhaps the offer of half a peanut butter and orange marmalade sandwich when you forgot your lunch. Most of us can't really remember the first time we noticed someone of the opposite sex and felt a tingle, a cell by cell ignition of a pandemonium of feelings telling us that we were "in like." Our first crush is enshrined in a pure-bred innocence we were allowed before life forced us to be emotionally mongrel because mongrels survive better in nature. It is understandable that we try to capture shards of that childlike innocence in our adult relationships, opening our lives to people who may stimulate the robust pleasure of love's presence. It is this openness that leaves us unprotected, easy quarry to the predator that lives off the relationship-vulnerable—the "Loser."

Inspiring insights can be gained by reading the titles of books aimed at women in the self-help section of any bookstore, before ever reading a page. There are the books aimed at rendering men helpless to the "feminine wiles" of beauty, social poise, and manipulative persuasion, as if women were trapping men like little chinchillas to be sewn together for a fur coat. Then there are titles on improving bad relationships, gaining intimacy when your partner doesn't want to be in a relationship, understanding male and female differences as if men and women were from two different planets, and books on the parameters of surviving divorce when the planets don't align. All these books are concerned with building a beautiful edifice of a relationship but ignore the simple question needed to pour a foundation: How does a woman know if the man she has is the one she wants?

We all like to make our own choices when it comes to relationships, use our own judgment in choosing a partner. It is a universal naïveté to believe we are good judges of other people. Combining this naïveté with the hope of achieving a fantasy relationship is like believing in winning the lottery. We are not the best judges of what is good for us in a relationship; our fantasies are not realistic. The lottery makes money by allowing a few big winners and a lot of losers. In the hands of many women, the act of choosing a man is overly subject to attachment needs, aesthetic appeal, and witty banter perceived as "chemistry." When options are shrouded by cryptic illusions, this choice is not calculated but capricious. In the hands of the uninformed, choosing a man will rely on whimsy and folly.

In the course of a dating life, few women experience enough repetition of the many problems of men to actually identify what should be avoided. The feeling of love and the need to be needed color the accurate perception of the person they are with at the time. Some women begin to develop better dating selection parameters later in their courtship careers, after many ego-wrenching relationships, maybe even a divorce or two. Other women never really develop limits and are destined to find themselves in the same situations with the same types of men.

Psychologists working with large numbers of single persons find the repetitive patterns in dating very apparent. Working with both single women and men allows the psychologist to hear both sides of the dating paradigm, the women acting out their fairy-tale fantasies and men acting out their less cerebral motivations. When trying to make a woman healthier in her relationship choices, many therapists try to help women through their own insecurities, and accept that their own issues can cloud their decision making. They use their academic and acquired knowledge of the mental processes of women and the psychology of relationships to enliven natural self-protective functions, intuitions women can use to avoid emotionally destructive connections. The problem is that all the insights women gain about themselves are often worthless in partner selection. It is not that women can't understand themselves, it is that men have learned ways to short-circuit women's intuition, to use women's needs and desires against them when decisions are being made. Women need to be taught about men, not themselves. They need to learn the male tricks, the hidden messages behind male behavior.

Early in any relationship there are signs foretelling of the bad news to come, signs of the short-circuiting male tricks. Many of these signs are obvious, some are less apparent. To the naive, these signs can be justified away, excused so as not to interfere with the fantasy of having met that "special guy." To the sophisticated, these signs say: DANGER, DO NOT ENTER, or in modern parlance, DON'T GO THERE. These prophetic signs are called "Red Flags."

What exactly is a Red Flag? A Red Flag is a warning, a notice that danger is looming over a relationship. A Red Flag is a steadfast proclamation to back off, get away, or keep it platonic. Red Flags are signs that right now, at this point in time, the person you are with has the "Loser potential" to make you run screaming to the freezer to consume a gallon and a half of double-chocolate-chunk ice cream. It may not mean that you abandon all hope forever of a relationship with this person, as people can change over time. At any point in time, each of us is more relationship ready than at other times. The change that people do make however, is better done alone, when the pain of loneliness strengthens motivation. Loving and caring about a person needing to change only maintains their status quo, their prospect of being a Loser forever. A Red Flag means you proceed with fully opened eyes and wait, before you invest your hard-earned ego and self-esteem into the man signaling you that there could be serious problems.

Red Flags are most important in the start-up phase of a relationship. In the start-up phase, both of you are trying to be on your best behavior. Both of you are presenting more of the ideal person you would like to be, with reality deemphasized, hidden in the dark cellar that you only show people when they get close to you. You are trying to sell the package by the best parts. Even if you've known someone as a friend for years, the rules change once the idea of a relationship begins. You go back to presenting only your good side. In the start-up phase of a relationship, you are most limited in the information you have about the other person. On the surface this looks like a great disadvantage. In fact, this start-up phase is your time of greatest advantage.

Being knowledgeable about what to look for in potential partners makes this the best time to judge who is sitting across the table from you. As a person tries to present their ideal self, small quirks often come through signaling disastrous times ahead. A person who has difficulties even when they are trying to be at their best is telling you that a monster lurks deep within the depths of the lake. The cues will be very subtle at this stage, but it will predict extreme behavior in the future. Being knowledgeable about the behaviors that we call

Red Flags at this early stage will help you identify the Loser, and help you move on to someone more deserving of your attentions.

By looking for Red Flags, you can learn how to determine the all-important Loser potential within the *first three dates* while your ego is still intact, when your judgment is not compromised by your fancies, when you haven't invested dreams, time, and lost opportunities. These assessment/profiling procedures can be used in the early stages of any relationship, giving you a clear picture of what may follow and what needs to be done.

What is the "Loser formula"? Bad upbringing + current life problems + bad experiences in dating + bad attitude = Loser potential. As we go through the Red Flags in this book, we will be talking about the way a man grew up, how he developed personality attributes that may not be relationship conducive, and how upbringing can create intimacy and sensitivity problems. We will be talking about how current life problems, particularly the inability to handle present problems, may make a man a bad candidate for a relationship. Some guys are not persistent Losers but presently act like Losers because the timing for a relationship is wrong. Relationship readiness is a timing issue as well as a personality issue. You will learn to assess timing. We will look at men's bad experiences with women, from their earliest days of dating to the present, and how these experiences might have shaped a Loser out of a guy that could have started on the right track. Finally, we will look at the current attitudes a man is showing you, and which ones might be problematic and develop into disasters if you decide to start a relationship. We are hoping by letting you know how men develop, you will realize that just because a man is a Loser in relationships may not mean he is a bad person overall. This is an area that confuses many women, because they can like parts of a man, overlooking that when he is in a relationship the guy is bad news. It's like having a fire in your living room. If confined to a fireplace, it is a good thing. If roaring uncontrollably in your couch, you've got a problem. Many men are wonderful when confined to the hearth of friendship, work, or even helping others. Get these same men in a relationship and they set your blood boiling, your emotions blazing, and they just plain burn your ass! Learning the "whys" and "hows" of Losers will make you less judgmental but more careful about getting singed.

How do you assess Loser potential? As the authors of this book, we have an unusual triad of experiences as psychologists. First, in our practices, we have heard the dating stories of thousands of single and divorced women of all ages. We've heard of the disappointments, the ways women are fooled, and the plights of relationships doomed by men whose personalities did not make them available for relationships. We have seen the marriages that work and the ones that are doomed from the start. Second, we have listened to the stories of men, some who have purposely deceived women and others who were unaware that they were incapable of bonding intimately with another human being. We also were able to make comparisons to the men that were good relationship material, and found that the relationship ability of men was quite predictable. Finally, to complete our triad of professional experiences, we have done extensive work in the law enforcement and forensic communities, profiling negative and deviant personalities, teaching how to ask the right questions in an interrogation, and sometimes predicting behavior before a person has even formed his intention. This combination of experiences and skills has been included in this book for the reader to be able to predict Loser potential. The information has been put in the form of a variety of tests that you can do after your dates to see if the man you are dating has the capacity for a relationship at this time in his life. The tests will look at background information about their upbringing, body language, verbal style and content, behavior on dates, how he handles confrontation, and even your intuitions. A narrative follows each test to let you know what behavior to expect from a guy that falls at different score levels. So go out on a few dates, put them to the test, and see what you've got. Call it "Profiling Made Easy" or "Loser-Buster 101," but it is basically a guide for the smart woman to assess Loser potential.

The book highlights twenty-five Red Flags to look for on your first few dates. Each chapter contains a test for the presence of a particular Red Flag. Finally, each chapter teaches how to break up with each of the Red Flag types so as to limit your exposure to annoyance and/or danger. These Red Flag types are not pure absolutes. Don't be surprised if many men fit into a number of these profiles, a sort of mixed bag of Loser qualities. This means they can come up with a number of ways to torture you. Pick the main type and follow the suggestions on leaving him. We also discuss how a situation might create a Red Flag all on its own.

We tried to make each chapter interesting and fun to read so if you want to read the book from start to finish first, you'll be entertained. You may then want to approach this book as a manual and pick it up after you or one of your friends goes out on a date. Put a guy to the test. Make the "date or dump" decision. *Red Flags* should be seen as a book you can use again and again.

Red Flags does not propose to take away freedom of choice but to arm a woman with better tools to make that choice, before she invests time and emotion in a man who is unworthy, before she invests love in a man who will not return it, before she invests one ounce of energy in a Loser. *Red Flags* gives a woman a reasonable chance to make the right choice in finding a man. It takes courtship from the realm of interplanetary differences and brings it back to earth.

Red Flags is the dating woman's best weapon against getting attached to someone who will take advantage of her, control her, abuse her, or reduce her self-esteem. It is the woman's guide to dating that has not been written; it says things about men on dates that have not been revealed to women. *Red Flags* is about men, written by men, giving the straight story about men to avoid. It is about the subtle and not so subtle signs to see if there is trouble ahead. *Red Flags* makes very clear what has been hinted about, overanalyzed, underexplained, and intuitively understood by grandmothers, mothers, coworkers, and best friends for years. *Red Flags* is the *divining rod for bad relationships, a mental inoculation against Losers.*

Dating can be some of the most difficult work that we do in life and some of the most enjoyable. If you can weed out the potential Losers, you will have a greater chance of finding that satisfying relationship that gives you energy to bring to other parts of your life. *Red Flags* will help you in this quest.

The Liar

*Did I Say a Porsche? A Hyundai Is
Sort of Like a Porsche, Isn't It?*

In the 1930s, a young Jerry Siegel, frustrated by his lack of success with women, fantasized what it would take to have women want him. He figured women would be throwing themselves at him if he could jump over buildings and throw cars around. The result was the creation of the comic book character Superman. In the years since, men have continued to be Jerry Siegels, constantly re-creating themselves in the image of Superman, except not only in their imaginations, but on their dates. That's why men can often seem like comic book characters on the first three dates.

Paula wanted to like Steve. She was tired of all her short-term relationships during the last four years. She was ready to try to settle in with one "nice" guy. Paula met Steve and his friends at a restaurant bar while she and her girlfriends were waiting for a table. He was so nice with his dirty blond hair, well-defined forearms, and slight country southern drawl so smooth and gentle—the perfect compliment to her long curly auburn hair and hard New York Rs. An exchange of numbers written on cocktail napkins, a couple of witty phone conversations cut short by supposed business calls on call-waiting, a rushed invitation to dinner, and Paula and Steve found themselves together in an Italian restaurant forcing a "get to know you" conversation.

"So where did you find that cute accent, Steve?" Paula reaches over and touches him on his forearm, just above the wrist, to let him know she approves.

"Well, I guess you could say I come from a long line of southern aristocrats. Lots of old money, you know, debutante balls, plantations and stuff." Steve seemed proud of his blue-blood background.

"So I guess this New York life must be very strange to you. Can't get good Italian food down south, can you?" Paula was trying to make conversation.

"Well, my mom was Italian originally from Brooklyn, so I sort of grew up Italian."

"How did she meet your father?" Paula was intrigued by the contrast.

"Well, Dad was in the air force, got stationed in Washington, and met Mom at a USO dance. They got married, settled outside of Baltimore, and had me. And we all lived happily ever after." Steve was happy to have tied it all up.

Paula was a little confused. "So, you grew up in Maryland and your dad was from . . ."

"Ohio. He was raised on a farm in Ohio. His mom died in childbirth, and his father had to raise eight children by himself."

"On a farm in Ohio?" There was a note of confusion in Paula's once melodious voice. "Now, where did you get that southern accent from?"

"Well, I went to college in South Carolina and it just sort of stuck."

"Then, who are the aristocrats? Who has the plantation?"

"Well, that's a long story. Let's see, how do I make this clear for you?" Paula became more aware that when Steve spoke his eyes either darted around the room or he looked down. "See, when I was down south in music school, studying classical voice, I looked up my family background and found out that my ancestry, prior to my dad and a couple of uncles, were southern plantation owners. After the Civil War, they were forced to move north because they angered a couple of Confederate generals when they helped slaves escape brutal slave lords. So they ended up just leaving their land and moving to Ohio to farm."

"Yeah, I guess those Confederate generals can ruin your day if you let them. So you sing. Sing me a beautiful love song." Paula was trying to change the topic and maintain her flirtatious charm.

"Well, I used to sing. See, I went to study voice because I had a great tenor voice, won a lot of recital competitions even though I was a kid, and I might have been one of the world's best, but after my third year at college I got vocal nodes and was told I'd never be able to sing again. So I studied marketing and now I'm in charge of a marketing department in a large computer company."

Needless to say, the longer Paula was around, the smaller the computer company became, and the department head became a struggling sales rep working on commission.

Yes, it's normal for men to exaggerate a little about themselves on the first three dates. You probably do it, too. But, when the exaggerations create the same sensations in your head as too much hot mustard on your pastrami and rye, you may be in the presence of a Red Flag.

Why do men lie and exaggerate at all? Don't they realize it would be better for them to be themselves? The second question is easiest to answer: "No, sort of, maybe a little!" If men realized it would be better to be themselves, they would exaggerate being average, feigning tremendous humility, fallibility, and embracing any other positive characteristic that would demonstrate self-realization and insight into personal faults. Some accomplished men actually do this because they realize it's never good to be too far above average, but it is good to be a little above average. Most men just try to reach the above average level with their lies. Men's number one fear in dating is they will look silly in front of women and be rejected. If they are better than other men, but not too much better, they believe the odds of rejection are reduced.

Which is the beginning of the answer of why men lie and exaggerate. People generally lie and exaggerate to *protect, project*, or *propel*. Lying to *protect* centers on not wanting someone to have information that might hurt them, such as being told they have lousy taste in clothing, they could lose a few pounds, or their grubworm-and-mushroom health soup was not exactly tasty. Lying and exaggerating to protect is frequently well meaning and more acceptable than other forms of lying, particularly in relationships without an established foundation.

Lying to *project* occurs when a person tries to throw blame for an unpleasant event onto someone or something else. It is human nature not to want to be connected to failures, losses, or circumstances that turn negative. If a couple of well-placed lies can project all blame and responsibility elsewhere, then the liar assumes life will be easier. This is the least acceptable form of lying.

Lying to *propel* is by far the most common on the first three dates. These lies or exaggerations are designed to make a person look better than he really is. Lies to propel lift someone from the ordinary to the sublime. The basic thinking is: "If I appear to be a more accomplished, richer, better catch of a man, she will be more interested in me and we can move on quicker, go farther, and her love will deepen." Many would argue that these types of lies are as inevitable in the first three dates as a male peacock fanning his feathers, a male gorilla pounding his chest, or a male fan at a live sporting event adjusting his crotch after "The Star-Spangled Banner."

This third type of lying has three major considerations: the tangibility of the lie, the amount of exaggeration, and the time frame. Lying or exaggerating about something highly tangible, such as the number of brothers and sisters is weird. You've got a Liar. Automatic Red Flag! Lying about something such as the number of places he's lived ("We moved every couple of years") when they moved only three times overall is not so strange. The latter is less tangible and could be just an expression of the frustration with a life of moving that seemed to happen "every couple of years." A person who makes $60,000 a year and says he makes a half a million is much worse than someone who exaggerates and says he makes $75,000 a year. The smaller exaggeration is more acceptable. Finally, lying about the past ("I wrote a book") is worse than the present ("I'm writing a book"), which is worse than the future ("I am going to write a book"). Look for these general tendencies when evaluating the negative impact of lies. Of course, there are exceptions to these tendencies, but they offer a good standard. What is important is that you look closely at the lies and be realistic as to how far out of the ordinary they are.

Paula overlooked Steve's gross exaggerations about his job and his lineage. She ignored her intuition to drop him even when he gave unusual details and implausible embellishments. She even ignored the grandiose fantasies of the "voice that could have been great." She ignored Steve's use of too many details that were intended to sidetrack her questions. Paula stuck it out with Steve through the tough first few dates. She always wanted to believe the best in people. She was tolerant of minor flaws. She thought she could make a big difference with this guy. Paula was a big-hearted girl. Besides, Steve had "nice buns."

After three months of missed promises, strange looks from people when she told them stories about her new boyfriend, and trying to force intimacy with someone who was incapable of being close to anybody, Paula broke off the relationship. All she wanted was a relationship based on trust and devoted caring. Trust is impossible with a Liar. The stories change too often. As far as caring, a person this insecure is so busy protecting himself, he just cannot be devoted to another.

The following test is a general guideline to use regarding lying on the first three dates. Rate a new guy with this test after the first date, then after three dates. Note any changes.

Trust is impossible with a liar

IS HE A LIAR?

Circle the number and add up the score

Family Background

He felt he could never earn his father's approval	2
Problems with the law	3
Father not present during development years (absent or uninvolved)	1

Work/School History

History of losing work because "boss was a jerk"	2
Working at a job below his intellectual potential	1

Friendships

Doesn't have a lot of close male friends	1
Friends he has seem to have a lot of problems or are heavy drinkers/drug users	2

Past Relationships

No contact with any past girlfriends or friends made during past relationships	1
Derogatory comments always made about girls from past relationships	1

Body Language

Eyes:

Looks you in the eye when talking to you, soft direct look when you talk (it is normal to look up when thinking about what to say)	−1
Can't look you in the eye when he is talking	1
Eyes dart around the room when he is talking	1
Looks down when he is talking	2

(test continues)

Dress/Hygiene

Makes up excuse if not dressed appropriately	1
Talks about better clothes at home or in past	2

Behavior

If the first date was blind or from a personal ad, did he:

Mildly exaggerate or mislead about his looks	1
Completely exaggerate or mislead about his looks	3
Report accurately his physical faults	−1

If first date was not a blind date, did he:

Tell little stories about how he used to look better	1
Tell fantastic stories of how he used to look better	2

If he says he will call you and forgets, does he:

Apologize and take responsibility	−2
Make up an elaborate excuse	1
Blame someone else	2
This is not a concern, he always does what he promises on time	−1

Conversation

Style:

Gives too much detail in his stories	1
He has a lot of practiced stories that are not spontaneous but he tries to make them seem spontaneous	2
There is a lack of specifics about family, friends, and personal background when he talks about himself	1

Content:

The facts of a story change from conversation to conversation	2
The facts of a story sometimes change in the midst of the same conversation	3
His stories are grandiose when drinking	1
His stories are grandiose when sober	3
He spends a little time trying to impress you with his accomplishments, job, who he knows, or financial status	−1
He spends a moderate amount of time trying to impress you with his accomplishments, job, who he knows, or financial status	1
He spends a lot of time trying to impress you with his accomplishments, job, who he knows, or financial status	2
He blames others for his lack of success	2

(test continues)

When Confronted

When questioned or confronted with a lie or exaggeration he:

Admits exaggeration, apologizes, and thanks you for the correction (like some guy will actually do this—get real!)	−5
Embellishes to make the story fit the new evidence	2
Never admits to being wrong	1
Gets immediately defensive and questions your motives	1
Gets angry and attacks your morals for doubting him	2

Your Impression

You think he was trying too hard	1
You feel a little cynical regarding some of his descriptions of himself	1
You feel like you have to defend your growing feelings	2
You feel he explains himself unnecessarily	1
You feel he is a little insecure	1
Total Score	

Score 10 and lower: No reason for concern at this point, he's about as honest as you can expect this early in a dating relationship

Score between 11 and 18: Yellow Flag—There's reason for caution

Score 19 and above: Red Flag—Loser antennae should be up; time to move on

Liar, Liar, Pants on Fire

When a man's score falls in the Yellow Flag category, you should be very careful to monitor future lies. Don't let him know your concern, but sit back and monitor the direction of his change on the next couple of dates. Perhaps when he is less afraid of rejection, he may ease up and become more truthful. Take the test again after another couple of dates and see if the scores go up or down. If there is a significant decline, and the connection is still strong, it could have a shot. If the scores stay the same or increase, you may be only a ten-cent cab ride from a very unique relationship hell. Get away.

If the man falls in the Red Flag category, you've got a Liar and it's time to move on. If you stay with a Liar, you can expect many things will happen to you. You will be made a fool of when you act on information that he gives you and it turns out to be wrong. When one woman was told by her boyfriend that his father had passed away, imagine her surprise when she confided in her boss, a one-time friend of the father, and was told that her boyfriend's dead father was still alive and wanted to see his son, but his son had refused. Or imagine how she felt when an acquaintance corrected her about her dream man not being the captain of the football team in high school but the class jerk. Or how she felt when finding out he was fired from his company, not promoted. You'll become very reticent to act, unsure of what you know.

Additionally, women who stay with a Liar find people stop believing *them*, too. They live through a string of broken promises, always finding excuses or blaming others for things that happen that may have been under their control. They are always defending their man, and this gets annoying to all involved. They start isolating themselves from family and friends. Cynicism becomes very strong; bitterness is the predominant emotion. Ever get behind one of those ladies at the bank who is screaming at her kids, calling the teller stupid, asking to see the manager, and making you a half hour late to meet your friends when you were going to be ten minutes early. Not exactly a Barbie moment, is it? People don't start off life that way. Make sure your Ken doesn't have this Red Flag, or the ATM cash machine may start to cringe when you approach.

Nifty Ways to Leave Your Loser

So you got this Loser and you want to know how to get rid of him. First rule: *Never tell him why!* Your goal is not to change him, not to make him feel emotions, not to get him to admit to anything or recognize a mistake. If you get into this kind of discussion, you will get a lot of explanations, then defensiveness, then anger. Remember that his number one fear is rejection. Put an animal in a fearful situation and you can expect attack. Unless you take delight in being shredded like panty hose in a Ginzu knife commercial, keep your desire to tell him *why* to yourself.

Focus on you, not him. "I'm just not developing the feelings I thought I might. I just can't get involved with you right now or we're both going to get hurt." Stay at the feelings level. Resist the urge to give concrete explanations. When he pressures you, do not explain further. Overexplanation is the biggest mistake women make in a breakup with a Liar. The less said the better. Just repeat the same thing over and over. Keep him from the blame. It's your feeling, not his problem. Men constantly talk with other men about how they can't understand women's feelings. It's a male-bonding thing. Take comfort in knowing that the next time he's cruising in the car with the guys, you gave him something to complain about between hockey scores and spitting out the window into oncoming traffic.

The Neglecter

If He Doesn't Call Back,
Tell Him to Hit the Road, Jack!

Violets have this amazing characteristic not shared by any other flower. Because violets contain a little iodine, their scent can only be absorbed temporarily. The flower continues to secrete the most beautiful perfume, but our capacity to sense it is saturated quickly, leaving us with only a flirtatious memory of the brilliance that had momentarily girdled our senses. Minutes later we regain the capacity to partake in the violets' sensual olfactory pleasure, only to be anesthetized again. Moments of glory shattered by reminders of our vexatious human limits. The impermanence of the violet truly intoxicates, making it perhaps the most favorable of all the floral scents. Many men want to be like violets, coming on with a panoply of nature's gifts, only to fade into the smell of the manure that fertilized their intentions. These men rush into your life and make you feel real good, then all of a sudden they disappear, sometimes resurfacing a little while later, sometimes never resurfacing. When you sense the male violet, recognize that it is as carnivorous as a Venus flytrap, as strangulating as poison ivy, and as quick-growing as spring dandelions.

*   *   *

After a marvelous first date Linda was smitten with Roy. She had fantasized the whole relationship after only one date: engaged in a year, wed in two. They both liked animals. Two children, a boy and a girl, three dogs, and two cats; it would be a very happy family. He was so attentive, so wonderful. How could it go anywhere but best friends, lovers, lifelong soulmates, partners? Roy left the date with exactly the same feeling, at least that is what he said: "This is the best date I've ever had. I think we found a match."

Twelve days later, Roy hadn't called. Linda couldn't believe it. What happened to the cool guy that went out on the date? What happened to "I'll call you, we've got to do this again, soon." What happened to the three dogs and two cats? Linda had pondered alone too long, so she decided to get his number from a mutual friend and call him.

"Roy, this is Linda from a couple of weeks ago. What've you been up to lately?"

"Oh, Linda, the sushi girl. Wow, I was planning on calling you tonight."

"Now, Roy, do you expect me to believe that after twelve days?"

"Yeah, we must be on the same wavelength. Really! I sure enjoyed our date. I've been real busy the last couple weeks though. I haven't called any of my friends for ages. I haven't even called my mother back, and she called over a week ago."

"Gee, I hope she didn't want you to take her to the doctor or something."

"So, what've you been up to, girl? How's life since the great sushi date?"

"I've been pretty good. Work's all right. I had to call Pat to get your number. He said you guys were out a couple of days ago. Where'd you go?"

"So that's how you got my number. Yeah, Pat's a good guy. I

don't get to see him much though. Have you heard about what happened to him and his last girlfriend?"

"No, I didn't even know he had a last girlfriend."

"She really went psycho on him when he tried to break up. She kept calling, haunting him. Then she disappeared for about three months. All of a sudden he's in this relationship with Kaitlin, and she resurfaces with a list of things she's missing. She tells him she doesn't remember getting her apartment key back from him, and she knows he's been sneaking into her place to steal things. Follows him to a restaurant party and confronts him right there in front of Kaitlin and his friends. He doesn't know anything about this stuff and is sure he gave her the key back long ago. But she doesn't take that as an answer and starts beating on him and accusing him of coming into her house and stealing things. It was a really bad scene."

"Knowing Pat, I suspect there're two sides to that story. I mean, he is sort of a player."

"Dream on, girl. Nothing deserves that kind of bullshit. So, how've you been? God, I miss talking to you."

"Like I said, I've been all right. Except there was this guy I hoped would call me, and he just blew me off."

"Hey, you could have called too. I don't remember my phone ringing."

"Roy, I didn't have your number. You knew that. I gave you mine and you were going to get a number change or something."

"Oh yeah. Well, you know, shit happens. I guess you'll never let me forget this until I make it up to you, so you'll just have to go out with me again this Saturday. I'll get tickets to the baseball game. I know you're a big fan. I'll even buy you a hot dog and a Cracker Jack or two."

"I'm not sure. . . ."

"I'll let you have the prizes. Box seats. They're only one

game out in the standings. I'm not going to let you say no. I'll
bug you everyday until you say yes."

"I should say no, just so you have to call to bug me."

"Noon on Saturday. I'll be at your apartment." Roy hangs up.
"Call first!"

Every guy knows that a woman wants a phone call after a
date to be told how marvelous she was and how he'll remember
her forever. If a guy doesn't call he is either not interested
or he is choosing to be a jerk. Sometimes a call the next day is
difficult because of schedule demands. But if you are waiting
by the phone so long that the music you heard that first night
has gone from "edge" to "retro," you may be rocking to the
beat of a Red Flag.

Imagine yourself in a world where telephones, faxes, and
e-mails didn't exist. A place where everyone communicated
through the mail, and people didn't mind the delay in feedback of a couple of days, even a week. How would you feel? If
you are like most people, you've gotten used to quick feedback and would feel pent-up with anticipation, anxious, maybe
even angry, like the world was too backward for you. Your actions would reflect this craze, maybe some jittery movements
in your body, pacing, displaying low frustration tolerance with
people. Others would view you as impatient, a person that
overexaggerates the importance of everything, and makes a
big deal out of nothing. You would be very different and separated from everyone. Until you adjusted, you would hate it.
That is exactly the way you will feel when you start to date the
Neglecter. And he will feel like you are in too much of a rush,
overexaggerate, and blow everything out of proportion.

Where did this come from? Somewhere during the Neglecter's youth he found he didn't have to function on anyone's
time schedule. Perhaps he was left alone a lot by his parents,
or one or both of his parents were very laid-back and didn't
feel any pressure to conform to time constraints. The Neglect-

er doesn't take commitments seriously and was probably allowed to quit activities in his early life. As an adult, he doesn't take established conventions of courtesy seriously and feels that if his actions hurt others, that is their problem, not his.

Now, this pattern would seem to suggest a bad work history, but that isn't always the case. The Neglecter frequently feels that work is the place for sticking to time constraints and meeting deadlines. In fact, you'll often hear this line from Neglecters: "I spend all day at work living on a time schedule, I'm not going to do that at home." Often they have a very pleasant personality because they have freed themselves from many of the human situations that precipitate personality problems. They are often good-looking because less-engaging individuals couldn't be this way and maintain a social life; therefore, only the attractive ever survive with this pattern.

If you date a Neglecter, you will constantly be on their time schedule regardless of what may be planned. At the root, the Neglecter believes that everyone is wrong and should "take things as they come." This is a positive attitude in moderation, but there is no moderation for the Neglecter. People work around this man and/or tend to never expect anything of him. He likes when people don't expect from him, because when he does the minimal, everyone makes a fuss. By lowering what the world expects, he quickly can become the center of attention whenever he wants. He is in control by refusal. Unfortunately, you can never depend on him for anything and he will never take you seriously because you are in essence one of those people who reflect the conventions of the outside world. So unless you want to walk through life like you're constantly wearing a pair of those alpha-rhythm goggles with the flashing lights, this is probably a bad choice for you.

Linda went out with Roy a number of times and even thought they were developing a relationship of sorts. He would call every once in a while, but there would be times when she would keep calling him and he wouldn't call back.

She would convince herself it was over. When he did call back, he acted matter-of-fact about being out of touch and criticized her for believing it was over. He told her he liked her but only seemed to call as a precursor to going out on a date, when *he* wanted a date.

Linda tried a couple of times to have a relationship talk, but Roy kept saying he liked what they had, and why change anything. He told her many times about his philosophy of taking things as they come and not making any major plans too far ahead. Linda was getting more and more frustrated. One day at lunch, a male coworker introduced Linda to someone from another company who was in a joint venture with her company. There were good vibes, and he asked her out. After the date, he called her that night to tell her how much he enjoyed her company. Then he called the next night just to talk. The initial attraction wasn't as strong as with Roy, but it grew as she got to know him. She had three dates by the time Roy called next. Roy asked her out, but she already had plans to go on a business trip. She told Roy she'd call him when she returned. Roy left a message while she was away. She didn't call him back.

Not every man that doesn't call back is a Neglecter. Use the test below to rate whether you are in the land of the Red Flag.

IS HE A NEGLECTER?

Circle the number and add up the score

Family Background

Left alone a lot as a child—had to entertain himself	1
One parent extremely laid-back	1
Both parents very laid-back	2
Never was a member on an organization (like Boy Scouts) or dropped out of them if he was a member	2

(test continues)

Work/School History

Feel work is the only place for time schedules	2
Always handed in schoolwork at the last minute or late	1
Doesn't like to talk about work at all when not there	1
Feels he is in a job, not a career	1

Friendships

Friends complain that he never seems to be on time	1
Friends don't seem to expect much of him or depend on him	3
Believes his friends are too uptight and need to relax	2
Friends seem to put more effort into keeping in touch than he does	2

Past Relationships

Past relationships just seem to fizzle, ending without a breakup scene	1
Makes no effort to keep in touch with friends from past relationships	1
Complains about feeling controlled a lot in past relationships	1
Complains about too many obligations in past relationships	3

Body Language

Very relaxed body posture from the start	1
Doesn't make efforts to touch you when time is right	1
Gets himself comfortable in a place without regard for your comfort	3

Dress/Hygiene

May not dress appropriately when asked to dress up	1
Seems to have an attitude that he will wear what he wants, whether appropriate or not	3

Behavior

Doesn't return call	
Once	1
Twice	2
Three or more times	4
Doesn't have a clue he should have called you after a date	2
Very different on phone than in person	2
Late for date	1
Misses date or changes at last minute	2
Cancels social commitments	1
Doesn't show up for social commitments	3
Doesn't respect your asking to be called	2

(test continues)

Behavior

Secretive about what he is doing	1
Gives mixed messages to keep you around	3
Gives you an honest answer	−2

Conversation

Calls you by a nickname that is very impersonal	1
Lots of excuses, but never apologies	2
Never tells you he would like to see you again	2
He gets short when you call him, as if you are interrupting something and he doesn't have time to talk to you	3
Compares you to others he doesn't call, or isn't courteous and tries to make you see it as just "his way"	4

When Confronted

Says you could have called him	1
Says you only had a couple of dates, that's not a commitment	5
Makes you feel like you are expecting too much of him	2
Tells you that if you don't back off, he doesn't want to see you	5

Your Impression

Seems very matter-of-fact about things	1
Concerned he might be too laid-back	1
You have no idea where you stand	2
Seems to be avoiding or guilty all the time	2
Seems to be hiding something	1
You feel like you want to shake him awake	2
	Total Score

Score 13 and lower: No reason for concern at this point
Score between 14 and 26: Yellow Flag—There's reason for caution
Score 27 and above: Red Flag—He'll forget you daily, until you leave him; bye-bye

You Got His Number

It is essential that if you have a guy in the Yellow Flag zone, you do not get attached. Do not figure that he will come around if you give a little more, particularly sexually. Do not continue to accept his apologies. After he's been confronted one or two times and doesn't straighten up, let him go. But first, you should confront him. When you do, look for an apology, even a small one. Never ask for an apology first; you want to see if he realizes he needs to give one. If he never apologizes, then you can point it out to him. His reaction will tell you a lot.

Next, it's time to do a little research. Look to see if he has the habits in the rest of his life of not living up to social commitments. Look to see if his friends consider him undependable. If they won't answer that question or waver a little, take that as a yes. Finally, look to see if he is very different with you alone than when he is around his friends. The Neglecter usually doesn't want his friends to think he likes anybody because that creates an expectation, particularly his female friends. If he's lovey-dovey alone and distant in front of friends, you've got "the man." The Neglecter will always be looking to avoid expectations.

If your man falls into the Red Flag zone, he has got to go. If you decide to hang around awhile because he has nice eyes you will start to see the time in your world revolve around him. Even if you decide to take the onus of calling all the time, he will control the length of the conversations, he will control when you can go out, and he will control the pace of the relationship. You will start to find yourself frustrated on many fronts. You will be frustrated never knowing if your plans will work out because he won't live up to the commitments. You will be frustrated because you never know how he is feeling about you; in fact, that will seem to change on a daily basis. You will be frustrated that he is constantly telling you to calm down, telling you that you're making everything a big deal. You won't feel you are being taken seriously, and he won't take it seriously when you tell him that.

Then, there's the bad news. You will be associated with him, thus people will start to see you as less dependable. You may find that friends won't invite you to places because they need to be on a time schedule and they are not sure you will be there.

Your friends will remark that you are either ignoring them or that you've changed and have become less close. And just when you're ready to drop him, he'll do something romantic that will put you back on the treadmill for another 5,000 calories. Your very essence will start to wither away until there is nothing left of your old life. This is one to get rid of now, before your existence gets so small that even a Wonderbra can't build it up.

Click Your Heels Three Times in Your Ruby-Red Slippers

The Neglecter may be the easiest Loser to get away from of all the Red Flag men. "You had the power to control him all the time, Dorothy." All you have to do is become him. Don't call him anymore and don't call back when he calls you. If he happens to catch you in, talk for a very short time in a very superficial manner and hang up quickly. Don't look for friendship. Don't look to explain. Just slide out of his life. Always be nice. Being nice is important for your spirit, to keep you feeling good. Always take care of yourself, but neglect him.

Sometimes, these guys figure that since they are losing you, and you are the best thing they've ever had, they decide to start giving you a lot of attention. *Do not fall for it.* It might be as tempting as stealing the remote control from a boyfriend during ESPN's Bass Fishing Weekend Championships, but you will not find him to be any different when he gets comfortable again. He doesn't need to be anyone you meet again on your yellow brick road. If he approaches you wanting to be more attentive, let him know that you've adapted the "wait and see" attitude and you're taking life as it comes. Right now, you're going to date around and maybe sometime in the distant future, life will bring you two back together again, but you'll wait and see. Enjoy this breakup. It may be one of the few you really can. Look for other violets, or other flowers, to sniff while he sneezes from the neglected spores of freshly cut emotional ragweed. If he only had a brain!

The Know-It-All

The Game for a Know-It-All Is
Jeopardy! *Beat Him to the Buzzer*

Aeschylus (525–456 B.C.) was one of ancient Greece's most brilliant men. Even in this day, almost two and a half millennia later, college students struggle studying the plays of Aeschylus such as *Agamemnon*, *Prometheus Bound*, and the *Libation Bearers*. But he was a very bald man. One day when strolling through the park, an eagle flying overhead was carrying a turtle dinner but needed to find a rock on which to drop it to crack open the shell. Aeschylus's head looked like a very good rock for just such a purpose. Although history books never recorded whether the eagle got his reptilian meal, we do know Aeschylus did not survive the encounter. Perhaps this was a message from God that we are all humbled before nature. Or perhaps the eagle just didn't want to listen to Aeschylus's brilliance anymore. Think how many times you have wanted to crack a turtle on the head of a guy who was acting like a Know-It-All.

Claire favored intelligence and a sense of humor in the men she chose for relationships. She liked good conversation and a worldliness that gave a man confidence. She met Hal at a happy hour through a girlfriend who had met him only once herself. They didn't talk to each other very much at that first meeting but enough for Hal to ask Claire's friend for Claire's phone number. On the phone, they talked for a long time and Claire was impressed that he seemed to be pretty well-rounded. An early movie that they both wanted to see and a late dinner was planned. Claire was very relaxed going into the date.

"What did you think about the movie? I thought it was great the way they wove the love story around the action." Claire thought she'd start the ice-breaking at the dinner table.

"Yeah, I guess. I just wish they made those movies a little more realistic. You know the odds of shooting out one tire at full speed must be five hundred to one. Two tires is next to impossible. If you look closely you can tell the different takes they did on the car chase scene. They didn't do a good job of matching background. I counted at least six different angles. That must have cost tens of thousands of dollars."

"It's a movie! You're supposed to suspend reality a little. Tell me about this restaurant we're going to now."

"Well, it's a smaller place with really great food cooked in an authentic Roman style. The staff knows me real well. I bet you didn't know the Romans have a different way of cooking from the rest of Italy. They tend to use all parts of an animal. They call it *quinto quarto*, or fifth quarter. They serve the pasta blended with these extra meat parts. It's actually a better approach than used in any other part of Italy."

"I didn't realize that about Roman food. Where did you get that from?"

"I make it my business to study just about anything I can, talk to people, and just know as much as I can. I love information. I also like to cook."

They enter the restaurant and Hal enthusiastically greets by first name a man who appears to be the owner. The owner responds politely but without signs of strong affiliation. They are seated at a table in a rather nondistinctive fashion, menus are placed in their hands, and they begin to look at them.

"Claire, here's an example of real Roman cooking that I think I should order for you. *Linguine alla carbonara.* It's one of my favorite pastas. A flat pasta with bacon. That's what *carbonara* means—'with bacon.' It was made because the Roman soldiers generally got the scraps of the pig after the citizens ate high on the hog. So they made this dish with little bits of bacon, because that's all they had."

"Actually, the story I know is that *carbonara* was named after the homeless street people in the city who had a dirty look. The ground pepper made the chef think the dish looked dirty like the street people."

"Nah, it's the bacon. Interesting story someone fed you, though."

"I got this story while I was an exchange student in Rome for six months. I actually went to the restaurant La Carbonara where the dish was invented. In Italy, they actually use pancetta not bacon, and 'with pancetta' in Italian would be *con pancetta.*"

"I guess they tell tourists different stories than you find in original cooking books. You should always be suspicious in a foreign country when a place says they invented something. I really prefer to cook French anyway."

"Great! I spent the other half of that year in Paris. . . ."

There was not a topic brought up that night that Hal didn't seem to have some information on. He was a willing listener as long as he could offer advice he felt she needed. Hal was even kind enough to correct the waiter's pronunciation when he thought menu items were incorrectly stated.

Everyone takes pride in having information others may not. It makes people feel a little special. But when you'd rather watch the World Wrestling Federation Death Match Marathon than hear one more expression of what your date knows, you are definitely in the same arena as a Red Flag.

The Know-It-All has a very interesting set of life patterns. He seems able to impress people on initial contact, since he is outgoing, generally fakes happiness, and rarely lets on that underlying his basic personality is a solid depressive note. The insecurity a Know-It-All feels can come from a number of places. High-achieving Know-It-Alls are usually insecure about their social skills, and the only way they interact with others is to present themselves as all-knowing. There is usually an *expressed* feeling of superiority over others. As far as the high-achieving Know-It-All is concerned, other people are stupid, uninformed, or just have no desire to improve themselves. The *suppressed* feeling is their lack of comfort in society and anger at the adolescent feeling of not fitting in. Yes, there may be life after high school, but it isn't always a different life. Isn't it comforting to know that a lot of jerks in high school stay jerks? And you could find some other high school's class jerk who is now an adult.

Low-achieving Know-It-Alls are insecure because they haven't measured up to society's standards of success: school grades, position, money, notoriety. The low-achieving Know-It-All may have been saddled with a very judgmental parent or two, who was always putting him down or calling him names. With the low-achieving Know-It-All there is usually a history of reduced success in school settings, possibly because of a lack of concentration or organizational skills. Their lives are usually unbalanced while growing up, and there is often a history of consistent marijuana, drug, or alcohol abuse in high school and college.

The Know-It-All places a higher value on intelligence than any other personal trait. A balanced individual recognizes that intelligence is only one of many traits that makes a person attractive or leads them to success. The Know-It-All thinks intelligence is so far above the other traits that it alone defines a person. Usually the Know-It-All has a higher than average intelligence, although the low-achieving Know-It-All thinks his intelligence is much higher than it really is. In order to prove intelligence, the Know-It-All will read or gather from the media lots of pieces of information and store it in his memory to be used at first opportunity to show off. If he doesn't know the information, he'll try to guess from what he does know. On the positive side, he seems better than the average person at reiterating the information he has collected. The Know-It-All's intellective abilities tend to run more along the lines of rote memory than intelligence that synthesizes ideas and concepts. That's why his guesses are often incorrect. A Know-It-All often has the words of tons of songs stored in his head but isn't able to sing a song any differently than the recording he memorized. He will do well on the multiple-choice tests of life, but doesn't do well with tests that ask him to put two ideas together—like romance and keeping his mouth shut.

It was a short-lived relationship for Claire and Hal. Once Hal started being confronted by Claire's friends at parties, she had the swift wisdom to get out. In the month and a half that they did date, Hal took Claire to a lot of new places and she saw things she might not have seen on her own or with most men. Unfortunately, the museum tours were accompanied by Hal's view of history, the trips to the city were of mostly obscure places that Hal knew, and the music that Hal introduced her to was of rather esoteric artists whose recordings were not very easy to find. Not that Claire minded the variety in her life, but a steady diet of caviar can make anyone start wishing for freezer-burned fish sticks.

On the surface, it would seem that recognizing a Know-It-All is easy, but in fact distinguishing between a guy with real smarts and a Know-It-All may actually be difficult. Use the test below to know whether or not you should start reaching for a good hard turtle.

IS HE A KNOW-IT-ALL?

*Circle the number and
add up the score*

Family Background

Family placed a high value on intelligence and education, pushed him in school	1
Parent(s) were very judgmental	2
Parent(s) called him bad names	3
Background was rather unbalanced, lots of double standards	2

Work/School History

Either high achiever or achieved well below intelligence level in high school	2
Excessive marijuana use when in high school	4
Talks about how he is better than people at his job	2

Friendships

Trouble maintaining long-term, same-sex friendships	1
Feels he is smarter than his friends	2
Puts his friends down	2
Minimizes his friends' career successes	2

Past Relationships

No contact with any of his past girlfriends or friends from those relationships	1
Girls tended to be the one to break up	1
Criticizes them for being less intelligent or stupid	3

Body Language

Eyes dart a lot	1
Takes liberties with protocol (puts feet on table, determines seats for everyone)	3
Doesn't smile when you first touch him	1
Seems physically disconnected when you talk	2

Dress/Hygiene

Showers, washes hands, brushes teeth slightly excessively	1
Criticizes others' clothes in comparison to his tastes	3

(test continues)

Behavior

Insists on ordering dinner for you	2
Corrects you or someone with you	
Once	1
Twice	3
Three or more times in an evening	5
Corrects or argues with a person in the person's area of expertise	5
Must have first word	1
Must have last word	2
Looking to give information but not receive	2
Does not volunteer to help even in an area he says he has an expertise	2
Criticizes others but doesn't do much himself	2
Acts like he knows everybody	2
Displays any signs of depression	1
Watches a lot of TV	2
Reads a lot of nonfiction, "fact-information" books	1

Conversation

Name-drops	1
Calls many people you meet stupid	2
Criticizes anyone you may have said was interesting	3
Never says "I don't know"	2
Never asks questions about something he doesn't know	2
Tells stories of how he was smarter than others	3
Starts sentences with "I bet you didn't know"	1
Starts a sentence with "Would you like to guess . . . ?"	1
Always has a "why" or "how"	3
Feeds you and others bits of information that are tangential to conversation	2
Tries to limit topic of conversation to something he knows	3
Tries to top yours and others' stories with his	3
Willing to learn from you	−4

When Confronted

Changes topic when you confront	1
Puts you down, or says, "Your life isn't a prime example, either"	3
Gets defensive	2
Says he will prove to you what he has been saying but never does	2
Wants to really understand what you are saying	−3

(test continues)

Your Impression	
He is the brightest guy you've met in a long time	1
He is a guy that needs encouragement, and his intelligence will get him far	1
He is pompous	3
He thinks he's better than most people	3
He feels he can't make a mistake	3
Feel he hasn't shared much that is personal but has talked a lot	2
Total Score	

Score 12 and lower: No reason for concern at this point
Score between 13 and 26: Yellow Flag—There's reason for caution
Score 27 and above: Red Flag—He doesn't *know* how to treat you; make him a dummy

It's Final *Jeopardy!* Time

If the score falls in the Yellow Flag category you must really look closely at whether you have a legitimately smart man or one who is a Know-It-All. There are actually very intelligent men who get a little nervous on dates and spray like a Mountain Dew after a ride on the Great American Scream Machine. Focus on whether he is interested in others' opinions and learning from other people. Men who are just plain smart really look for learning opportunities and usually feel they can learn something from everyone. Not so for the Know-It-All. Also, look closely for signs of depression. Is the guy over-critical of others? Does he complain a lot? Is everybody doing something wrong? Does he seem to spend a lot of time alone doing little or nothing? Finally, look at the guy's background. Does he have the kind of education and experience that would have exposed him to firsthand knowledge about different parts of life? Is he living his life now with a passion for knowledge? Is he well-traveled or experienced to have gained all the information he claims? The Know-It-All can sneak up on you, so look closely at his behavior before it gets too far.

If the man falls in the Red Flag category, ask him to tell you a little about trains, then tell him to find one. Sticking around will put you on the tracks of a nightmare relationship. Know-It-Alls turn people off and then everyone starts playing the avoidance game. You may grow used to him, or perhaps less judgmental, but people with a choice whether to interact will stop including you. The Know-It-All will usually have some difficulty holding a job if he is in one where he can be fired. You may end up being the only means of support between his jobs. Then the depression! The Know-It-All's depression will start to work on you. When someone is constantly saying negative things, you start getting negative feelings about yourself. Many Know-It-All daters start getting some of the same Know-It-All characteristics. Remember when your parents told you to choose your friends wisely because you start to become like them? Time to listen.

The high-achieving Know-It-All poses an even bigger challenge. He may have a job from which he can't be fired. He may be able to provide you with things that are a little above the ordinary. He may even have a prestigious lifestyle. If you have overvalued intelligence all your life, this may be enticing. People like to have the high-profile lifestyle, but you can quickly become ornamental in the life of a high-achieving Know-It-All. Your opinions will hold little value with your man, and your mutual friends may begin to accept the same attitude. You probably won't know what is happening to you, but you can always just ask your boyfriend. He'll know!

For Him the Buzzer Tolls

You will leave this relationship "the dumb one" who is "naive" and "unrealistic about the world." That's what the Know-It-All will tell anyone who will listen to him. He's got to have a woman of intelligence, and you're not it. You'll be insensitive and uncaring, regardless of how much you try to be the opposite. And after a month or two, he will say he left you for someone more his own speed—prettier, sexier, or brighter than you. Makes you want to be as gentle as you can with this slob, huh?

Leaving a Know-It-All is like leaving a bad dream—just wake up, go to the bathroom, splash some water on your face, and forget it. Use what he will give you ("You and I are very different socially, intellectually, and emotionally"). Be brief, to the point ("It's time for us to go our separate ways"), be gracious ("I thank you for all the good times"), and get out of there ("But this needs to be a clean break, good-bye"). There is no room to soften this breakup and do not under any circumstance stay around to take some of the abuse he will project on you for his miserable life. Find a girlfriend or a nonromantic male friend that didn't like the guy and have them take you out that night and celebrate. Hear from someone else what kind of Loser you were dating. Then go home and turn on the Discovery Channel and learn about the mating rituals of the giant Galapagos turtles. You too can know it all.

The Time Teaser

Absence Makes the Libido Wander

In December 1973, right before Christmas, a writer for the *Tonight* show wrote a joke for Johnny Carson's monologue that suggested there was a toilet paper shortage in America. Apparently, this was in response to a government official stating that government-issue toilet paper was scarce, not the soft kind the public used. Immediately, millions of people started stocking up on toilet paper, hoarding it for fear that they might be reusing wrapping paper to cleanse their fannies after Christmas dinner. As people rushed to leave their fellow Americans high and wet, so to speak, a real shortage was created, forcing many stores to have to ration toilet paper. Johnny Carson retracted his joke four days later, but the damage had been done, creating a nationwide disappearance of the soft multi-ply's. It took close to a month before the stores were able to restock, probably making many families resourceful in their elimination aftermath, perhaps reducing private libraries of books that would never have been read again anyway. Many men create these same kinds of shortages with the time they are willing to give to a relationship. Women who use their resourcefulness to stay with these men are flushed away like freshly squeezed Charmin.

Sharon met Barry in the volleyball league run by the community program at the high school. He was a good player, team captain, and his team gave her team a whomping like they'd never seen before. Sharon flirted a little between games because she liked Barry's style. While at the net together in the last game, Barry suggested a bet that if his team won by ten points, Sharon would have to let him take her to dinner the next night. Sharon agreed. Barry was serving for game point, a rocket shot right into Sharon's chest. She missed it, not on purpose, but she let Barry think that maybe it was intended. It was going to be a spontaneous evening of dinner and whatever ideas they came up with afterward. Free and relaxed. Barry showed up at Sharon's door about twenty-five minutes late.

"Shar, I'm really sorry. I got tied up with an emergency down at the office. One of my coworkers needed me to bail him out on a project. Comes to me about at three o'clock with this proposal in complete disarray, so I jumped in and took over. I'm sorry. I guess I just miscalculated the amount of time it would take."

"No problem. As long as you get me back for my next date in three hours, I won't hold it against you. Just kidding. Don't worry about it."

"Okay, let's go. Ahh, dinner. I didn't get a chance to make any reservations. Is there anywhere in particular you'd like to go?"

"How about La Bergerie?"

"Great. Where's that?"

"It's this little place in Paris, on the Ile St-Louis. Always wanted to go there."

"Guess you want me to make the choice, huh?"

"You won the date with those powerful shots of yours, serving into this poor peasant girl's bosom."

Barry was enjoying the repartee, but his mind seemed focused elsewhere.

"Okay, I got it. We'll go down to this place my friend owns. I haven't seen him in a while and he's always calling me and asking me to come down."

As they get into the car, Barry's cellular phone rings.

"Aren't you going to get that?"

"Nah, it's probably just one of the many friends I haven't had a chance to get back to because I've been so busy. They'll just ask me to do something tomorrow and I'll have to turn them down. Besides, you and I have to get to know each other."

"All booked up tomorrow?"

"Yeah, I've got a racquetball game in the morning about eight, then I hope I'll be able to get some time to run back to the office and finish what I don't get done later on tonight. At noon, I have a board meeting for the community pool. At two, I'm supposed to meet with the committee for the fund-raiser for the alumni club. I wish I hadn't agreed to be the chair of that thing. Then at four-thirty, I have the Saturday afternoon softball league. I have a dinner meeting at six-thirty with a couple people on a new business plan I put together to see if I can start bringing in more money. Then at night, I need to stop over at my parents' house for a few minutes because it's my sister's birthday, and I want to catch her before she goes to sleep."

"Yeah, Saturday's usually a day of rest for me too."

"It's better than being bored. I can't stand sitting around and doing nothing."

"Yeah, there's nothing worse than a day with no demands where all you have to do is sit at the beach, make idle talk with friends, and drink piña coladas."

The date was pleasant enough but somewhat short; after all, Barry had let Sharon know early on that he was going back to the office. Sharon wished they would be able to spend more time together, she really wasn't busy the whole weekend.

Barry graciously offered Sharon the option to come watch him play softball.

Most people like somewhat active lives. The great philosopher Bertrand Russell said that "at least half the sins of mankind are caused by the fear of boredom." But when a man's life is so active that flossing would throw him an hour off schedule, you may fall into the huge cavity of a Red Flag.

There is an old adage that if you want to get something done give it to the busiest person you can find and he will somehow get it completed. There is great truth to the idea that busy people tend to accomplish a lot. Mostly because these men focus their lives on accomplishment and fueling their various passions. Unfortunately, this same attitude does not carry over into their relationships, and they frequently are not very attentive to their partners. These Time Teasers' dating lives are like young women switching radio stations in their car. They get a lot of little pieces of a relationship but never hear the full song. And there is a lot of static along the way.

Ambition comes from a variety of places in a man's life, thus it is difficult to define any one or two patterns that will most likely breed the Time Teaser. Some have a past where they have to be strongly self-reliant because of poor families or the early departure of their parents. Some built ambition through their need to please and get positive feedback. Some fear boredom so strongly that they would rather stress themselves out than take a moment to relax and risk having nothing to do. And still others led lives where many events occurred that were of crisis proportions, thus making them believe that everything was urgent. Self-worth for the Time Teaser is measurable, based on the levels of accomplishment. There is usually a strong achievement-based fantasy life, and sometimes they put relationships with women in the category of achievements rather than relationships.

The Time Teaser learns to manage time with a number of

devices designed toward being able to fit more things into a day. They almost always have a tendency to overestimate their ability to accomplish something in a limited amount of time and that often makes them late for events such as dates, which take a lower priority. The concept of lower priority is strongly functional here, as they tend to give the most priority to anything that has an urgent quality to it, whether it is important or not. Relationships tend not to have an urgent quality until they are troubled, then it's often too late.

Time Teasers are joiners, ending up in a myriad of clubs or teams, and tend to fall quickly into leadership roles because they are very goal-oriented. Leadership roles unfortunately create more urgency and necessity on attendance. They feel that the concept of maintaining balance means doing a variety of things, perhaps professional as well as humanitarian. Big hearts are not usually a problem, nor is generosity. Many Time Teasers will give money to a number of charities or to their women, missing the boat that time is the bigger commodity in a relationship. In fact, the Time Teaser's boat is completely guided by its captain, which happens not to be you. You will go to a lot of his events, but your life will tend to be very vicarious as you watch him go about the many things he has scheduled. You will be the consummate audience, although most likely he will allow you to participate in his nightly nap in front of the TV set after he's exhausted. These men like a nice lap to lay their head.

Barry and Sharon went out for quite a while. They spent less time alone than most couples and more time doing a lot of activities. Sharon liked being his girlfriend. It was sort of a whirlwind romance, but it had to work around the numerous activities in Barry's life. Sharon tended to become a master at working her schedule to fit the times Barry was free. It worked well for almost a year, and they started making plans to get engaged. After all, Barry was a big-hearted guy, ambitious, and had a lot of the qualities Sharon liked. At least when he was around.

After their engagement, Sharon started noticing that Barry

was not really spending any more time with her, even though they had made a commitment together. They struggled trying to set dates for the wedding, looking at catering halls, and even having an engagement party because Barry's calendar was always filled. He didn't seem to want to slow up as Sharon suspected he would. Sharon came to the realization that even though she was with someone, as far as being committed to a relationship, she was basically still alone. Resentment started and Barry didn't afford the time to solve the problem. They started counseling, but scheduling got a little too hectic. It took two months to get their third session in and by that time it was too late. The breakup was not easy, but Sharon learned something new about the man she wanted to find, and Barry had repeated an old pattern that he continued for many years. A couple of broken relationships later, he would get help. He put the energy into therapy and changed rather quickly. I guess it was the right time.

As the Time Teaser is usually in no way vicious, and often has a number of good qualities, the signs are not going to be as apparent as many others in this book. The test below will help you discover on the first three dates whether your guy needs a little seasoning.

IS HE A TIME TEASER?

Circle the number and add up the score

Family Background

Got a lot of attention for achievements when young	1
Parent(s) owned their own business or were high-level managers	1
Family was poor and he had to go to work early	1
Expected to care for parent(s) as an adult	1
Competitive with brothers in achievements	2

(test continues)

Work/School History

Paid for part of college with own money	1
Works harder than others at work	1
Puts in a lot of time at work, rarely goes home on schedule	2
Believes most people do not work very hard	2
Seems highly passionate about work projects or earning money	1

Friendships

Maintains a lot of friendships, almost too many to keep up with	2
Reputation among friends for being late	2
Tends to be the guy a lot of people lean on or always get involved	2
The party thrower of his group of friends	1
Tends to overestimate food and drink amounts for get-togethers	2

Past Relationships

All fizzled after a period of time, he will say mutual or they left him	2
Lingering phone calls from past girlfriends, checking up on him	1
Will blame some guy for stealing girls, or girls for being unfaithful	2

Body Language

High activity level, tends to be moving at most times	2
When stops and sits for a while will tend to fall asleep	2
Looking around a lot to see if he knows somebody	1

Dress/Hygiene

Tends to dress in similar patterns every day, not as much variety in dress	1
Does not have "hang around" clothes, either a little dressy or a complete mess	2
Forgets stages in morning grooming routine, particularly if razor, vitamins, toothbrush, etc., in bathroom are rearranged	2

Behavior

Frequently late	1
Spends money rather than gives time	3
Member of a lot of organizations or groups	2
Knows a lot about what everyone is doing around him	1
Tends toward leadership roles in organizations	3
Focuses on urgency of events, rather than importance	4
Finds it hard to say no to people wanting his time	3
Passionate about more than one project at a time	2

(test continues)

Behavior

Has another project immediately behind the one he is presently working on	3
Dates have to be activity-oriented	2

Conversation

Talks a lot about work	1
Talks about busy schedule	2
Cellular phone and/or beeper get overused	3
Will use cellular phone in restaurant when with you	4
Asks a lot about who you have dated	1
Has difficulty listening to you because his mind is wandering	3
You feel the conversation is one-sided, like he thinks your life is boring	3

When Confronted

Says he's only one person and can't be expected to do everything	3
Promises more time with you without a real plan of how	2
Promises more time by saying when something else happens he'll be freed up	3
Admits time is a problem and is planning to get outside help to fix it	−3

Your Impression

Focused on money and accomplishments	1
Dating seems goal-oriented	3
Does everything in a big way	3
Good intentions not always followed through on	3
Seems to feel relaxing and doing nothing is a waste of time	2
Total Score	

Score 11 and lower: No reason for concern at this point
Score between 12 and 23: Yellow Flag—There's reason for caution
Score 24 and above: Red Flag—Don't have the time; don't spend another dime

When "Tick" Should Not Have a "Tock"

So, you got a guy in the Yellow Flag category and you really like him, now what do you do? This is another one of those where you have to be very careful, because the lack of glaring flaws can make you get attached to these guys quickly. Particularly if you like men who are ambitious and passionate about what they are doing. The first step with a guy in this category is to let him know the concern you are having in no uncertain terms. Do not complain or sound like you just want him to give you attention, because in male-speak that means: "I need to pat her on the head temporarily, she's having one of those moody girl things." Say, "I am a little concerned that your priorities make a relationship very difficult, and I don't want to get too involved with anyone who has difficulty relaxing and makes me nag him for time." He will aptly point out the time you are spending together—mostly fit in around other things. Or he may offer the temporary solution of "let's go away together, just the two of us." Don't fall for either, although the latter may be pretty tempting. As the relationship develops, let him know the lifestyle you want involves inclusion and joint decision making regarding time. Set aside a day or two a week where you will always spend together taking a French class or eating Chinese food. If he doesn't seem to change or keeps switching your weekly get-togethers, you've got a bigger problem and should read below.

If the test shows you are with a Red Flag Time Teaser, time has run out, and you should too. The girl that stays with this type of guy will constantly be nagging and turning into the person they never wanted to become. The relationship will be a compendium of always being late, a change of plans and going to some couples events alone because an important meeting has come up. You'll miss out on a lot of life waiting around, and with many of these men, if you are not there when they are waiting they think you've lost interest and give you up. You may be accused of trying to interfere in his career or make him less successful. Then you will be told you don't understand the pressures he is under trying to "make it." It's not worth it.

Women in marriages with these men say they are more alone now than they ever were when they were single. And being a single parent with a husband is not a pleasant image.

These women usually have fantasies of running away or starting some kind of exciting life on their own, without their husbands. Their husbands confuse earning money with contributing to the family, two very different ideas but not mutually exclusive. You can avoid the whole rush by backing out early on and finding someone with the time to give you.

It's Crying Time Again

Out with the old, in with the new. Since you are being left alone a lot, get yourself, or keep yourself, in an active social life before you leave. This type of breakup has the potential to hurt you more than him, because these guys are not bad, just inattentive. This is also the guy who might learn enough from the breakup to be revisited six months later, but not sooner because change takes time.

Let him know the issue of time has put you in a bad position, and you do not want to be tied up waiting for him anymore. If he says he will change, let him know he can keep in touch, but you are broken up at this point. If he gets mean, cut it off completely. If he's considerate or quiet, you can keep him around, just do not date him and never get romantic until a good period of time has passed and you have seen a consistent attitude change. He's heard this before, he just hasn't figured it out yet. He has to realize that time management is not adding another day planner but letting go of one. In the meantime, five golden contracts, four softball leagues, three civic groups, two Turtle Waxes, and a *Playboy* magazine with pear brandy will have to suffice for what his true love could have given him.

The Cheater

High-Risk Romance:
Do Not *Try This One at Home*

There is a fable about a scorpion that lived on a desert island. This scorpion had stung and poisoned all the other small animals and reptiles on the island, killing all the competition for the bountiful buffet of spiders and insects. A frog swam across the channel from the mainland every couple of days to feast on the plentiful flies and bugs on the island, and was able to easily hop away from the scorpion when threatened. Having killed all potential companions the scorpion got very lonely. So one day he approached the frog and said, "Mr. Frog, I cannot swim and I am lonely. If I could get to the mainland, you could have this wonderful island all for yourself. Would you let me ride on your back as you swim across the channel?" Tempted by the offer to have the island to himself, the frog thought for a second, then responded, "I am not so stupid. You have killed all the other animals on the island. You would sting me too." The scorpion responded, "Ah, but I cannot sting you, Mr. Frog, because if I sting you I will drown." This made sense to the frog so he agreed. He entered the water and let the scorpion on his back. Halfway across the channel, the frog sensed a prick in his back and began to feel the poison seep into his body. As he was dying in the water, he turned to the scorpion and said, "Now we will both die. Why did you sting me knowing you cannot swim?" The scorpion replies, "Because I am a scorpion." The man who cheats on a spouse, fiancée, or girlfriend is basically a scorpion destined to fulfill his destiny again and again. If necessary, he will destroy himself in the process to fulfill his urges to cheat on a relationship. A guy with this Red Flag is guaranteed to fit into another category also, so you've got double the problems with this toad. There are fourteen hundred different species of scorpions in this world, a paltry number in comparison to the number of different types of Cheaters. All of them have a poisonous sting.

Mark was the first to greet Virginia when she started to work in the DA's office. He was very kind and offered to give her the real scoop on the different judges, how to get around the bosses, and how to get something accomplished without making waves. Virginia appreciated the help and thought nothing of it when Mark suggested they "do lunch" because she knew he was married with a child. She was even going to pick up the bill because of all the help he'd given her, making her adjustment easier.

"I really appreciate all the help you've given me since I got here. You really have been quite the gentleman."

"I always like to help a beautiful lady. So what do you do with yourself on the weekends?"

"Well, I go out with my friends, usually. Sometimes we go dancing, sometimes we just hang out. I'm not sure what I'm going to do this weekend. It will probably be one of those spontaneous, last-minute things. And what does the family man do on the weekends?"

"Are you telling me a girl like you doesn't have a steady boyfriend? That's too hard to believe."

"It's amazing, isn't it? And I have all the 'power' clothes. I don't even want to get near a Y chromosome right now. It's summer and I want to be free to do what I want."

"Yeah, I like that feeling too. I am really looking forward to this summer. It's going to be great having parties on the boat with the guys."

"With the guys? Doesn't your wife like being out on the water? I wish I had a boat. I'd be out all the time."

"My marriage is over. We're getting separated as soon as I get an apartment. I'd be out now except we wanted our son to finish the school year."

"Wow, Mark. I didn't mean to pry. I'm sorry to hear—"

"Don't worry. It's all for the best. I only married her because she got pregnant. I knew she was a psycho. I just tried so hard to make it work. But now it's time for the fun. It's summertime and the weather is hot, and I know how to have a good time. We'll have to hang out together this summer. The boat goes in this weekend."

"This must be hard for you. How long were you married?"

"Too long. Enough about that, it's over. Tell you what. Since you and your girlfriends don't have any plans this weekend, how about if I get a couple of guys together and we have the season's first boat party?"

Virginia doesn't know what to say. She stumbles on her thoughts for a couple of seconds.

"Virginia, it's no big thing. Just a group of people getting together. We'll have fun. We'll drive over to the island and lay out in the sun, then go to a beach club. It's going to be a group of us. Your friends will like my friends. I need to get away."

Virginia reluctantly agreed and a couple of her girlfriends met a couple of his guy friends and they had a great day in the sun. They did it a few more times in the next month, and after a while, she and Mark had become really good friends. Mark was a lot of fun and really knew how to make people laugh.

He seemed very sincere and caring. The wheels of possibility started turning.

Some women say that guys who have been married or engaged have a better sense of what a relationship is really like—a better sense of what commitment is all about. It makes sense for men who have been divorced awhile, because they are making an informed choice between being married and being single. But when a guy thinks monogamy is a board game from his youth, do not pass go, you're playing with a Red Flag.

Why do men cheat? Is it really because their wives don't understand them? No!! Men cheat for a variety of reasons, all of which foreshadow problems in any or all of their relationships. The decision to cheat is removed from the problems in their past or present relationships, removed from the nature of their partners. Cheaters use their past bad relationships and bad partners as an excuse to try to motivate you to compete with another woman. Cheating is a moral decision, not a result of external forces.

Probably the most common internal reason men cheat is an inability to delay gratification coupled with an attitude of entitlement. The Cheater may have grown up as one of two extreme types: spoiled or deprived.

The spoiled child is used to getting what he wants, when he wants it. His parents will work to make him happy by supplying him with toys, attention, and assorted goodies. They respond to his boredom with their creativity, constantly trying to devise new ways to make him happy. The parents blame everyone else if the child has problems. Problems in school, school's problem. Problems with other children, other children's problem. As a result, the child becomes spoiled. He does not learn how to deal with frustration. He does not learn to make himself happy. He never looks inward for satisfaction but looks elsewhere for excitement. He is used to this excitement being provided for him by others. His values become corrupt. He has the intellectual knowledge of right and wrong, but not the courage of his convictions. Having had everything handed to him, he develops a powerful sense of entitlement. He does not develop inner strength. Since he has led a privileged life, he assumes that he deserves privilege. He starts to believe that he is special, above others. He believes that the rules and ethics of society apply to the "little" people, not to him. His desires are paramount; nothing else matters.

One problem of an indulged childhood results from the paradoxical effect of having too much pleasure provided too easily. Humans are designed to habituate to the stimuli around them. In other words, we quickly get used to the things to which we are constantly exposed. This is so we can be aware of new things that enter into our awareness. This is instinctual. It allowed our ancestors to survive in a dangerous world where new things might be new threats. Long-term appreciation comes from having to work a long time to attain something. The spoiled child becomes a jaded adult. He cannot appreciate anything he has for very long. Only novelty can provide him with fun and excitement. He becomes addicted to sex for the sake of sexual pleasure and novelty. Relationships quickly lose their luster. He gets used to them and has to move on to the next adventure, the next toy. He cheats. On his island he will kill all potential companions, or do something else to them that makes them destroy themselves.

The boy who grows up in a deprived environment gets to the same place via a different road. He sees other children getting things he cannot. They seem to have an easier life. They have possessions they can be proud of, and he sees his lack of possessions as a defect in himself. His self-esteem suffers. He may come to believe others look down on him. In fact, poor children are often teased by their peers. Children can be cruel. As an adolescent, the Cheater may see other boys with more money "getting all the girls." They feel isolated and alone and blame their disadvantaged status.

As time goes on for this deprived child, he starts to become jealous. He will fantasize about the things he wants, the things he deserves. He promises himself that someday he will have the type of life that he should have had all along. He promises himself that he will not be deprived ever again.

Some of these men grow up to be workaholics who can never accumulate enough wealth. Others grow up craving power and may find themselves as leaders of business, or possibly politicians. Some find an escape from their past in being able to "have" any woman they want. They become Cheaters. Unlike their spoiled counterparts, however, it is not the fun of sex that is the main attraction. These Cheaters are addicted to the power of frequent, novel sex with a variety of partners. Women are a rung on the power ladder, the privilege of their work.

Either way, the Cheater can't get enough. He wants what he wants when he wants it and sincerely believes he's entitled to it. He succumbs easily to temptation and puts himself in tempting situations. The Cheater is always on the hunt. Scorpions eat spiders, bugs, and any living thing they can fit in their mouth. The Cheater is a scorpion. What do you expect from something that eats spiders?

Understand that almost all men have fantasies that border on the wild side. Values and ethics keep these men from acting on fantasies that they know are destructive. The Cheater does not incorporate these values as his own. He is aware of them. He certainly knows right from wrong. He is even aware that most would view his behavior as reprehensible. But far from being remorseful for what he does, he is proud of himself. He sees other men as "suckers" for following a social norm that deprives them of pleasure. He may even see himself as somehow above these rules. A predator is not bound by the rules of the flock. You become the prey. His wife and family become victims.

The Cheater is a specific type of sexual addict. Like most addicts, failed attempts are made at times to control their unacceptable behavior. Often these attempts are made when they are caught red-handed, or put in the painful situation of having hurt someone that they do care about. Addictions, however, are more powerful than other emotions. The Cheater cannot stop himself for love. Promises, determination, and willpower will not curtail his behavior for long. The Cheater may try, but soon the urge grows and his resolve breaks down. His thoughts become self-centered around his goal of conquest. "I deserve the excitement." "I'm entitled to a little fun." "No one is going to tell me how to act." Feelings of remorse quickly turn to thoughts of anger. Determination to abstain becomes determination to conquer. The cycle of cheating continues. Like other addicts, it will only be when he hits bottom that the Cheater will change. Like all addicts he needs to be kept away from his drug of choice while he is recovering. Most Cheaters never agree to these terms. It's hard to negotiate terms with a scorpion.

Why are some woman attracted to the Cheater? Mystery can be exciting, and the Cheater's attempts to cover his behavior can be mysterious. The Cheater knows how to turn on the charm. His charm is his spear in his hunt for big game. Unfortunately some women may confuse it for Cupid's arrow. For some women, the Cheater may trigger a fantasy of proving to themselves how special they are by being the one to satisfy this previously insatiable man. If they are "woman enough," he will not need another. This underlying thought, most often dormant and subconscious, is the underlying motivation for staying too long with the Cheater. What these women don't understand is that the Cheater is not looking for a woman. He is not looking for a relationship. He is looking for power through sexual conquest. And once conquered, repeated invasion of one's own territory is pointless. In other words, you are only good until he has conquered you.

There is a final characteristic of the Cheater that should make him even more revolting. Much of what is described above is similar to Red Flag #10, the Sex Guzzler, but the Cheater has an added dimension that makes him even more insidious. He needs to have a stable relationship in order to feel the thrill of cheating. He needs to be fooling someone. He likes the adventure of the escape, the cover-up, and the lies. He will tell people he hates the sneaking around, and truly he believes this himself. But after a divorce, when he is free to be a tomcat, he will work to build a relationship. He wants that one girl. Then he can start to cheat again. Want to give him a ride across the channel on *your* back?

The boat trips continued throughout the summer with the numbers of people always changing. Later in the summer, Virginia agreed to go on the boat alone with Mark to go over to the beach club and meet some of their friends. The friends weren't there, and Virginia and Mark were suddenly alone on a date. Dating was a lot of fun for Virginia. Mark really knew how to treat a woman and knew how to listen. She soon became aware that Mark hadn't left his house as he said he had planned. She found out that all of Mark's friends that had gone out with her and her girlfriends were also married. Virginia got suspicious but was starting to really like Mark, so she adopted a wait-and-see attitude.

Mark kept putting off leaving his wife with progressive milestones—her birthday, his son's birthday, family vacations, grandparents' visits—that would be always a month away. Virginia found out from one of her coworkers who didn't know of their relationship that Mark's wife was pregnant. Mark suggested he intended to tell Virginia but was waiting for the right time. He said he wasn't even sure it was his child. He said he would leave his wife right after the baby was born. Virginia had felt the scorpion sting. It took a while to get the poison out of her system.

The Cheater is one of the easiest Red Flags to detect. Take the test below to help you.

IS HE A CHEATER?

Circle the number and add up the score

Family Background

Grew up in deprived/poor household	1
Grew up overindulged by mother	2
Only child	1
Center of attention	2
Father kept mother in subservient role	2
Father disrespectful of mother	2

Work/School History

Had teachers/boss "wrapped around his finger"	1
Charms way into promotion	2
Works in sales-related field	1

Friendships

Many acquaintances	1
More female than male friends	1
Tries to keep you away from his friends	3

Past Relationships

Cheated in past relationship	6
Seems to have no time between relationships when he is single	3
Is in another relationship when he starts dating you	4

Body Language

Eyes dart	2
Eyes look up to the right a lot	1
Eyes look at your breasts or legs	2
Eyes always looking at other women	3
Looks down when he talks	2
Invades personal space before you do	3
Touches you early in conversation before you do	3

(test continues)

Dress/Hygiene

Dresses sharply most of time	1
Well-groomed	1
Accents dress with jewelry	1
Wears cologne most of time	1

Behavior

Secretive about what he does with his time	2
Secretive about his friends and family	3
Secretive about where he lives	4
Gives beeper number as best way to get in touch with him	3
Gets many pages when you are with him and does not comment on them	3
Turns pager off, stating he wants to focus only on you	2
Asks you not to identify self as girlfriend when calling him at work	3

Conversation

Does not talk about family or friends	2
Talks about all of his "toys/gadgets" like a little boy	1
Has a lot of practiced stories and jokes	2
Seems rehearsed	2
Brings up broken relationship talk in first date	3
Makes sexual innuendo early in date	3
Tells sexual jokes that are mildly offensive	2

When Confronted

Never admits being wrong	1
Minimizes your feelings	2
Embellishes to make a story fit new evidence	3
Gets angry and dismisses you	1

Your Impression

He is keeping a secret	3
He is willing to tell you whatever you want to hear	2
He is insincere	2
Total Score	

Score 15 and lower: No reason for concern at this point
Score between 16 and 30: Yellow Flag—There's reason for caution
Score 31 and above: Red Flag—Don't cheat yourself; throw in the cards

You've Got to Know When to Hold 'Em . . . Know When to Fold 'Em

If your date scores in the Yellow Flag range, you don't necessarily need to hire a private eye. While he may seem to be a man of mystery, he is possibly just holding back from you at the present. It is possible he is just shy and needs some time to warm up. He may have been hurt in a previous relationship and is in a self-protective mode. He may just not be sure. Maybe you scare him, in a good way. But it's a gamble to stay with this guy.

No matter the reason, if he is not a Cheater, he will let down his guard. Since he has nothing to hide, he will eventually let you in. The fog of mystery will clear to reveal whatever potential exists between the two of you. You might want to gently let him know that you expect more sharing of information. Ask him outright if he is married or engaged. If he responds by closing off more or lying to you, you've got the bad guy. If he responds by saying he's married, but . . . , you've got the bad guy. Time to put the cards on the table and cash out.

Beware the Red Flagger! Cheaters cannot give you or any woman what they want and need in a relationship. Cheaters do not change easily, quickly, or while in a relationship. No matter how romantic the idea of changing a man might be, all that will happen is his poison will seep into your body. Cheaters have built a very strong habit of lying and have perfected the poker face. Try to turn your hurt into anger so you can quickly dump him. If that anger turns inward and you blame yourself for not being woman enough to hold on to him, you're lost. This is a stacked deck and you are not going to win. Let the test above be your map. If your date falls in the Red Flag range, he's not a landmark, he's a dumping site.

Know When to Walk Away . . . Know When to Run

One of the best ways to get a Cheater to leave is to let him know you believe he is cheating. His style is to move on quickly to a less suspecting victim or convince you that you're wrong. The only exception would be if he thought you knew he was cheating but were willing to tolerate it. This would be the fulfillment of one of his fantasies: having a stable relationship for when he was in the mood, and being able to go on the hunt when the desire struck. Eventually the Cheater tires of this also. You're dumped if you do, dumped if you don't. Best to dump him. Don't let him get any false ideas. Tell him clearly that you believe he is cheating. Be emphatic when you state that cheating in a relationship will never be part of your life. In response to his smooth excuses, respond that you have already made up your mind, and he is wasting his time trying to convince you otherwise. Tell him you fully expect that he will never contact you again. Now is the time to get up and walk away without looking back.

If the guy tries to keep in contact with you or pursue you, it's time to get nasty—real nasty. Give him the steps you will be taking to get him out of your life if he persists, such as contacting his wife, contacting his workplace, taping phone conversations, charging him with sexual harassment if you work with him, and so on, and so on. Make sure he knows that you will take no action if he doesn't contact you again. Do not feel sorry for this jerk, do not be afraid of him, make him pay. Remember, the addict has to hit bottom before he will stop. Help him find the bottom if he doesn't leave you alone. It's your game. You're got all four aces in your hand. Time to cash in your chips and move to a new table.

The Pacifier

*If He Promises the Moon,
Don't Accept Uranus*

First they come up with an idea that can exploit a basic human trait such as greed, wanting something for nothing, or even wanting to help others. The "outside man," or "roper," locates a "mark," and the con game is on. The roper gets the confidence of the mark, then introduces him to the "inside man." The inside man tells the mark a story of how he can make a fortune, help catch a crook, or get something free. He delivers the "convincer," which is usually an amount of money the con men have put in that must be increased by the mark's money. Time for the sting. The mark is put on the "send" to get the money from a bank or a loan, by selling a business, or even by stealing it. Once the con men get the money, the "blowoff" starts, which is the way to get rid of the mark. One of the more effective blowoffs is called the "cackle bladder," when an actor/gunman, usually playing a cop, mobster, or irate loser, pretends to kill someone involved in the scam. In the rush, everyone disappears. It is estimated that hundreds of millions of dollars will be given to con men in any given year by people hoping to get insider information, get a free trip or low-cost stereo speakers, find discounted home improvements, win a foreign lottery, or help a bank examiner catch a dishonest teller, or by elderly persons wanting to build up an annuity for their grandchildren. The best victims are people who are convinced they are too smart to be conned, too aware. The con game in dating is different because you are dealing with one person, but basically it's the same process. Promises are made that you are going to get the relationship you want and the "sting" comes when you believe him. And to make it harder to identify the dating con, sometimes the con man himself doesn't know he is part of the scam.

Jane and David met doing volunteer work for the local civic improvement group. They were painting a shelter for wayward girls when they got paired up as work partners. What a better way to meet a guy than doing good for other people, thought Jane. In psychology, they call it a halo effect when one good quality makes a person believe everything about the person is good. Their first date was wonderful. He made a promise to take Jane out to a concert on the second date but ended up going with his brother instead. He apologized and they went out on a different night. He promised to meet her for lunch one day the next week but seemed to have forgotten about it when they talked later. They were meeting for another date to go to a fund-raiser when Jane opened the door and was beaten over the head with the halo she had created.

"David! You're not exactly dressed to go to a fund-raiser. Where's your suit or tux or whatever you're supposed to be wearing? What gives?"

"You're going to kill me, Jane. I was on the way to pick up the tickets Wednesday and it hit me. I wasn't sure I really wanted to go to this thing. So I turned around and went home to think about it."

"We talked on Wednesday night. You didn't say a thing. I've got a new dress and everything."

"Well, I didn't want to tell you until I was sure I knew what I wanted to do. I hadn't made up my mind when I talked to you. I figured I could always go and get tickets. I didn't want to upset you until I knew."

"What are you talking about? I bought this purse for this dress."

"By the time I decided to get tickets it was too late."

"Call! Why didn't you call?!"

"If I called, you wouldn't have seen me tonight. I want to be with you tonight. I just couldn't bear the fund-raiser. With all the money we've saved we'll get to have fun for a couple of weeks or even take a trip if you want. I'm going to make this up to you. I mean, wouldn't you rather do a couple of nights at the theater or go to a bed-and-breakfast for a weekend?"

"You're not dressed for the theater, David."

"I didn't mean tonight, but soon. The important thing is we have a great night together. I mean, the only reason I mentioned this stupid event was to spend time with you. We don't need a reason to spend time together. By the way, I don't think I have ever seen a woman look better than you do tonight. But I feel that way every time I see you."

"David, you've caught me completely off-guard. I don't know what to say. I don't think . . ."

"Come on, Jane. Don't give up on us. Put on some jeans. Let's go out and have a great time. I have some cool ideas of how we can spend the evening so you won't even think about that . . . uh . . . where was it we were going? See, I'm so excited I already forgot."

"You forgot before."

"Let's not be negative. We're going to have a great night tonight. Hey, if you don't have a great time, you never have to see me again. We might as well have fun. I suspect it would be better than sitting at home and ruminating about what we didn't do tonight."

"I should . . ."

"You should go put on some jeans. Meet me halfway. I will make it up to you."

Jane did meet him halfway and they went out that night and actually had a great time. Between a full moon, a quick pace of fun events, and a fast-talking guy that was good at making you believe in yourself and him, Jane decided that it wasn't a big deal to miss an event now and then. Besides, David promised it would never happen again. The fund-raiser wasn't the biggest thing Jane was missing that night.

No one wants to believe that they are being conned. Guys sometimes do make promises with good intentions and plans don't work out. But if canceled plans are happening more frequently than psychic hotline commercials on late-night cable TV's stupid movie channel, you may be the "mark" for a Red Flag.

Make no mistake, the genesis of a Pacifier is nurture, not nature. The Pacifier comes from a home that had general tension and possibly major turmoil. The possibilities for this are numerous; the tension could come from high expectations of his parents, fights between his parents, or comparisons to his brothers and sisters. Whatever the source, the Pacifier learns early in life that people want to believe spoken words. They learn early that marketing is 90 percent of sales. They learn early that perception of substance sustains lack of substance for a long period of time. The Pacifier told his parents something would happen and he got out of trouble, sometimes temporarily, sometimes permanently. He learned to say the words that would calm things down or do the minimum to make things better. If the turmoil was created entirely by one parent, he may have had a good role model for being a Pacifier, as his other parent probably developed the skills of pacifying to the level of an art.

School brought with it whole new challenges for the Pacifier. He learned how to emphasize his good points and create a "halo effect" with the teacher. He would find the symbolic apple the teacher wanted and give it to her whenever he needed the benefit of the doubt. He didn't become a top student that way, but he did get by, sometimes very well, with much less work than other students who got the same grades. Most kids who tried to get away with this kind of manipulation and con would get names like "brownnoser" or "ass-kisser," but the Pacifier knew how to play the other kids too, so they admired his skills instead of rejecting them.

As an adult, the Pacifier is the ultimate networker. He has that knack for always being in the right place at the right time. He makes promises in his relationships shrouded in compliments and motivational talk. He knows how to stir up your inner belief in yourself, and thus him. You believe in him, and when he doesn't deliver, he has a way of convincing you he will deliver double next time. God gave women the Pacifier to frustrate them to the point of needing to scream and break things. It could be worse, God gave men golf. *Fore!*

Jane stayed with David a couple of months, even though he had a less than 50 percent record of following through on promises. They had planned to go away to a wonderful lodge for Valentine's Day weekend with a few other couples. Everyone was to meet at Jane's house. David was the last to show and announced that he wasn't going to be able to go for "personal reasons." Jane got upset. Jane's friends refer to what transpired next between her and David as the Valentine's Day Massacre. Their relationship didn't survive.

Before you line your date up against the wall in your basement, give him the following test to see if he is a Pacifier.

IS HE A PACIFIER?

Circle the number and add up the score

Family Background

Grew up in deprived household	1
Tension and or fighting in house while growing up	1

(test continues)

Family Background

History of verbal abuse in family	2
Parents compared children frequently	2
Parents divorced or separated before he moved out of house	1
Father or mother was an alcoholic	2

Work/School History

Low to average student who did minimum to get by	1
Had teachers/boss "wrapped around his finger"	2
Charms way into promotions	2
Works in sales-related field	2
Excellent networker	2
Manages to get other people to make up for his slack	3

Friendships

Has many acquaintances	1
Knows a lot about the lives of his acquaintances/friends	1
Friends have a variety of skills/connections that he makes use of	2
Most of his socializing with friends occurs when he needs/wants something from them	4

Past Relationships

Exaggerates reasons for breakups	2
Talks too positively about past relationships	2
States he is still friends with past girlfriends but you never see him have contact with them	2
Tells long, complex, confusing stories about past relationships	2

Body Language

Eyes dart	1
Eyes look up to the right a lot	1
Looks down when he talks	1
Tilts head to left or right when he is talking to you	1
Smiles a lot when he is talking	1
Touches your shoulder or forearm to emphasize point	1

Dress/Hygiene

Dress is often unpredictable	1
Has explanation for his mode of dress on any particular occasion	2
Has wide range of clothing from formal to work outfits	1
Knows exactly how to dress for any occasion	1

(test continues)

Behavior

Calls you a nickname without asking you	2
Late for date	1
Makes dates very romantic	1
Changes plans a lot at the last minute	2

Conversation

Talks fast	1
Too much flattery	2
Insincere flattery	2
Doesn't listen before talking again	2
Makes a lot of excuses for behavior you do not like	3
Makes a lot of promises	3
Paints a rosy picture of future life with him	2
Gives too much detail when he talks	2
Can evoke strong positive emotion	2
Motivationally spurring you to do things with him	2

When Confronted

Never admits to being wrong	1
Embellishes to make story fit the new evidence	2
Tells stories that distract you from the point you were trying to make	2
Quickly suggests doing something "fun" and forgetting about what was bothering you	2
Promises he will "make it up to you"	2
Continues same behavior without regard to your confrontation	2

Your Impression

He seems to be all fluff, no substance	2
Compliments seem insincere	1
Always seems to want to convince you of something	2
Seems to be "slick"	2
Cannot "pin him down"	2
Total Score	

Score 10 and lower: No reason for concern at this point
Score between 11 and 20: Yellow Flag—There's reason for caution
Score 21 and above: Red Flag—He's one big broken promise; throw him away

Taking the "Sting" Out

If your man scored in the Yellow Flag range, time is the only answer to determine whether you have a Pacifier. Chances are you need to look further at his life and background to see if he has developed bad patterns or is just in a period when he shouldn't be making promises. There are periods in everyone's life when it is more hectic or a number of different things occur at once, and they should not be promising anything new, because they are too unsure of day-to-day activities. Generally, the stressors during this period are somewhat obvious and you can wait for them to subside before you make a final decision. Once they subside, if he still keeps missing or changing plans with you, take a close look: He's a Pacifier and you'll want to remember him so you don't make the same mistake again after you leave.

If he is already in the Red Flag range, you are probably barely able to read this chapter because the anger and frustration have welled up inside you like an allergic reaction to a beesting. If you stay with this guy, you are going to constantly be in a bad mood, and on edge. You will never know what the future of your relationship is going to be, and you will vacillate between extreme emotions like love and hate so much that your friends will start carrying voodoo charms to protect themselves against the evil spirits that certainly must have overtaken your body. This is a really bad guy to date for your own mental health. If you want commitment, better to find a guy who doesn't make you feel like you need to be committed.

The "Blowoff"

The level of insight in a Pacifier is slightly thinner than the shelf paper in your mother's cupboards. It also serves a lesser purpose. In this breakup, do not expect him to have an honest sense of enlightenment from your reasoning. You can expect that he will agree with you, try to make you believe he understands, and try very hard to talk you out of it.

For all the relationship books you have read, the Victoria's Secret lingerie and perfume you have purchased, the cooking lessons you took to make his favorite meal, the act of leaving will probably be the first time you have ever gotten his honest attention about wanting more out of the relationship. He will promise to straighten up and will even become very good at keeping his promises for a period of time. The concern is the Pacifier will do what he has to do to get your confidence back. His basic nature will not change unless he has an extended period alone or in therapy. This is very deep-rooted and not under his conscious control. Because he is so good at this game, he will be able to convince most women to try again after they make the initial expressions that they will leave. You must not fall for this con. Remember, the Pacifier may not even know that he is conning you. He is so good, he has himself believing he will become a perfect human being. He needs to be alone to change. He needs to start over with someone else. You need your life back. Tell him why and end it. When he tries to resell himself to you later, let him know you are actively in another relationship or enjoying the dating scene. Lie if it is not true. Just make sure you do not return.

The best part about being conned is that if you are smart, you become inoculated to another con man. You learn. It's a type of learning that you don't particularly benefit from sharing with a lot of people, except your close friends. Some people look down on people who are conned. It's sort of like a nose job. You're better for it in the mirror, but you don't need to share the process with everybody. So let this little Pacifier snot go, and don't let everyone else's nose get in your business.

The Leech

Some Guys Just Ate Too Much of That Paste in Elementary School

It seems that every few years the pharmaceutical companies come out with a new psychotropic medication that is touted as a miracle drug capable of curing a major mental illness like depression, anxiety, impotence, or some other emotional pain. Even Sigmund Freud fell victim to the belief in a miracle drug that almost cost him his career before it had even started. (Did you think you'd get to read a book written by psychologists without at least one mention of Freud?) When Siggy was starting out, he wanted to make a name for himself quickly, both in order to gain money for research and for love. Financial means would allow him to marry his fiancée, Martha. He stumbled on a drug called cocaine, from the coca plant and used by South American Indian tribes for rituals. The prohibitive cost (about $1.27 a gram) almost ended his research, but he risked all to begin to use the drug as an anesthetic for eye problems. Meanwhile, he started ingesting some himself and found it cured lethargy and gave him energy and a whole bunch of other things. He started experimenting on his friends, family, and patients to cure everything from fatigue, severe pain, depression, and even indigestion. He found they all enjoyed this wonderful new miracle drug that seemed to lift their spirits and give them the edge they needed in their lives. More important, he saw himself going down in history as the physician that brought the curative properties of cocaine to light in the medical world, and this would make him rich and famous. When the addictive qualities became apparent and the death of one of his friends was hastened by a cocaine addiction, Freud was shattered. The medical community said he set the "third scourge" loose on the earth. (The first two being alcohol and morphia. Some might argue his later discovery of psychoanalysis could be the fourth scourge on the earth.) Siggy made the terrible mistake people often do, believing one thing can cure all, that there is a magical substance that will make the whole world right. Men do this also, but instead of it being a substance, they depend on a woman as their drug. If you happen to be the lucky woman they become dependent on, you will be convinced there is another scourge on the earth.

Laura had only been working at the company for three weeks when Jeff got up the nerve to ask her out. Their first date was a lunch in a wonderful little Italian restaurant. As they left, Laura's boss told her to take an extra hour. Jeff confessed later that he had made the arrangement with her boss, betting a Cuban cigar on a basketball game against an extra hour with Laura. He won. Laura thought that was charming, in a male sort of way. A couple of days later they decided to try a nighttime date. Jeff showed up with a beautiful bouquet.

"The flowers are very nice. The colors go together so well. Did you pick them out yourself?"

"I guess I should say yes, but honestly I asked a couple of the secretaries to get them on the way back from lunch. Then I wasn't real happy with them, so I took Muriel down with me to the florist and had her help pick out the rest.

Muriel is really good with colors. In fact, I brought a camera. Let me get a shot of you by the flowers. Sort of a first-real-date commemorative."

"I'm not too big into pictures. Besides it'll probably end up on the bulletin board at work. Where are we heading tonight?"

"I have us booked on the Riverboat for a dinner cruise. Actually they'll probably take a picture; I'll make sure they don't since you don't like them. It is such a nice night, I thought we'd spend a little time on the water."

"That sounds wonderful. I always wanted to do that. In fact, we were talking about it at work just the other day." Laura gives a questioning look.

"Just a lucky guess. I saw it on TV and the girl in the commercial looked like it should have been you. So now it will be you."

"That's sweet, I think. Haven't seen the commercial. Hope it wasn't Wilma Flintstone or something. Anyway, let's go."

They leave and get into Jeff's car.

"So tell me, if you could go anywhere in the world, where would it be?"

"Gee, I don't know. That sort of came out of nowhere. How about the Riverboat restaurant cruise?"

"Good answer. I think I'd go to the Greek Isles. I was thinking of going this fall actually."

"That sounds great. You should go. I don't get to go anywhere too much since a little trip after I graduated from college. Money's tight for a single girl. I sort of miss traveling. It was always one of my goals, but I've been too busy with student loans."

"Well, maybe that will change soon. I've got a lot of frequent flyer miles from the company sending me everywhere."

"Right now I don't see much changing. I can't even find the time to get my oil changed in my car. The inspection's overdue, it hasn't had a tune-up in almost a year, it's started to knock a little, and I can't find the time to get it anywhere."

"No biggie. I can have my mechanic come to work tomorrow and pick it up. He's good and cheap. Does it for me all the time. In fact, he does a lot of the gang down at the office. No worry."

"He picks it up at work. That's really cool. Can I call him?"

"Well, he knows me. I'll take care of it."

"You're just a regular knight in shining armor, aren't you?"

"Did'ya think I was going to let you be a damsel in distress too long? I'll see he has it ready for your 12:30 lunch."

"Oh, my schedule got shifted. I now have a 12:00 lunch."

"Damn, I just had mine adjusted to 12:30. I can get it switched back. Well, I'll see that it's ready by 12:00, then."

"Good thing I didn't tell you I was cold last winter, you'd be trapping little furry animals."

"If you were cold last winter . . ."

That night Jeff ordered the same thing to eat that Laura did. They danced and had a pretty decent time. Jeff wrote Laura a six-page letter after this date telling her how glad he was that he asked her out, and how much he liked the date. The next day he took care of her car, which had to be picked up at lunchtime, and another half-hour basketball bet. Laura didn't know what they were betting on. She didn't realize there was even a game on, and she's a real basketball fan. It wasn't basketball that Jeff was playing this time, and Laura wasn't a fan of his new game.

It is very nice when someone is attentive to us. It can lift our whole day if it is the right person, at the right time, in the right way. But when the attention starts to become a hard pill to swallow, you may be looking for the cure for a Red Flag.

There is a pitiful quality to anyone who wants so much to become dependent on another. We hear so much of the pitiful women whose dependency leads them to become perennial victims, blossoming every year in a new relationship that is abusive. Dependent men get less press because they tend to be less recognizable. They work hard to maintain one-way relationships that offer them little except the feeling of being attached. When one relationship ends they work very hard at finding another, so they may again survive. Being a Leech is not easy because you must partially destroy that which is feeding you. The man who is the Leech will destroy the exact relationship he so desires.

Dependency solves four very important life problems for the Leech. First, the Leech's self-esteem is highly tied into relationship needs. He cannot feel whole or complete until he is connected to someone in some intimate fashion. It is possible that he is very successful in many other parts of his life, but it is the relationship realm that controls most of his thoughts and, in essence, becomes the ultimate goal of his life. Without it, he truly cannot feel successful, and thus can never feel good about himself. Because of this lowered self-esteem, he is often willing to be a chameleon regarding his own desires, coloring himself to fit you and what you want. Alas, a chameleon is just a lizard that changes color when he is frightened, which may make many women's hearts jump, but not usually with amorous pulsation.

Second, dependency solves a problem for the Leech, who "lacks a life" and needs some infusion of excitement or maybe even close friendships. Guys that seem to have a lack of intimacy in other parts of their life, or perhaps have a too-close relationship with their mother, may tend to need this new woman to stimulate a change. Their regular life may have become very mundane, rutted, and they lack the sufficient motivation to change it for themselves. A new relationship can give them the motivation to change, since throughout their life it has been easier to do for others than for themselves.

Strongly connected to this may be their inability to dream about personal achievement without a person with whom to share accomplishments. The Leech may put everything on hold until he has a companion. No travel, making any major purchases, even buying new clothes, until he finds out what his future companion may want. Since men are so connected to their dreams, being unable to proceed makes them reach a desperation state and thus creates dependency behavior. Many men who are single and become obsessed with their work end up in this cycle where they save everything they make, waiting for the day when they can "come out of storage." They look around to attach, becoming a Leech to the next person they find. You feel you found a successful man in the place you'd least expect, like a sale at your favorite store. It was a sale all right, but the man you found this time is half-off.

Finally, dependency solves the problem of loneliness. Any professional who has worked with dependent women who end up in abusive relationships hears the same phrase: "I'd rather be miserable than be alone." Being truly comfortable living by oneself is a difficult state for most humans to learn to accept. In modern times, many individuals who live alone end up cohabitating on weekends after only a few dates. It's nice to wake up next to someone, to sleep side by side, to share a morning ritual. It is one of the most amazing parts of human nature to begin to recognize the ways humans will allow themselves to be demeaned, or will self-deprecate just not to be alone.

A major factor in many dependent men is an obsessiveness that makes them think constantly about something they want or something in which they are involved. They work out plans, build scenarios, go through conversations, build dreams—in essence live life before it occurs. It is exactly this obsessiveness that makes this a very difficult relationship to both maintain and/or dissolve.

Laura was a very understanding girl and thought she could overlook some of the desperate nature of her relationship with Jeff. They had some great times together, but he kept moving the relationship too fast. She felt strangled by his attentions and thought she needed to account for every moment of her day. This started to wear on her, until the pressure built so high that she started feeling very disorganized in her own life. By the time three months had come, Laura knew everyone Jeff had ever met, Jeff was introducing her as the girl he was going to marry, and Laura started to feel like a fake, like she was part of the audience in an infomercial. Although Laura became convinced she needed to break up the relationship after only three months, it took her six months to finally break it off because Jeff's reactions were so severe at the slightest hint of dissolution. Laura learned the principle of doubling: her therapy to get over the negative effects of the relationship lasted twice as long as the breakup.

If you want to give blood, call the Red Cross, don't let a Leech suck the life out of you. Latch on to this test if you have even the slightest suspicion you are possibly dating this Loser.

IS HE A LEECH?

Circle the number and add up the score

Family Background

Older brother that was very outgoing	1
Was mother's favorite	2
Family describes him as quiet when growing up	1

Work/School History

Doesn't seem satisfied with accomplishments, even when he has done well	2
Sets next goal quickly after achieving something	1
Likes mentoring, particularly having someone look up to him	1

Friendships

Seems to be willing to ignore friends completely for you	2
Stops all other social life without you	3
One of friend's wives is his closet female friend	1
Didn't like hanging out with friends if he wasn't a "couple"	3
All his friends know everything about you the first time you meet them	2

(test continues)

Past Relationships

Gets dumped in just about every past relationship	2
Past girlfriends describe him as a too nice guy or too dependent	4
Knows about what all of his ex's are doing	1

Body Language

Sits a little too close to you and is always facing you even when it isn't called for	1
Won't leave your side at a party	2
Starts copying your mannerisms	4

Dress/Hygiene

Goes out and immediately buys something new to wear or a new cologne when you say you like the way it looks	2
Seems like every outfit he owns some girl bought for him	1

Behavior

Tries to cut you off from friends	1
Offers to help you with your problems	1
Tries to accelerate the relationship	2
Calls two or three times a day	1
Calls four or more times a day	3
Wants a lot of pictures	2
Writes long letters to you between dates	3
Panics if you are late	1
Gives up work or another important activity just to do something you want (without telling you)	1
Changes daily schedule to meet with you, without telling you	1
Anything new you introduce him to becomes center of his life	3
Wants you to make all decisions on what to do	3
Buys you anything you say you want	2
Orders the same as you in a restaurant	1

Conversation

Tells you he dreams about you	1
Tells you he thinks about you all the time	2
Starts trying to talk like you	4
Talks like you've been together for a year after only a couple of dates	4
Talks about goals that he has included you in	3
Introduces you as the girl he is going to marry after only a few dates	4
Projects you into commercials, ads, movie roles, etc.	5

(test continues)

When Confronted

When asked to back off, he can't do it	4
Panics at the hint that you don't want to move at his pace	2
Breaks the limits you set when you ask him to call less	4

Your Impression

Seems a little shy about taking risks	1
Never seems to be comfortable	2
He tries too hard to fit in	2
You suspect his self-esteem is not very good	2
Seems like his life was on hold before you	2
You have become the center of his life very quickly	3
Ready to be your boyfriend after first date	2
Total Score	

Score 12 and lower: No reason for concern at this point
Score between 13 and 24: Yellow Flag—There's reason for caution
Score 25 and above: Red Flag—He's a bloodsucker; drain this one now

Don't Touch Your Nose with Krazy Glue on Your Fingers

If your new man falls in the Yellow Flag category, you've got a potentially sticky situation on your hands. Remember, leeches used to be used in medicine all the time and even now doctors will use a leech to relieve a congested infection if it is less invasive than other techniques available to them. Some moderate leeching could be good. You may be the type of person that wants someone a little dependent and attentive to you, so a Yellow Flag may not seem so bad. The key is to strike a level of comfort with this Leech so that he knows you're going to give the relationship a legitimate shot. Talk with him about taking the relationship slowly so you can enjoy every step of it. Set some limits on the number of calls you expect and the type of contact you like. As you make a low-self-esteem guy more comfortable, the Leeching should decrease a little and you may end up with someone who becomes a good partner. If Leeching seems to increase over time and exceeds your comfort level, be very careful; there is the strong possibility of it developing into a disastrous situation that will control every part of your life.

If your man falls in the Red Flag category, be aware you are in for a real problem if you stay. The longer you are around a Leech, the harder it will be to break up. The relationship will have a lot of good times and you may enjoy the security of knowing the guy is there for you, but the dependency will start to choke you. You will begin to lose your old life and begin to feel that you have to account for every part of your day. The Leech may question every one of your decisions, want to know your every move, and will never actually let you know what he really thinks. Your pity for his insecurity will turn into anger at his dependency. You will begin to think of him as less than a real man. Many women find they actually get a little abusive just trying to distance themselves from him. He will take your abusiveness as his fault and either apologize or send you flowers, making you feel even worse. You may begin to question yourself and finally find that you are losing your own identity. You will feel it. If you Krazy Glue your finger to your nose, you're gonna lose a little skin. Remember, Leeches survive by sucking the blood out of the host. You will watch the life drain out of you if you stay with this guy. Stay away and watch an old Dracula movie if you have a deep desire to make bloodcurdling screams. Vampires are better bloodsuckers, and most of the recent ones in the movies are better looking than any Leech anyway.

Breaking Free from Relationship Flypaper

You've got a major problem. This is one of those relationship breakups that you cannot delay. If you tend to procrastinate, tell a couple of friends to help keep you on track. You've got to do this as soon as you can, or else it will get stickier.

If you allow anything other than a complete breakup, you can use the principle of doubling. In other words, if you try to remain friends, it will take twice as long to break up as the time you spent in the relationship. You've got to do this one face-to-face and not after a date. Set aside a separate time when you will discuss the breakup. Realize you'll get the crying, begging, maybe a suicidal statement, offers to change, everything that he can throw at you not to ruin his life and dreams. Sometimes it is advisable to forewarn one of his close friends to be there with him after you tell him you don't want to see him anymore. Do not—do NOT—discuss reasons. Take the blame. You are not ready for this relationship. Period!!!! Do not talk about some other guy or you will create something for the Leech to obsess about. Expect that you will get a lot of phone calls, new ideas of how it can work, and a couple of letters. Ask the guy to please not make you have to turn into a bitch just to get rid of the relationship. Tell him you do not want to be friends because you think the close contact will make it too difficult. Do not initiate contact to find out how he is doing and try not to socialize with his friends. If you do, inform them that if he finds out, it will be hard on him. This will be painful, but it is the Band-Aid that has to be ripped off, not extracted slowly. He's probably got plenty of glue left in him and there will be another miracle cure elsewhere.

The Show-off

*Beneath the Colorful Tail of
the Peacock Lies Nothing More
than a Big Turkey*

Does size matter? It seems so in pheasants. The brightly colored male pheasant is adorned with fleshy face ornaments and spurs on his leg that look like thorns on a rosebush, only bigger. Both the ornaments and leg spurs attract a female. The leg spurs also help the pheasant fight to keep the female it has attracted. Sometimes pheasants will fight to the death. Female pheasants seemed to prefer cocks with big spurs! When researchers wanted to test this phenomenon, they created artificially long spurs for some of the less endowed fowl. Sure enough, it worked. The males with the biggest spurs got the most females. In the animal world it is called "display behavior." Male chimps swagger and shake tree branches. Roosters crow. Peacocks unfurl beautiful plumage. Pheasants grow big ones, or strap on big ones. The "strap on spurs" of man can be seen in the fancy cars, the gold chains, the annoying name-dropping, and anything else done for the purpose of attracting women. Men build their muscles, buy their toys, and do whatever they can to impress. They try to elongate their financial necks like a swan, but often underneath the show there is nothing more than an ugly duckling.

Judy's friends described him as a "good catch." They had met Larry at work. He came in on a temporary consulting assignment and impressed Judy's friends as rich and successful. They described him as a good-looking man who dressed impeccably and seemed to have an air of self-confidence. They knew Judy was *looking*, and arranged for the two to spend an evening together at an office party that was being held in a nice restaurant. Like many women, Judy did not like blind dates. But she was determined to "put the work" into meeting Mr. Right. She picked out an evening outfit just short of formal. Stylish in red and black. She believed it projected competence, independence, and sensuality, letting a man know up front that she was an independent woman who could take care of herself. She felt it put her on more even footing. She headed off to the restaurant with much determination.

Judy's friends met her at the door. Allison and LeeAnn each had that gleeful look of someone who believes she found you the perfect Christmas present. With some giggling and reassurance, they escorted her into the dining hall and approached a tall dark-haired man in a black pin-striped suit.

"You must be Judy. I'm Larry. Your friends told me such wonderful things about you."

"It is a pleasure, Larry."

Judy's friends disappeared into the crowd. Judy held out her hand, and Larry shook it, holding it for a couple extra seconds. He was perfectly groomed, every hair in place. His tie, expensive-looking silk, sported a diamond tie tack. On his wrist there was a gold ID bracelet and a large braided gold chain. He had at least two rings. Judy was never much for jewelry on a man, but she liked this look on him.

"So, Larry, my friends weren't clear on what you do for their company."

"Oh, I own my own reengineering firm. When companies get in trouble, they call me to set them straight. Don knew he'd better get some help, and so I'm onboard to show them how to get back on track."

"Who's Don?"

"Your friends' boss, the president of Alianico. He's pretty lucky too. I just finished a big job, or I wouldn't have been available. I'm really in demand now. Charging whatever I like and getting it!"

"Sounds like you're doing very well."

"It's good to be king."

"So what does the king do for fun?"

"Well, I like scuba diving. I went diving in the Cayman Islands a few months ago. I had a few days to kill between jobs and a friend flew me down in his private jet. Great trip! I should show you some pictures. I have them in the car."

"Let me guess—a Jaguar."

"Gotta have a car. That's quite perceptive, or did your friends tell you?"

"I think the gold Jaguar pin on your suit was a little hint. They don't make those for Sentras."

"Then we'll have to work on getting you a different car. I have friends who can make ridiculous deals on any car you want. For the cost of a Sentra we could put you in a 'power car.'"

"I think I'll wait on that until I get my scuba certification. Hate to put that wet gear in a Ferrari."

"That would be a shame. I've actually test-driven one of those a couple of times. So what do you do in your spare time?"

"Oh, nothing as exciting as jet-setting. I do some volunteer work at the Ronald McDonald house. Other than that, I like to see movies and the occasional play."

"Volunteer work is so noble. I don't have time for that, but there is always a large deduction for charities on my return. If you like movies I'm sure I can get us on the set of the new Woody Allen film they're doing."

"Really, you're just ready to jump in and help any way you can, aren't you? That would be interesting, though."

"Most women who date me get the opportunity to do things they have only dreamed about doing."

"I'm glad you're not bashful, Larry. Humility never becomes a man."

"Boy, you sure are pretty when you're being sarcastic."

"Keep bragging and you'll see more than sarcasm."

"Ooooh! You're a feisty little cat aren't you? Did I tell you about the time I went into a lion's cage with a lion tamer? I've got pictures of that too."

"No doubt you left them in your villa in the French Riviera."

"Actually, Italian Riviera. But the lion pictures are in my wallet. Let me show you. . . ."

Most men want to be proud of their possessions and accomplishments. In reality, what a man has achieved in the past is one reflection of who he is in the present. In a healthy individual, the things a man has done for himself can foreshadow his ability to contribute to a partnership. But if the man you are dating does more strutting than a rooster on Viagra in a brand-new hen house, you may be in the incubator, hatching a Red Flag!

Bragging is perhaps one of the most common things men do, especially in the beginning of a relationship. Men may use bragging to attract a woman. While this still stems from insecurity, it can be a less serious problem. Getting a woman's attention, starting a conversation, and presenting oneself in an interesting manner, all while facing the fear of rejection, is stressful for most men.

Bragging may be used to cover up these perceived inadequacies. If a man can get you focused on his accomplishments, you may not notice his defects. To some extent, we are all insecure and looking for ways to prove ourselves. Our possessions and accomplishments are concrete things that we can display like trophies. The more insecure, the greater the desire to lead with the display case. For men, there are a lot of other peacocks with bigger and more colorful tails, and worse yet, pheasants with bigger spurs.

For the Show-off, bragging is a way of life. These men are often unreachable in the context of a relationship. Transcending insecurity, the Show-off sees himself only through the things and accomplishments he has acquired. He has no depth, and connecting with him on an emotional basis is a frustratingly impossible task. The Show-off forms relationships with women who can either be viewed as trophies themselves or serve as an audience for their achievements. These men are unlikely to change. They don't want to, don't know how to, and don't think they should. Stay away.

What do women find attractive about the Show-off? In the long-term, not much. In the beginning, the prospect of associating with fame and fortune has a certain fantasy appeal. The man may come across as interesting. In fact, he may really be interesting. His possessions and money may be a break from the ordinary. The places he frequents can offer an interesting change of pace. But in the end, most of us like to spend our time with people who make us feel good, and the Show-off does not qualify.

Egged on by friends looking for a vicarious thrill, Judy went out with Larry a number of times. She got to ride in a fancy sports car. She learned exactly how much sports cars cost. She got to dine in fancy restaurants. She learned the names of the owners, the chef, how much the restaurant cost, who financed it, its weekly intake, break-even points, and how her Show-off was partially responsible for the restaurant's success. She got to see them film some of that Woody Allen movie. She flew in a private plane, drove a speedboat, even went backstage at one of the plays she attended.

What she didn't get to do was be herself. Larry was too busy bragging to notice her, anyway. She was a warm body with a nod, a smile, and a vocabulary that he wanted limited to: "Oh, wow!" As for Larry, she didn't really know him. She knew about his things, about his accomplishments, about the famous people he had met, but she did not know *him*. She was not sure there was a *him* to know. When she looked at him, she imagined a big furry sheepdog that, once sheared, might be nothing but a scrawny mutt.

By the time Judy broke up with Larry she felt there was no relationship depth, so there was no pain. She tried hard to get close to him, but he kept running away from intimacy. He was too insecure and scared. The only ones disappointed seemed to be her friends. They had enjoyed hearing about Judy's glamorous dates with the Show-off. They focused on the expensive items and lavish places he took her. Judy was happy to entertain her friends with an interesting tale. But enough was enough. If her friends needed entertainment, they could see a movie. When it came to intimacy, this peacock was just plain chicken. She plucked the last life out of the relationship with a "Dear Larry" letter.

The test below is designed to help you see if your relationship is running foul.

IS HE A SHOW-OFF?

Circle the number and add up the score

Family Background

Is an only child	2
Parents were demanding	1
Grew up in overindulged household	3
Grew up in deprived household	3
Parents compared him with his siblings	2
Had high-achieving older siblings	2

(test continues)

Work/School History

Brags about his alma mater	2
Exaggerates accomplishments in school	2
Brags about achievements at work	2
Exaggerates importance of position at work	2

Friendships

Brags about friends' jobs, possessions, positions of power	2
Does not seem to do a lot with friends	3
When you meet his friends they do not seem as close to him as he described	3

Past Relationships

Brags about the women he has dated	3
Unclear as to reason past relationships did not work out	2

Body Language

Flexes muscles a lot, stretches a lot	2
Looks at himself frequently in mirrors/other reflective substances	3
Eyes dart around looking at people or objects	2

Dress/Hygiene

Sharply dressed	1
Lets you know he is sharply dressed	2
Tells you brand names of clothing	2
Tells you prices of clothing	3
Overdressed for date	1
Wears a lot of jewelry	1
Constantly adjusting clothes	1
Hair perfectly groomed	1
Spends time readjusting hair	2

Behavior

Takes you to flashy or expensive places	1
Takes you to "hot" or talked about places	2
Takes you to sophisticated places	2
Knows chef/owner/staff of places he takes you	2
Makes sure you know he knows the owner and why	2

(test continues)

Conversation

Talks about his possessions	1
Virtually gives you an inventory of his possessions	3
Tells you brand name of his possessions	2
Tells you why his possessions are superior	3
Talks about income	1
Alludes to amount of income	2
Tells you amount of income	3
Puts down people with lesser incomes	4
Talks about accomplishments	1
Humorous stories where he can make fun of himself	−1
Humorous stories where he is victorious	1
Nonhumorous stories where he is victorious	2
Never-ending stories that blend together	2
Responds to your conversation	
With admiration and questions	−1
With examples of similar things he has done	1
With one-upmanship of things he has done better	3
Name-drops	
Occasionally	1
Annoyingly	2
Seems to know everyone of importance in the world	3

When Confronted

Apologizes and admits to being partially wrong	−1
Shows insight into behavior	−2
Gets defensive and questions your motives	2
Continues same behavior without regard to your confirmation	2

Your Impression

Comes across as braggart	3
Seems to be covering insecurity through bragging	2
Seems to use bragging to avoid intimacy	2
Total Score	

Score 15 and lower: No reason for concern at this point
Score between 16 and 30: Yellow Flag—There's reason for caution
Score 31 and above: Red Flag—You've got a turkey; cook his goose

Is This Goose Cooked?

Showing off is probably the oldest and most common negative trait seen in males. (Leaving the toilet seat up had to wait for the invention of the toilet.) So a Yellow Flag is not necessarily a cause for alarm. Some minor bragging and showing off is almost to be expected. It is genetically determined. Men are raised to be competitive. They have been taught that their role is one of provider. They have been instructed that their responsibility as a male in a relationship includes problem solving and protecting the family unit. They want to prove that they are up to this task.

Showing you what they have been able to acquire, how well they can compete in the marketplace, and what they can do to solve problems, is part of the male courting ritual. When the healthy male shows off, it is an invitation into his world. After all, if he is not competent and capable, why would you want him?

After a few dates look for this behavior to diminish. It will still pop up, but only occasionally. His behavior will round out and he will be willing to share some of his weaknesses and failings. He will really let you into his world, and want to move into yours. Don't expect him to hide his achievements in the sand. He'll still want you to see him as competent and capable. That's good, healthy self-esteem. If this doesn't happen, set the timer on the relationship oven. The bird is getting done quickly.

A man who falls into the Red Flag category is no longer involved in typical male courtship behavior. His showing off and bragging are not an invitation to join into a partnership. It's just the opposite. His acquisition of money and glory help him to keep the world at bay. Very insecure underneath his plumage, the Show-off is afraid to let you in. Accomplishments and possessions have become narcotic. He became an addict years ago. Each acquisition, each dollar, each celebrity whose name he can drop, whispers in his ear that he is okay. More than okay, better, perhaps even the best. All the Show-off has to do is make sure people see only the outside. The inside is not decorated as nicely. It's your turn in the game of Duck, Duck, Goose and you're out of ducks. Run!

Get the Flock Out of There

Though it might be tempting to tell him you conferred with the United Nations on this breakup, don't. No reason to stoop to his level. Besides, he's just being himself, whatever that may be at this time. Don't bring his bragging into it. It is unlikely he sees himself this way, and it is not your job to change him. Whether over dinner, in a letter, or on the phone, tell him that your time with him has been interesting and memorable. He'll believe you. Tell him that you are looking for a different lifestyle than the one he lives. You can't keep up with him. While it was nice being with him, you see your future going in a different direction. When he points out that you will never meet anyone like him, acknowledge this to be true. Do not say, "And I hope I don't." Repeat that you are looking for someone different. When he asks what that difference is, you can honestly say someone who is more conventional.

Don't expect the Show-off to be happy about this breakup. He does like to get his way. Inside he knows he wasn't close to you, but he figures that's your fault. He will probably tell others that he dumped you. No problem, you know the truth. He'll fill his life with adventure and find a new trophy to let her hair flow from the passenger seat of his sports car. There's always another female pheasant who will fall for his huge strap on spurs. Polly want a cracker?

The Player

Floats Like a Butterfly, Stings Like a Bee; Tell Him to Buzz Off

In southern France, northern Spain, and northern Italy they were called the troubadours. In northern France during the twelfth to fourteenth centuries, they were trouvères, groups of traveling lyric poet/singers, who found great favor with the aristocratic feudal courts and eventually the middle class as well. The troubadours were prized for the originality of their metaphor. The trouvères were prized for their abilities to use traditional themes and cliché phrases, giving pleasure from familiarity rather than originality. The function was the same, relating stories of love intended to woo the ladies and entertain all who listened. Their creative work did much to develop the literature and music of France, but it should be known they sang the same songs over and over, just constantly moving around to find a different audience. The modern version of the troubadours and trouvères has become much more base: men who repeat the same stories to entertain and woo women, moving from person to person. Like the trouvères, a lot of clichés roll off their tongues, but for some reason the poetry is missing in their approach. It may not surprise you to know that few of these modern-day Players have made a strong study of French lyric art.

Eric was as smooth as a freshly detailed Jaguar when he introduced himself and handed Pam a note. They were sitting a couple of tables away at a bistro. Pam was having dinner with her family, Eric with a male friend. Singles tend to notice each other in a restaurant, so Pam had studied Eric a little before he approached. The note was very basic: "I don't usually do this but I had to take a chance that you might be single. I was drawn to your smile and your very cute ways. It was quite a pleasant disruption to my meal. My name is Eric. I would rather talk to you than dream of you. Please call, 555-1616." Taken by Eric's charm and silky boldness, Pam called and set up a date. Eric said he was a cop, so she felt safe. It didn't hurt that he had major blue eyes, either.

"That was quite bold of you to hand me a note in front of my parents. I would jump out of a plane before I'd do that to a guy in a restaurant."

"When I was a kid I used to love the movie *Pinocchio*. I used to listen to the record over and over. You know what song got me the most?"

Pam pauses for a second. "I don't know . . . 'Dad, I Want a Nose Job'?"

Eric almost cuts Pam off. " 'When You Wish Upon a Star.' It let me know that everything good in life starts with a dream, with a wish. I learned that the most important thing in life was to dream and then act. Even if it gets you in trouble, like it did Pinocchio, you have to act. Pinocchio got to be a real boy. He got his wish. I always act on my dreams."

"So you were seeing stars in that restaurant. I thought you had a table away from the window." Pam laughs at her own wittiness.

"I saw the only star I needed to see, and that was your smile." Eric notices Pam's face being a little suspicious. "So I'm

a little corny. I guess I'm still a little kid when it comes to believing in dreams coming true. You like Disney?"

"Yeah. I think my favorite Disney movie is *Beauty and the
Beast*. I just think it is so charming when Belle says to . . ."

"You must have done some theater or some modeling. You
have the greenest eyes. You must have done some modeling."

"Just for my mirror. I had to try on about thirty different
outfits before . . ."

"If you ever want to try, I know some people that could
probably help you. It starts with a dream. I really think you can
make anything happen that you can dream about. I heard this
great joke for the first time today."

Eric proceeds to tell a very funny joke that seems well re-
hearsed. He laughs at the joke after he tells the punch line
and in the middle where it is a little funny, almost as if helping
it be funny. He picks up with the conversation while Pam is
laughing.

"So turnabout is fair play. Why did you call after getting this
letter from a mysterious stranger?"

"I saw it as a great opportunity to bum a free meal. Don't
get that much these days." Eric laughs briefly at Pam's line.
Then gets a hurt-little-boy look on his face.

"Gee, I thought we were going to hold hands and play on
the swing set after we ate. But all you want is the food."

"I thought all you cops did was chase little boys and girls
away from the park after dark."

"Nah, sometimes we watch. Depends on how little they are.
Yesterday I was making this arrest . . ."

Eric goes into another very funny cop story where he ends
up saving the day after a series of bungles. After the story is
over Pam makes an observation.

"Cops always seem to have a lot of fun at work."

"You gotta live every moment. You never know what could
happen. That's why you have to dream."

"You're not going to break into song, are you?"

Eric told more stories as they sat there that night. In some he was the dupe and able to laugh at himself, in some he was the hero achieving almost superhuman feats. He kept complimenting Pam on everything from her smile to her teeth to her taste in clothes. There was never a dull or awkward moment.

It is always wonderful when a conversation can flow effortlessly from one topic to the next. A lack of clumsiness may seem a good sign, but on the first couple of dates clumsiness is almost sacred. It is expected. If the first few dates' conversation seems as canned as a ten-year-old tin of SpaghettiOs, you may be opening the lid on a Red Flag.

Most men are drawn toward games when they are young. Whether a boy is better at kickball or hits the baseball farther often determines the male pecking order in elementary school. Ability at games is venerated in the preadolescent. As women's sports become a central part of female development, we notice that girls also respect game ability in other girls but still don't revere it in the way boys do. As men achieve better game abilities, they also increase their confidence level. Confidence is attractive in males, further encouraging the better game players to take risks. The more confidence, the more important gaining the proper technique to win at games becomes, to maintain a level of ability. Better technique creates even better abilities. Thus, the game ability cycle self-perpetuates.

As boys get older, the types of games that are revered begin to include the ability to attract women. The trophies change from cast human miniatures atop gaudy fake-gold pedestals to life-size flesh figures on pedestals of fantasy. The "home run" describes not only the addition of a point toward a team goal, but rounding the bases with the local Marilyn Monroe, Heather Locklear, or Pamela Lee. Boys again realize that to be the better Player at this new challenge, they must develop method. The proper love technique is the Holy Grail that will make him unstoppable.

Yes, there is a technique to dating successfully, depending on your view of success. Suave and debonair is traditionally what a man views as successful—having the right lines, making a woman feel special, like a real woman. Psychological research suggests women rate a sense of humor as the most highly valued personality trait in a male. Make a woman laugh and she loosens up, you have a better chance. Confidence is second highest. Many men know this instinctually, so they are willing to sacrifice the spontaneity that would come from interaction for the success that can come from a more organized approach, a technically more precise approach. In their approach they have set jokes, set ways to demonstrate their confident self.

As they become more successful, they gain real confidence in their technique. They start to be identified by their peers as a great Player, and enjoy the recognition of their special art. Often these Players work in jobs where there is a male-oriented social group and unspoken social rules that determine a hierarchy. Success in gaining the favors of women is greatly admired. They may study the techniques of great lovers in movies, almost believing they are a Bond—James Bond—in modern form. They dig into your fantasies and your dreams of being a Bond girl, or your dreams of being the best you can be, your fantasy self. They make you feel good about being you, make you laugh, make you believe in yourself. Compliments, great humor, stories of intrigue—swept away on a cloud of possibility, you form a different kind of "bond," and usually get the double-0 without the seven.

Pam felt wonderful after the first couple of dates with Eric. They were a lot of fun, held surprises, and, most importantly, Pam felt she could be herself, and that did a lot for her self-esteem. Eric was very much what she was looking for in a guy, a manly type of man, and she started dreaming that she had found the shining armor dude who would rescue her from the dating scene.

After the initial relationship surge, Pam started to notice

that their time together was dwindling away. Eric always had a great story behind his new lack of time; often he seemed to be doing something important or living up to a commitment or some other commendable activity. She knew he'd settle down as they started to get closer; that is, until Pam and Eric went to a wedding of one of Pam's close friends.

Eric showed up late as usual, and in the middle of the reception he seemed a little on edge. When Eric went up to get a drink, a girl that Pam used to go out to clubs with came over to her and started asking questions about Eric. At first, Pam thought this girl was just admiring her boyfriend, but after the questions got more personal, the other girl told Pam that Eric had been in clubs a lot and had been hitting on mutual acquaintances as recently as last night. When Pam confronted Eric, he joked with the line, "Guess I'm snagged." Pam didn't want to leave it at that, so he started being more emphatic. He responded, "Look, babe, I didn't make any commitments to you. I don't see a ring on your finger." Pam did not catch the bouquet, but she did catch a ride home with someone else.

Just like the troubadours and trouvères, the Player knows the themes you want to hear, the metaphors that will weave a warm woolen sweater around your heart. Before you swoon for the poetry of these roving serial gigolos, perhaps you'll want to put your date to the following test.

IS HE A PLAYER?

*Circle the number and
add up the score*

Family Background

Competitive relationship with brother	2
Only boy with older sister	1
Family is very into appearances, from parents to children	3

(test continues)

Work/School History

Very sports-oriented in high school	2
Dated a lot in high school	2
Dated the prettiest and most popular girls in high school	3
Works in a testosterone-centered workplace (locker-room mentality)	3

Friendships

Male friends are very party-oriented	2
Male friends tend to meet a lot of new women and few seem to stick	3
Male friends have a number of groups of women to play around with	3
Male friends have a set social pattern of getting together on weekends (meet at the firehouse, dorm, certain bars)	2
Male friends have signals designed to inform the others to back off someone they are interested in	4
Male friends have many inside jokes or their own language dealing with women	2
Male friends make signs behind a girl's back when they are doing well on a pickup	4
Friends tell stories of "girls of the past" or "wild times" openly	4
Male friends make bets on success with women	5

Past Relationships

Usually the "dumper" in past relationships	3
A large number of short-term relationships	2
Doesn't want to talk about past	1
Never says anything negative about past relationships	1
Acts real modest about past relationships	1

Body Language

Very forward, relaxed, and too open	1
Grabs hand or arm very early in acquaintance as part of conversation	2
Hands on other parts of your body early	3
Closes personal space early	3
Puts arm around you very early	2

Dress/Hygiene

Clothes designed to show off best body features	2
Spends a lot of time on hair grooming	3
Has the purposely unshaven look or similar unique grunge/relaxed look	3
Works hard at unique facial hair	2

(test continues)

Behavior

Plays the little boy routine, asks you to take care of him	3
Sets a very romantic scene	1
After first few dates seems to come and go a lot, never sure when he'll show up	3
Repeats himself a lot after a couple of dates or does same actions over again	2
Will try to show you he is your fantasy guy whenever you tell him what you like in men	3

Conversation

Seems to know what to say without thinking	1
Positive about everything, like a motivational speaker	2
Uses a lot of clichés	3
Uses repeating phrases to appear motivational	4
Jokes are very well rehearsed	2
Never leaves a quiet moment	3
Has stories with a lot of excitement, where he is the hero or the goat	4
Has a lot of jokes on tap	2
Has stories that lead to "guiding principles" of his life	3
Brings up the hurt of relationship breakup	2
Compliments excessively	1
Seems like he is listening almost too intently	1

When Confronted

Totally denies being a player	1
States that he was a player once but has changed	3
Starts complimenting you as soon as you confront him	3
Says he can walk away if you'd like	3

Your Impression

You are a consumable	4
You are highly attracted but know he is wrong for you	4
You know he is not the committed type, but maybe he'll change	5
He'll always be a lot of fun, especially in bed	4
	Total Score

Score 13 and lower: No reason for concern at this point
Score between 14 and 24: Yellow Flag—There's reason for caution
Score 25 and above: Red Flag—Don't play with matches like this one; go home a winner

Singing the Lyrics Does Not Mean You Feel the Music

If the guy you are seeing falls in the Yellow Flag category, you need to move to the information-gathering mode first, then the confrontation mode. This guy is going to try to look very sincere and caring about everything because he suspects that is what you want him to be in your fantasy. Bring the conversation into the very sincere mode and see if he knows what he is talking about. Talk about the sincere work he may say he is doing and ask pointed informational questions to see if he has the answer. If he tells you he works with children who are terminally ill in his spare time, see if he knows where the office of the Make-A-Wish Foundation or the local hospitals that work with these children are. See if his knowledge goes beyond the normal saw-a-show-on-cable-TV variety.

Players try to see more than one person at a time, making up elaborate stories for why they are busy. Check out what he is doing on the days he is not seeing you. Call at the last minute and see if he'd like you to join him on his philanthropic missions. Call him at work when he cancels a date with you because of work, and see if his work buddies make up an excuse for why he can't talk to you. The guy that says he is doing volunteer work or working on an emergency problem at the office and is really at the clubs or with someone else will leave a trail of Liars (see Red Flag #1). If you strongly suspect his sincerity, lay it out for him. Be in control when you do. Lay down a couple of things you won't let happen, like being lied to and played for a fool. If he is truly insincere, he will either try too hard to prove he is for real or he won't call again. As with all Yellow Flag situations, always be a little distant until you are satisfied intellectually, not emotionally, that you don't have a Player.

If the Red Flag personality has come through on this test, you've got a Player. It's time for this Loser to find a different sandbox. If he's a great lover and you want to keep him

around, do not get attached. Instead, just make him an occasional "stop, drop, and roll" and keep looking for someone
with some emotional depth. Treat him like elevator music,
something to keep the silence away. Getting attached to this
person will lead to many nights of disappointment and eventually being made a fool of when you are told "there was really
never a commitment." Remember, the goal of the Player is
success in the game as seen by other men. The only way he
can guarantee that is to share his experiences with the other
boys. Your sexual relationship becomes a spectator sport to
be shared on darts night, bowling night, between innings,
or while switching the triple-X-rated movies on the stag-night
VCR. After a breakup, many of his friends may admit to you
what a jerk he was with the hope of repeating some of the
same activities they heard about in such great detail. Respect,
by the way, will not be one of the activities they wish to engage in. Unless your idea of being a sex symbol is being a
poster child for those bad blonde jokes, you'll want to pass on
these future offers.

Pulling the Plug on Karaoke Romance

If your *emotions* run along the lines of getting revenge, you
are quite normal. You've been used! This is a bad situation
and that guy should be stopped. If your *actions* run along the
lines of getting revenge, you are heading for major trouble because you are at too great a disadvantage. Remember, the
worse you make him look, the dumber you look. If you try to
convince everyone that he was so obviously a Player, people
will ask, Why'd you date him in the first place? Why did you
have expectations? The more fuss you make, the more the
men will be wowwed at his ability to control women. The next
logical step is to have everyone painting you as a "psycho,"
which will be quite easy to do because you will have to esca-

late your behavior just to get people to listen to you. You are not in a winning situation. If you conduct yourself with dignity after you find out he's a jerk, you will obtain the only victory left to you. The better you act, the worse he looks for taking advantage of you. Your only chance to exact small amounts of revenge is much after the breakup. Tell anyone who asks what to expect from this Player.

Once you've made the decision to break up, it must be focused and involve no contact. He may work very hard to try to win you back, probably using sex as bait if that was a good part of your relationship. Do not get involved in talking about looking for a commitment; do not tell him that you were just using him; do not tell him he is a Player. This is not a great debate but a breakup of a relationship. The Player is one of the few Losers for whom it may be useful to try to put off with lines like "I'm going away for a month" or "I have to focus on work right now, call me in a month." Maybe you can say you just want to be friends right now, you can't get involved. Then, do not return his calls and get off the phone immediately if he calls and you pick up ("I'm sorry I can't talk now, I'm not alone"). There is no possibility of damaging his ego, you can't reach into another galaxy, where his ego resides. Romance to him is karaoke: he does not make the music, he just sings the words. Rest assured you will be replaced quicker than an inkless pen, cleaned out quicker than a mud stain on his low-riding jeans, and he will replenish his tank as easily as driving into the full-service gas line. Most important, your heart will no longer be hanging in a wood-paneled lodge, the trophy of a man who considers slaying feminine trust and optimism a great hunt.

The Sex Guzzler

*The Way to Your Heart Is
Not Through Your Pants*

Chanoyu, better known as the Japanese tea ceremony, is a lusciously rich tradition that focuses a person on the four principles of the tearoom: harmony (*wa*), reverence (*kei*), purity (*sei*), and tranquility (*jaku*). It is a tradition of cleansing, setting an environment, and enjoying the senses that seem long lost in the impatient society of today. There is tradition in the way the hands are cleansed, the way the tea is prepared, the treatment of the tools and the pot for making tea. The tea comes as a reward at the end of the ceremony, after the soul has been cleansed; *wa, kei, sei,* and *jaku* have been established; and the more wondrous parts of the inner universe have been opened. Women particularly have found that the calming effects of an hour or two in *chanoyu* can have weeks of calming effects on their lives, giving them more patience and a better appreciation of their day-to-day activities. Healthy dating is similar to a tea ceremony with many rituals that are observed to bring about comfort and closeness. Many men, however, believe the lower rewards should come slightly ahead of the acts of the soul, heart, or any higher parts of the anatomy. Tea now, principles later. After all, why worry about washing your hands, boiling the water, using the right pottery, and all that other jazz when you could just pick up a Snapple on the way to a ball game. For some reason, women don't seem to report the same calming effects from the male dating rituals as the traditional *chanoyu*.

There was something sexy about Rob when Anne met him at a club. He had a confidence about him that women often found attractive. His first words to her were "You're killing me with that dress," and from there they struck up a conversation. Usually, Anne was not very optimistic about meeting the right kind of guy in this setting, but there was something quite unusual about Rob. She felt immediately comfortable. He wasn't afraid to be exactly himself.

"I'm just getting over one of those breakups. You know the ones that just stick with you wherever you go. We've all had them."

"Breakup? Not me. Men just fall at my feet and beg. Never gets to me." Anne laughs at her own sarcasm. "What happened, Rob?"

"Nothing really bad. We just wanted different things out of life. We had great times together. Some really great times. I'm just feeling sorry for myself."

"Yeah, I went through one of those recently. My boyfriend had a real hard time staying faithful. I knew I should have gotten a cocker spaniel instead."

"We men are such jerks. We don't know what we have when we've got it. I can't imagine cheating on someone that looks like you."

"Yeah, imagine that, a hot chick like me." Anne laughs. "Even the girls on *Melrose Place* get cheated on and they're just like me. I guess I was a little too boring for him."

"Well, variety is the spice of life, but that doesn't mean you have to change partners. After all, you just have to be more creative in bed. I mean, I can see you've got a little wild side in you. No reason to go elsewhere if you've got that. People just need to have more fun in bed, keep the right perspective. I can't believe I'm talking this way to someone I just met. You've got one of those beautiful faces that makes a guy just want to tell everything."

Rob softly touches Anne on the elbow as he offers to buy her a drink. She accepts. He leans a little closer when he makes the drink offer just so he's sure she'll hear him, then stays closer when she retreats.

"So, Rob, sounds like you're a little on the rebound."

"Nah, I'm over it really. Can't cry over the spilled stuff, you know. Back in the old days this would set me on a binge, you know, partying all the time, drinking too much. No more. I'm getting too old for that."

"Partying all the time sounds better than a sharp stick in the eye. Besides, you don't seem so old."

"I didn't say I'm too old for everything, but I sure have slowed up from the ten times a night stud I used to be. Just kidding, I'm lucky if it's ten times a year."

"Only ten times a night. You must be starting after two in the morning."

"I knew there was a wild side. What about you? Your guy sticking to those pretty ribs?"

"Nah, he was a loser. Didn't talk much, didn't listen much after a while, either."

"Well, there's no relationship if you don't relate."

"I should have seen it coming. I have no sense of when I'm putting my heart in danger."

"Now don't be getting that attitude. Life is about taking risks. You've got to go for it, give your all, then get up and try again if it doesn't work. You've got to jump back in there. You've got too much going for you. You have a great personality, a good sense of humor, and you're about a twenty-five on a ten-point scale. You're going to find a guy who won't be able to get enough. He'll be keeping you up for weeks at a time."

"Imagine how much concealer I'd have to use on my eyes then. If that happens, you should buy some stock in Maybelline."

"If!! What do you mean if? You've gotta make it happen. You could have your choice of any guy in here. Any of us would drink your bathwater. Remember you've gotta take risks."

"You obviously haven't seen my bathwater."

A healthy sex life is an important part of any good relationship. And on the average, men do have stronger desires to push that part of a relationship early. But when the topic of sex in your conversation gets more copy than a scandal in the royal family gets in an English tabloid, you are bowing to the throne of a Red Flag.

If tea didn't have some tasteful thirst-quenching qualities, we'd be burning tea leaves instead of steeping them; and, if sex wasn't a pleasant human activity, there would be very few babies around. But as in the tea ceremony, much of the relaxation and lasting pleasure from tea can be lost if the only intent is to guzzle. Relationships that guzzle sex tend to offer very little lasting quality as well. The Sex Guzzler is only around as long as the sex is fresh and new.

For the Sex Guzzler, the sex is the only thing he's interested in about a relationship, and usually he'll let you know that early. Some women just don't listen hard enough because they may be missing that kind of attention. The Sex Guzzler knows that women have sexual frustrations and fantasies and uses that as the cornerstone of his approach to making a woman feel like she is getting close to him. The Sex Guzzler lacks the capacity for real intimacy. His only goal is to give a woman enough attention and excitement to keep her around and available to him. At first, he creates variety by trying new sexual techniques, later the variety is created by finding a new partner. Women often feel these types of men leave unexpectedly, at the peak of closeness, not realizing they were never really close to them at all.

The Sex Guzzler can appear very similar to the Player (Red Flag #9), but there are some basic differences. The Player's goal is not only sex, but the surrender of a woman, making the woman fall in love. It builds his ego. The Sex Guzzler wants either a one-night stand or to make a woman a sex slave so she will do anything he wants. There is no desire to control the woman's interest or make the woman fall in love, except toward the goal of enslaving her to sex. The Player focuses on charming a woman only to increase his ability to manipulate her. The Sex Guzzler focuses on eliciting sexual passion or sexual experimentation. To the Player, romance is a game and he will work on one woman until she gives in. To the Sex Guzzler, sex is an imperative, a fix, and he will move on very quickly if he is not getting what he thinks he needs.

In the movie *9 1/2 Weeks*, Mickey Rourke played one version of this type of Loser. He kept a woman captive to her own sexual desires but never really told her anything about himself. He would make her crawl and beg for sex, drip candle wax over her naked body, bring in other partners, engage every whim and fantasy. When you try to get closer to him, the relationship is over. There is no desire to have anything more, no feeling that doesn't start below the belt.

Anne got entrapped by Rob and started spending a lot of time with him in a fantasy-type of sexual relationship. She confronted him a couple of times on the fact that he didn't like to hold her after sex. In fact, he preferred that she sleep in another room. When they were at her house, he would leave almost immediately after sex. At first, her self-esteem had a positive jolt from the idea that she could have such a fantasy man, then as he became less and less involved in her personally, her self-esteem took a nosedive. Yet she stayed.

Anne planned for Rob to meet her parents during a holiday gathering at her parents' home. He reluctantly agreed three weeks before, but Anne felt a little uncomfortable about his reaction to the suggestion. She put it out of her mind. They had a great three weeks of sex and Anne was sure the holidays were not an issue. The day before, Rob told her he wasn't going, indicating that he didn't want to meet her parents because he didn't want to have to live up to their expectations. When Anne questioned what expectations he was talking about, she was informed that their relationship wasn't leading anywhere but was just a fun thing. She cried most of that holiday season, but Anne was good at turning a negative into a positive. Holidays provide a lot of good comfort food, and no matter how big the FDA labels were about nutritional value, Anne had no guilt eating months' worth of two-hour sessions at the gym.

If you wish your man had an FDA label, try giving him this test before you get too involved.

IS HE A SEX GUZZLER?

Circle the number and add up the score

Due to similar patterns on test #9, score test #9 first, if the score on test #9 was:	
In the Yellow Flag range	7
In the Red Flag range	10
Family Background	
Spoiled by mother	1
Mother rejected or was too busy for him	5
Mother is dominated by father	2
Mother has low self-esteem	2

(test continues)

Work/School History

Covered in test #9	—

Friendships

Has reputation as a major womanizer	4
Talks about how all men are out for only one thing	2

Past Relationships

History of not being faithful (may be hard to discover)	5
Talks about past relationships' sex lives	3

Body Language

You find him looking you over a couple of times throughout the evening	3

Dress/Hygiene

Flashy dress	2
Gold jewelry, rings, neck chains, and bracelets	2

Behavior

Touches you very quickly on the first date and frequently	2
Rubs your skin on first date before he should	3
Makes you feel comfortable discussing anything	2
Insists on your drinking at his cost	2
Tends to drink a lot himself	2

Conversation

False modesty about sexual experience	1
No modesty about sexual experience	4
Talks about life being an adventure and the need to takes risks	2
Relates to relationship woes, hinting that he is better	3
Brings up sexual matters early in first meeting, sneaks it into conversation	3
Compliments excessively and in generalities about sexual attraction	2
Talks about your "wild side" or your fantasies	4
Gives you credit when you don't deserve it	2
Talks about significant drug or alcohol history in his past that has changed	3
Talks about how wild he was in the past	4
Relates incidents of sexual exploration early in dating	4
Dates centered on sexual situations	5

(test continues)

When Confronted	
Says you can leave anytime if you don't like the way he treats you	2
Tries to stop you from leaving by controlling you sexually	5
Your Impression	
Unsure he wants more than just sex	4
Feel like he is trying to control you	3
Seems too charming	2
Total Score	

Score 18 and lower: No reason for concern at this point
Score between 19 and 29: Yellow Flag—There's reason for caution, don't get drawn in
Score 30 and above: Red Flag—He wants you to put out; put him out

Obsession and Confusion Both End the Same

If you've got the Yellow Flag from your man on this test, it's time to experiment. Start making sure he wants to be part of your life by constantly inviting him to places with you and asking a lot of questions about his life. See if he wants to be included in your life or tries to remain outside. See if he includes you in his life or tries to remain a mystery. Don't tell him it is important to you; see if he does it naturally. Some girls actually tell a guy they can't have sex for a couple of weeks for medical reasons, then see if the guy still hangs around as much. It's not really lying because the medical reason is your mental well-being. This is one of those guys that you have to constantly reassess. Experiment a little and give him a post-test.

If you found a Red Flagger, then you need to decide what you want and what you are capable of at the time. Before embarking on any analysis of this type of man you should make a good assortment of your perceived needs, feelings, and ability to pigeonhole your life. If you want a wild sexual experience and can keep your distance without wanting more of a relationship, you shouldn't even bother testing for the Red and Yellow Flags. Be honest with your abilities to keep your distance and only react after you've assessed yourself.

A good Sex Guzzler will draw you into his world and can make you like him. You can start to become obsessed with the sex and care little for other things in your life. If you start to find yourself confused or losing a sense of responsibility for other things, you may be becoming a Guzzler yourself. This is definitely the time to get out. If you start becoming obsessed with trying to get information about him that he hasn't been willing to share, it's time to get out. If you become obsessed and confused about why he isn't wanting more from the relationship and keep trying to get him to make more of a commitment of affection for you, then it is time to get out. This is one of the hardest Losers for you to make the decision to leave, but it is important that you do it as early in the connection as you can. The longer you're a Guzzler, the more time you will need to spend in detox.

Take a Run from the Wild Side

There are few things more obvious than how to get rid of this guy. It is so simple: shut him off. Let him know that you won't be having sex with him again for a while, until your relationship builds further emotionally. He will stick it out for a couple of weeks, but then he'll be gone. However, many women can't stick it out, particularly if it has been a great sexual experience. If you find cutting off the sex too difficult, then you must take further steps.

Invite him to meet your parents, your friends, ask him to become a greater part of your life outside the bedroom (living room, coffee table, kitchen floor, etc.). Demand to meet his parents and friends. If he goes along with that then it is time to have a relationship talk, putting some demands on him. If he is a true Sex Guzzler, he will say yes at first, figuring he can get a few more weeks out of you, then he will start backing out of things.

When the backing out starts, and you are ready to get away, let him know you are interested in someone else who wants to share his whole life with you, and you choose to have sex with only one guy at a time. He may panic and make a bunch of false promises, but recognize you've already seen his true colors; it is time to go.

If you are the jealous type, maybe you should never leave this guy because he will have a new sex slave in a matter of a couple of club visits. He doesn't worry about rejection; it's simply a numbers game to find someone he can sexually control. The Internet is full of videos of Sex Guzzlers who take it one step further and tape their encounters with messages from women who want to be on the screen next. Get over your jealousy or you too may end up a star of movie night at the firehouse. However, you'd have to come up with one of those porn names like Wanda More or Gia Spot. Think about it.

The Abuser

The Poster Child for Losers

In Stockholm in 1973, the police interrupted Clark Olofsson and Jan-Erik Olsson attempting to rob a bank. They took hostages. During the over-130-hour hostage situation, a female bank employee started feeling a strong attachment to her captors. She started to identify with them and started feeling they were looking out for her, protecting her. She started to feel that the people who were trying to negotiate her release were wrong. She had romantic feelings toward one of her captors. After their release, all of the hostages refused to testify against the men who held them captive. They had developed positive feelings about their captors! Several months after the incident, the female bank employee got engaged to Olsson during a prison visit. Perhaps this just seems like one girl very strongly attracted to Losers. Yet, psychologists find empathic responses for captors happen frequently to hostages. The phenomenon has been since deemed the Stockholm Syndrome, the tendency of persons taken hostage to identify with their captors. Not all women are lucky enough to have their Loser come blasting into their lives to take them hostage. But abusive men find this quirk of nature as inspiring as a hot fudge sundae on a dateless Saturday night.

Jamie found Vic very charming. He was a man who had a lot of confidence and control over his world. He was extremely attentive, sent her roses after their first two dates, opened doors for her, and refused to even consider letting her pay a bill. Vic wanted to know everything about her and was very willing to share information about himself. Having recently been in some very bad relationships and even taking a total break from dating for a year, Jamie especially liked being treated well. Vic had been married for a very short time before, but said he was just too young to understand what marriage meant. He was such a gentleman and a guy who knew how to be a man. She couldn't imagine this relationship not working out. Although only on a third date, Jamie knew he was a keeper.

It was a nice fall Saturday and some of Vic's friends were gathering at a bar to watch a Florida versus Miami college football game. Jamie wanted to spend the day outdoors, but Vic nixed that idea. After all, it was a matchup of the two greatest college football teams in the game, according to Vic. He insisted on going and was very insistent on wanting Jamie to be with him because it was a "couples thing." Jamie hadn't been part of a couple in a while and it felt nice to have a guy consider her that way. The bar was taken over by his group of friends and their girlfriends. They sat at the bar a few chairs away from the others.

"So, Vic, how is it you started following teams that are more than a thousand miles away from where you live and went to school?"

"I love these schools, particularly Miami. They just have the right football attitude. They don't take nothing from anybody. That's how football is supposed to be played."

"My brother says they have a reputation for running up the score and talking trash!"

"Just because a team's good, people have to cut them down. Trash-talking is part of the game. It's the psychology of football. And only fans of pansy teams accuse other teams of running up the score. Your brother is not going to like anyone you go out with, and I guess that's what a brother is supposed to do."

"He didn't say he didn't like you. Only that your teams are the barbarians, pillagers, and thugs of college football." Jamie smiles.

He lightens. "He must be an Ivy League fan or worse, a fan of some Catholic college like Notre Dame, the Fightin' Rosary boys."

A married couple that stops at their seats to say hello interrupts them. Vic says hello to both of them and introduces Jamie. He talks only to the guy. Jamie and the girl have a quick conversation.

"So are you Vic's new girlfriend?"

"We've actually only gone out a couple of times."

The girl gets a strange look on her face. "Well, you're going to see a different side of him today if Miami starts losing."

"What do you mean? Does he turn into Godzilla or something?"

There is a hesitation. "Let's just say, Vic has a temper when things don't go his way."

"Oh, men and their sports. Maybe if they spent a little more time in shoe stores, we could civilize them."

"You think that's all it is?" She laughs. "Jamie, if you want to come over and talk, I'm right over there, or call me sometime if you need to talk about Vic." She writes down her number, puts it on the bar, and leaves with her husband.

Vic looks at the number. "What's that all about?"

"I don't know. She seems like a nice girl."

"Jeanne is a major whack job. I don't know how Kurt puts up with her. She's a terrible liar and is always meddling in other people's business. One of those bitches who's always trying to start trouble."

Jamie is a little taken aback by Vic's tone. "You really don't like this girl. Did she do anything to you?"

"Nah, she can't get to me. I don't do anything that she can latch on to. I just can't stand when I bring someone new around and these meddlesome bitches want to stick their noses in." He takes the paper with the phone number and rips it up.

Vic notices Jamie's concerned facial expression. Jamie was frozen, not knowing what to say.

"I'm really sorry, Jamie. I lost it there for a second. I just don't like it when people treat others with a lack of respect. That's what I like about you, you aren't anything like that busybody."

They had a good rest of the afternoon and evening. Vic treated her extremely well, in fact almost fawned over her. Lots of compliments, lots of attention, and his team won so he was in a great mood.

Picasso said: "There are only two types of women—goddesses and doormats." Hopefully, he was wrong, forgetting the entire middle of the continuum. Psychologists who work with women find that women who are treated as either goddesses or doormats are often treated in the opposite way by the same person. On the surface, it would seem great to have a man who is aggressive and confident around others, but kind and attentive toward you. The extremes of these behaviors, however, can be a sign that there is serious danger in front of you. Since men don't come with warning labels, you need to be particularly aware of the packaging of this Red Flag.

Sixteen percent of women are abused each year in their relationships. A woman is nine times more likely to be assaulted in her home than on the street. And in the time it took you to read the last two sentences another woman has been abused. There is no humorous side to the man that abuses women; nothing can be said to atone for this kind of Loser. Dating one, or being in a long-term relationship with an Abuser is real hell. It is important to be able to discover this man quickly and get away fast.

Men who have been abused are more likely to be Abusers. If a man talks about a childhood in which he was abused or saw his mother abused, you need to start looking further. There are many men from these pasts who don't turn out to be Abusers, but this should be an immediate sign to be on alert. A history of alcohol or drug abuse is also a marker to be aware of, whether on the part of the man or by his parents. Needless to say, if there is any history of him being abusive to a spouse or girlfriend in the past, you should have nine out of ten toes out the door before he finishes telling you. He will try to minimize the abuse. You should be gone before he starts rationalizing.

At the beginning of a relationship, this man will often try to expedite the steps in the relationship process. He will be in full gallop, talking about commitment or living together long before you have experienced with other men. He will try to show you he is in control, try to control you with money, or try to control your time. There may be signs that he doesn't want you to talk to certain people, as if he is trying to pick your friends. Jealousy is often an early sign in this relationship. He may need to know about everyone in your life. By the third date, you might see signs that he does not easily take "no" for an answer, and definitely will not take rejection. Remember the philosophy of the Red Flag: If you see something very early in a relationship, when a person is trying to be on their best behavior, there is probably a boiling cauldron below that will burn you badly.

This Loser believes women are inferior and sees himself as better than other men. The Abuser views the woman he is with below his negative view of the rest of the gender. He looks at the world through comparisons, and you never measure up. In order to abuse, the Abuser must rationalize your worthiness to be hit. This is done by making you more stupid, crazy, inconsiderate, uncontrolled, underhanded, despicable, etc.—in essence everything he is, but doesn't realize he is. He becomes especially nice after abuse and is overly nice while he is locking you into the relationship because he needs to show you that he is good and only you make him bad. There is much written about the chronic Abuser and the means by which women are trapped into identifying with the aggressor. This is one bank in which you don't want to make any deposits.

In the course of a six-month relationship Vic hit Jamie two or three times, always tried to intimidate her, and made her feel she was insignificant and would never get another man. She tried to break up a number of times, but Vic kept stalking her, promising never to do it again and sending her flowers. Once, he threatened to kill her during a breakup. She finally told her parents. They made her get an order of protection. Vic tried stalking and intimidating Jamie to go out with him again, but her father intervened and contacted a friend in the police department. Vic was arrested and spent the night in jail. Jamie was lucky her mother and father were strong. The whole incident would have been much worse if she was alone.

If you have even the slightest hint in the course of dating that something isn't right, that he might be an Abuser, give the guy the following test.

IS HE AN ABUSER?

*Circle the number and
add up the score*

Family Background

History of being physically abused by father or mother	3
History of father being physically abusive to mother	3
History of parent(s) calling him names	2
History of father calling mother bad names	2
History of alcohol abuse by father	3
Paints his family as better than yours	3
Excuses father's mistreatment of his mother	5
Mother spoiled him, did everything for him	2
Parents in stereotypical gender roles	2
Acts in a demeaning manner toward mother or sisters	4

Work/School History

Constantly talks about how his bosses and teachers are stupid	2
Paints himself as more valuable at work than anyone else	3
Feels peers are incompetent or don't know how to work hard	4
Gets angry about work issues	2
Remembers himself as better in high school than he was	3

Friendships

Says his friends are better than yours	4
Tells stories to show how his friends are worse than him	2
Compares you unfavorably to his friends' wives and girlfriends	4
Keeps you separate from his friends, especially ones you say you like	3

Past Relationships

Abusive in a past relationship	10
Minimizes his abuse in past relationships	10
Says that women purposely tried to make him angry	5
You are aware that he was very jealous in past relationships	3
Says his ex-girlfriends were all crazy	3
Degrades any other woman he was with	5
Talks about how much better you are than they	3
Tells you they were "control freaks"	3
Has stalked a past girlfriend	10

(test continues)

Body Language

You see him try to dominate others with his physical presence	3
Must always sit with his back to a wall so he can see the room	1
Physically cuts you off with his body from members of the opposite sex	3

Dress/Hygiene

Spends time looking at himself in mirror	1
Talks to mirror	3

Behavior

Does not accept a no answer	2
Seems like he always gets his way	2
Alternates periods of being really great with periods of moodiness	2
You observe a physical or verbal abusiveness to someone	6
Blames bad behavior of past on alcohol or drugs	10
Talks about how others try to control him	5
You observe symbolic signs of aggression (i.e., ripping up a picture, destroying someone's possessions)	5
Tries to quicken the pace of the relationship	3
Gets too nice after anger	5
Tries to control money too much	2
His behavior startles you because it comes out of nowhere, quick change to anger	5
Tries to buy you things to placate you	3

Conversation

Expresses jealousy	2
Talks as if he sees women as inferior, or too superior	2
Tries to pick who you talk to or are friends with	2
Calls other women stupid or crazy	3
Rationalizes a lot	1
Blames others for his failures	3
Expresses fantasized aggression (e.g., I'd like to rip off his head)	3
Tries too hard to be nice and complimentary on first few dates	2
Demeans women	3
Demeans mother	4

When Confronted

Attacks you	3
Points out all your weaknesses	5

(test continues)

When Confronted	
Gets angry	5
Walks away	5
Demeans you by calling you names	10
Your Impression	
Has a quick temper	6
You have to be careful not to anger him	4
Seems too nice at times	2
Does not respect your work	4
	Total Score

Score 12 and lower: No reason for concern at this point
Score between 13 and 21: Yellow Flag—There's reason for caution; be very careful
Score 22 and above: Red Flag—You got the king of Losers; run away

Do Not Volunteer

If the guy you are dating scored in the Yellow Flag range, it is better to assume you've got an Abuser than not. Your job at this point is to look for evidence to get him in the Red Flag range. This is a dangerous pattern, and caution requires that you be sure. Your goal is to work as hard as you can to see if you can get him over the line. If after all your diligent efforts you do *not* end up with a Red Flag score, then you can consider dating under the proviso that you go as slowly as possible and always reevaluate until you know him extremely well. The other Yellow Flags in this book suggest confrontation, perhaps patience, perhaps other virtues on your part. This one does not, it requires extreme discretion because of the inherent dangers of being caught in this all-too-common pattern.

If your date falls in the Red Flag range, get out as quickly as you can. This is potentially an extremely volatile situation, and you need as much space as possible, as quickly as possible. If you were thinking of a trip, take it. If you've only been out a couple of times and had wanted to date someone else, do it now. Get away. The process of being trapped in this situation happens slowly, and it takes all your self-esteem, pride, and dignity with it. Therapists that work with abused women tell them that the first time you are abused you are a victim, the second time you are a volunteer. If you've already been abused, seek some help. Do not become a volunteer.

The other concern comes if this has happened to you more than once. If you have been involved with more than one abusive man and continued the relationship past the point where others may have thought you shouldn't, you may have some inherent personality characteristics that put you at risk. You do not want to go through your life attracting these predators. Get yourself in counseling and make sure that the pattern does not persist.

Make Sure the Door Shuts Behind You

The scary part of leaving an Abuser is the statistics that show that leaving can be the most violent time. Women who are killed in abusive relationships are usually killed when attempting to leave. The Abuser so hates rejection, has made you so beneath him, that the idea of you on your own makes his skin crawl. He is already prone to very serious emotions, and very strong ones. He may want to control you in the only way he can, by hurting you. Therefore:

DO NOT ATTEMPT TO DO THIS ALONE

You are at risk and should have someone with you at all times. This is not a time to feel independent. The person with you should preferably be male, a person with equal or higher prestige than the Abuser, and someone who can remain very calm when faced with tough circumstances. It should not be a guy with whom he accused you of having a relationship while you were together. A clear message needs to be given that you are leaving, and you will not be alone. He needs to know that he will face consequences if he does not act appropriately. You should not try insight with him. Do not give him hope; in fact, talk as little as possible. "I do not want to date. There is no reason to discuss why. Please do not contact me." In shorter-term relationships, it usually isn't a problem. If you have let the relationship go a while, expect that you may have to go the route of the police. Do not make any contact with him if he stalks. Just go through the police process and keep someone with you.

There is an amazing sense of freedom when escaping an abusive relationship, but if you have been dating more than a couple of weeks, you are not ready to date someone else. Spend two or three months or more of not seeing anyone romantically before you try to set up a new relationship. You need the recovery time even if you think you don't. You will be too erratic if you date right away and drive a new partner crazy. Don't turn into some guy's Red Flag. We haven't written the book for men . . . yet.

The Criticizer

If You Can't Do Anything Right,
You've Found Mr. Wrong

The critics were out for blood. "It is impossible that a more inept, moronic, or humorless show has ever appeared on the home tube" (UPI). "A masterpiece of banality!" (*Variety*). "The worst new show of the season. It's hard to know where to begin to criticize the program. It's best to begin by switching channels" (*Detroit News*). The critics welcomed this show on September 26, 1964, with as many negative adjectives as they could find. It was sure to be a failure since no written word seemed to be positive. Undaunted, that show persevered for three seasons and ninety-eight episodes. The first year it placed 19 out of 117 shows. On occasion, it even beat out the television mainstay *I Love Lucy*. Eleven years later the show was brought back for a two-part special. The special got an impressive 52 Nielsen share, ranking it in the top five for the week. A second special was broadcast only a few months later. It continues to rerun in syndication more than thirty years later! People just plain liked it despite what the critics said. *Gilligan's Island* was a hit that most of us still remember fondly, although few of us would want to admit to watching it today. As England's prime minister Benjamin Disraeli (1804–1881) noted: "You know who critics are? The men who have failed in literature and art." The problem is that criticism is better at poisoning the mind than expressing the heart. If the guy you're with criticizes your every move, he's a show to cancel!

Julie wasn't thinking about men or dating or anything except breathing hard and sweating. She had just added weights to her jogging workout and was finding the activity difficult, but she was determined. She was taking charge of her life both mentally and physically. Julie was viewing her current situation as a challenge.

She was startled when she heard a voice to her right say, "You're doing that wrong."

"I beg your pardon?"

"Forgive me if I startled you. But I noticed that you were using your hand weights, well, like a beginner. If they aren't used correctly not only do you not get the full benefit of the activity, but you could actually hurt yourself. Here, let me show you. Don't pull them like you're lifting a suitcase. Fully extend your arms down, then alternate raising the arm that is opposite of the foot you have forward. Make sure you raise your elbow at the upswing too."

"Thank you, uh . . ."

"Rich. I'm glad to help. You look like you have so much potential, I just had to help you get on the right road with those hand weights."

"My name is Julie. Not to sound corny, but do you come here often?"

"Ah, the trite pickup line. In answer to your question, yes. I come here often and have never seen you before."

"I'm not trying to pick you up. In fact, I'm sorry to be bothering you now. Excuse me."

"Wait, my apologies. It is I who should be trying to pick you up. I am not a stupid man, nor am I blind. To let the opportunity of meeting such a spirited, intelligent, and, might I say, beautiful woman pass me by would be really doltish. Please, let me start again. I'm Richard."

"Flattery, and so well expressed. Good save. Apology accepted."

"I'm a troubleshooter for that computer company across the street. I try to get some exercise every day. It's good for the body, and today for my eyes too. You?"

"More flattery. You're on a roll. I'm an investment manager at the bank next to your company, and I'm somewhat new to the exercise gig. I have my work cut out for me."

"You don't look bad to me. Get a little expert coaching and you can completely change whatever you want. Like if you wanted to thin your thighs, for example, you could do that in a little over a month."

"It sounds as if you're volunteering for the job."

"Sounds like 'gym talk' for hinting for a date. But you don't spend enough time in the gym to talk the talk."

"I'm new at exercise. I have my doctorate in flirting."

"Then if you think you are up for a rigorous instructor, I'm your man."

"How about if we finish up by power walking to the café at the end of Grand Street, and do lunch?"

"Well, I guess you've had a good workout, for a beginner. Lunch is good."

Julie ordered a burger at first, but her new coach reminded her that diet is as important as exercise. She then set out to eat a chef salad.

"Julie, you must know a lot about money, right?"

"Yes. You need some investment advice?"

"No, not really, but if I were investing in the wrong stock or something, you'd be nice enough to tell me, wouldn't you?"

"I guess so. You want to share your portfolio or something?"

"No, I just noticed you're using your fork all wrong and I feel that I should tell you for your own good. Probably nobody else has felt comfortable pointing this out to you."

"Rich, which dressing would you like me to put on my salad? I'd like to pick one that matches your suit just in case you lose control of your mouth again."

Julie and Rich had a nice lunch from that point on. He was a unique individual who seemed to be very capable of flattering in one sentence and criticizing in the next. There was enough of a spark for Julie to go further with dating, but she was smart enough to be aware of the problems with both flattery and criticism.

Criticism is a part of life. It reflects the fact that we are all imperfect beings who periodically make mistakes. The ability to accept criticism is a sign of maturity. Accepting and acting on constructive, well-intended criticism can help us grow as individuals. But if the guy you're with offers enough criticism to fill the *New York Times* movie review section, look out, you may be turning the page on a Red Flag!

Why does a man criticize? It can be as innocent as wanting to help a friend be more efficient. In the context of a relationship, it might be an attempt to give direction: asking for something in a more pleasing fashion. Criticism is not a bad characteristic when given in very small doses. If the Criticizer's self-esteem problems are small, then much of his criticism can be reasonable, albeit annoying. As he becomes more confident in the relationship, the criticism may fade to a normal level.

When criticism is a mask for low self-esteem, the problem becomes large. The Criticizer may use criticism to build himself up. When he criticizes, he positions his knowledge and confidence above yours. Criticizing also reflects attention from the Criticizer, which can be particularly useful if he is under stress or his actions are being questioned. By putting others on the defensive, the Criticizer takes the advantage. Little by little, the confidence, control, and self-esteem of his partner are drained. He becomes an emotional vampire, while you become a pale and sickly unwilling servant.

The Criticizer often has a childhood deficient in warmth and praise. He often has an overcritical parent who never allowed him a feeling of confidence. As a result, he grew up overcompensating for being told he was wrong, could be better, and never finding validation. To avoid the pain of criticism, he becomes a critic. The best defense is a good offense. Unfortunately, this style precludes intimacy. This suits the Criticizer just fine. He likes the distance. Pleasure with no responsibility, all while appearing to be responsible, is the goal of the Criticizer. He wants other people to do most of the work in life so that he can sit back to complain and criticize. The Criticizer does little to produce, he only comments on the labor of others. He does not spend a year to build a building, he spends a day to tear it down.

Criticism in the hands of this Loser is the means for a power trip. For the Criticizer, a relationship is an opportunity to feel superior and more powerful than his partner. This feeling becomes his major motivation. Criticism in the hands of a Criticizer can be quite cruel. He relishes in the pain inflicted, while hiding behind the shield of it being "for your own good." Surprise! It's not your good he is concerned about but his.

Why are women attracted to men who criticize? In the beginning, their critiques are often within civil bounds. They are careful not to hurt, or if they do, are quick to apologize. They come across as confident and intelligent. They seem to genuinely care. They make a woman feel that they are sincere in wanting to help them and come across as capable of doing so. They hide the criticism in a lot of flattery. In the beginning stages, they tap into a woman's desire to be taken care of by a strong, competent man. They capitalize on the supposed maturity of a woman to be able to accept criticism. Often the Criticizer will find a woman who does not want to make a lot of decisions, a woman who wants to be a follower. By the time a woman realizes who she is involved with, much of her strength and self-confidence are gone. She is too unsure of herself to make the break. She fears she will not have what it takes to survive on her own. If you're with a Criticizer, remember *Gilligan's Island* is still running after thirty years. That's a good record of survival for a show that was so ridiculous and got such criticism. Go down to the lagoon and catch a boat out of there, "little buddy."

Julie dated Rich for a while even though she felt a subtle discomfort with him. He seemed to take his job as coach very seriously. He expanded his role of coach to more than just exercise. He seemed to know how she should dress. How she should deal with her coworkers. How she should talk with her mother. She even learned that she was disciplining her cat wrong. The way Rich criticized changed too. What started out as suggestions became either commands or put-downs. In the beginning, Julie protested angrily. Rich often apologized for the way he said things but pointed out that it was for her own good. Some of his advice was helpful. She did not want to seem like someone who could not handle criticism, but she started to feel continually drained around Rich. She was confused.

One day, as if she had awoken from a long sleep, Julie realized that if she was in need of all the criticism that Rich offered, she really needed to make some major changes. She did. Rich never understood how she could be so stupid to dump him.

The time to leave the Criticizer is early, before the relationship has begun. The test below will help you make that decision.

IS HE A CRITICIZER?

	Circle the number and add up the score
Family Background	
Parents divorced	1
History of parents fighting	1
Father uninvolved or cold	2

(test continues)

Family Background

History of verbal abuse in family	2
Does not have close relationship with family	2
Has close relationship with one or more family members	−1

Work/School History

Complains about incompetence of coworkers/boss	2
Complains about quality of his school or professors	1
Seems to have few friends at work	1
Seems to be involved in conflicts at work	3

Friendships

Does not have a lot of friends	1
Has reasonable number of healthy male and female relationships	−1
Criticizes friends he does have	2

Past Relationships

Talks negatively about faults of past girlfriends	2
Talks nonjudgmentally about past girlfriends	−1

Body Language

Stiff authoritarian body language	2
Seems to look down on you	3
Scowls	1
Rolls eyes	2
Frowns frequently	1

Dress/Hygiene

Tends to be impeccable	1
Shows off with the way he dresses	2
Constantly adjusts clothes to make them "look right"	1

Behavior

Makes suggestions about what you should or should not do	3
Two or more criticisms	
Over a week	2
Over a day	4
Over a date	6
Over a short period of time (i.e., when he first sees you for the evening)	8

(test continues)

Behavior

Criticizes small, unimportant issues	5
Criticizes in a cruel fashion	8
Criticizes from out of blue when discussion might lead to him not getting his way	6

Conversation

Compliments you	−1
Compliments are followed by criticism	4
Criticism followed by compliment	5
Unable to compliment without then criticizing something	5
Number of criticisms	
Equals number of compliments	3
Are greater than number of compliments	5
Does not compliment you	2
Criticizes your friends	4
Criticizes your family	4

When Confronted

Apologizes and admits to being partially wrong	−1
Shows insight into his behavior	−1
Gets defensive and questions your motives	2
Never admits being wrong	3
Attacks you and finds fault with your statement	3
Continues same behavior without regard to your confrontation	2

Your Impression

Seems to enjoy criticizing you	2
Seems very practiced at criticizing	2
Seems to use criticism as way to control a situation	3
Seems to use criticism to cover up insecurity	3
Seems to use criticism to avoid intimacy	3
	Total Score

Score 15 and lower: No reason for concern at this point
Score between 16 and 35: Yellow Flag—There's reason for caution
Score 36 and above: Red Flag—He's a disaster waiting to happen; evacuate

Is the Wrecking Ball Aimed at Your Head?

From childhood, you have been taught that a mature person can take constructive criticism. You were told that getting defensive or angry is a sign of insecurity. Those who criticize tell you they are only doing it for your own good. There's the problem. You can't always tell by the critique the motives of the critic.

The man who scores in the Yellow Flag range may be someone worth considering. He might be a competent person with excellent self-esteem. His motives may be genuine, and after you get to know him, he may just want to help you be the best you can be.

What he won't be is cruel. He will not criticize you in front of your friends. He won't criticize petty things. He will stop when you tell him to stop. His criticisms will be geared toward helping you, not helping him. That is a key difference. Would he help you do something that he wishes you would not do at all? Since you are important to him, he should be able to put his needs after yours. If you have a guy in the Yellow Flag range, look for the nature of his criticisms, whether he will stop, and who he is helping. The man who scores in the Yellow Flag range will also be able to accept criticism. He won't get defensive and will change accordingly. If you see these Yellow Flag signs but don't see him showing acceptance, he is no longer just a Yellow Flag.

The Criticizer who scores in the Red Flag range is a wrecking ball aimed at your head. For him, criticism is not an instrument of change but destruction. He has a clear agenda to strip you of your confidence and independence, to confuse you, and to rob you of your self-esteem. He needs someone to blame for all his miseries, to fail where he doesn't try. A few good shots and your relationship looks like one of those buildings they tear down with explosives. Beware of the cloud of dust when you leave.

No Reruns for This Loser

Breaking up with the Criticizer is important, and the sooner the better. Considering what he has taken from you, you might want to get back as much of it as possible. You will have a lot of rebuilding to do and you can start with him. Tell him point-blank that you are ending the relationship to escape his continual criticism. You have realized that this criticism is not for your own good, it is destructive, and you owe it to yourself to leave it behind.

Remember that you won't get him to change his mind or his ways. Your assertions are for yourself. You need to hear yourself say them to regain self-respect and rebuild confidence. He will try to turn this around, criticizing you for not handling his criticism as well as you should, for being insecure and critical of him. Don't fall for it. You might want to do this in a place you can leave, because there is potential that he will get vicious. Emphasize that you are no longer open to his suggestions. You have decided to do it your way, and your way does not include him.

It is possible, once he sees that you are serious, that he will offer to change. Don't soften. Thank him for the sentiment but let him know your mind is made up. State clearly that this is a well thought out decision and you will not back down. Now say good-bye and leave.

It is very important that you get yourself in counseling as soon as possible if you have had a long-term relationship with a Criticizer. Our egos are not strong enough to handle the droning torture of the Criticizer without major damage. You will not believe how long it can take you to recover from years of criticism. You are probably unaware of the many changes his emotional battering has caused. After you rediscover yourself, go to a movie or a play and remember, it's better to see the show alone than with a critic. Who knows, maybe someone will even listen to your opinion.

The Rescuer

*The Handout Today May Be
Choking You Tomorrow*

In the early sixteenth century, Dr. Johann Faust strove to become legendary as an alchemist, fortune-teller, and magician. He succeeded, although he may not have approved of what the legends said about him. In the fourth decade after his death, a narrative was written recognizing his tremendous abilities. So powerful was the story, it inspired a number of other poems and narratives: a classic, two-part, nineteenth-century poetic drama by Goethe; a couple of plays; and even the American musical *Damn Yankees*. The latter stories were all much more complicated than the original. The original sixteenth-century writing was a very simple tale of a doctor named Faust who made a deal with Mephistopheles, better known in our time as Satan. Mephistopheles granted Faust twenty-four years of great power and pleasure in exchange for his soul at the end of that time. In some of the tales of Faust, he is swept off to Mephistopheles' underworld. In others, he escapes by repenting at the last moment. In all, there is a warning about the meaning of gifts. Some men have the devil in them when they offer to lend you money or help you out of trouble. They'll play to your heart but they want your soul. If you give into the temptation of one of these Rescuers, you are accepting a plane ticket with free luxury accommodations and all you have to do is listen to a pitch for a lifelong time-share . . . in hell.

Marie had such a beautiful way about her. She was so trusting and believed the best in everyone. Unfortunately, she ran into some hard times because she trusted the wrong person. She had intermingled her finances with her live-in ex-boyfriend and ended up with serious credit-card debt, overdue rent, utility bills, phone bills, and everything else he left town to avoid. Marie thought it was strange that a grown man had no credit rating and she had to put everything in her name. If she'd only listened to her friends.

Tom was an unlikely lunch companion, but a male co-worker felt Marie should talk to him because Tom was good with money and might have a few suggestions for how Marie could dig herself out of the hole she was in. Marie agreed to meet him, with her coworker as a chaperone. The last thing she wanted was to build a new romance. She was a little leery of men right now. Much to Marie's dismay, her coworker left after introducing them so they could be alone to talk. Tom had a pleasant smile and such a nice manner about him. His presence alone seemed to calm Marie. She felt an immediate bond of trust.

"Marie, I feel so bad for you. I've heard of a lot of guys like that. It's a wonder women ever trust men. Please order something. Let me buy you lunch."

"Tom, I'm not sure I'm comfortable letting you buy me lunch. I usually don't eat at expensive places like this."

"That's just the reason I should buy you lunch. Look, Marie, I have the money. I work to be able to buy a beautiful woman lunch. Don't insult me."

"Tom, that's very sweet, but I got myself all worked up

telling you my story. On top of that, I don't even like eating in front of someone I don't know. I get nervous. I keep thinking I'm going to forget how to chew. I think I'll pass on lunch."

"I think it's time I helped you get over these problems, and we'll start with lunch." Tom calls the waiter over and orders two chef salads. "They have a big chef salad, and if you don't finish it you can take it home and you won't have to worry about dinner tonight. Already you'll have saved money."

"You're not big on the word no, are you?"

"I understand no when I need to, but I'm not big on letting problems take over your life. Particularly someone who gives so much to other people. You deserve better and you're going to get it."

"I'm going to get it, huh? Are you a fortune-teller, doing astrology charts, reading tea leaves, or are you connected to the Big Guy upstairs?"

"I'm all the connection you need, Ms. Marie. Here's the plan. We're going to start by letting me call all your creditors and get a cash buyout number. I'll be able to talk them down to taking fifty cents on the dollar. That'll knock your bills down to half."

"Tom, I don't need you to do this, I can make the calls. But I wouldn't have the cash anyway."

"Nah, you're too nice. They'll take advantage of you. It's better to have a man's voice when you're talking to these creditors."

"Tom, I'm not comfortable with this. We just . . ."

"Marie, I know what I'm doing. Once we get the buyout figure, I'll lay the money out for you and we'll clear up your credit report."

"No, Tom. I can't even consider that possibility."

"It's just going to be a loan. I know you have a job and can pay it back. I'm going to clear this up. It's the only way it can work."

"This is not right, Tom. It doesn't make sense."

"Marie, I give money to charity every month and never see any of the good it does. I make a good living and spend it on stupid things just to pretend I'm working for a reason. Finally, I can see my money do some good, see it go for something worthwhile, and you're going to deprive me of that when you could use it? *That* doesn't make sense."

Marie had resignation in her face. She had been under so much pressure, even something insane like depending on a stranger was sounding reasonable. Tom noticed her pondering.

"Now, you say your car is falling apart. I have a plan for that too. I have this friend . . ."

By the end of lunch, Tom had solutions for every one of Marie's problems, including the harassing collection agency phone calls, the parents who wanted her to move home, the problem with her boss, and the ring around her toilet bowl from too much iron in the water. Marie was always the nurturing one in relationships, so she rationalized that maybe it was time someone took care of her for a while. When she got back to the office she thanked her coworker and told him she had fun. Tom was a nice guy and definitely not a date from hell. . . . So she thought.

We all appreciate a helping hand. It's nice to know you have someone who takes an interest in your problems and who you can count on. However, when the help has more strings attached than a marionette production of *Ali Baba and the Forty Thieves*, you may be getting roped in by a Red Flag.

Natural selection has chosen the male for the role as provider and problem solver. While society has made gender-specific roles less defined, many male-female differences still linger. Thus, men see themselves as anthropologically bound to provide and protect. In a long-term relationship, the couple works to complement each other's strengths and weaknesses and balance nature's tendencies. A partnership is formed and responsibilities are differentiated based on abilities. Man's primal urges transition into a healthy life role of mutuality.

The Rescuer pushes his role as protector/provider/problem solver. He is looking for a quick fix, a masculine high, the testosterone pump. He will enjoy helping you more than you enjoy being helped. His true motive is to help himself to the buffet table of your emotions. If your trays are filled with problems, he becomes more of a necessity in your life.

Most of us expect appreciation in return when helping someone. This is not as noble as the pure altruistic acts of someone like Mother Teresa, but it is human. This is not to say that we cannot at the same time be motivated by the good feeling of helping others. It's just that the desire to be liked, respected, or noticed lingers in the background. What is the harm in getting a pat on the back in exchange for our trouble? We get a good feeling that is a combination of an altruistic high and a mild amount of recognition. The Rescuer completely loses sight of helping for its own sake. For him, it is a complex mixture of solving his own insecurity, wanting to feel like a man, wanting to be liked, and wanting control. The more he does, the more he will expect you to like him, praise him, admire him, be affectionate, and give in to his decisions regarding the relationship. It is an enslaving process that any feudal lord would envy. And you'll be jousting to keep your own identity.

The Rescuer is usually a very insecure man who cannot accept his faults and shortcomings. He has trouble appreciating his good points and working at self-growth. The problem is the intangibility of the things that make us who we are. Our values, beliefs, experiences, and personality lie within us. We must have some insight to see them and a sense of security to appreciate them. This is the basis of self-worth.

The Rescuer tries to cut out the middleman. He looks to make his self-worth tangible without insight and security.

What the Rescuer can do, what he has done, what he will do for you are clearly measurable. You can touch an oil change. You can quantify an interest-free loan. You can see a paint job. The man who always helps overcomes his fear that you will see right through him by building a tangible wall of gifts and acts. He no longer worries about being exposed because he has taken the easy way out. He believes he can control how you will judge him because his case has been presented in black and white. He is his own lawyer. And after you are with him awhile, you will understand why there are so many lawyer jokes.

The Rescuer has yet another unhealthy purpose. He would like to create a dependency. Since the Rescuer is plagued with insecurity and does not see why you would want him, he wants to make sure you need him. What better way to do this than to get you started on that slippery slope of accepting his gracious offers to help you out. The sophisticated Rescuer will start out making small, seemingly innocuous offers. These offers will progress in size and scope. Little by little he will draw you in until you are at his mercy. And he will expect you to thank him for it.

Marie and Tom started dating and it quickly became apparent to Marie that she had made a mistake. They had little in common except the resolution of her problems, and that seemed to be what he wanted to talk about most of the time. Her attempts to keep it on the friendship level were met with guilt trips. He kept trying to help her out more and more and would never take no for an answer. Marie got to the point that she wouldn't share problems with him for fear that he would come up with solutions. To make matters worse, he kept trying to take over regular functions in Marie's household. When she refused, he'd remind her that she screwed up before and would probably screw up again without his assistance. He said it in a nice way, though. The devil talks in rhymes that are pleasant to hear.

Marie borrowed money from her parents to pay off her debt to him, and then borrowed some courage from a self-help book and left Tom. He was crushed, but she got stronger because of it. In her next relationship she was a little too strong and independent, but in the one after that she found a balance between good independence and good dependence. Her favorite opera now is by a French composer named Charles François Gounod—*Faust*.

The test below can help you determine if you're dating a guy who plans to rescue you into a flaming oblivion.

IS HE A RESCUER?

Circle the number and add up the score

Family Background

Parents kept to traditional gender roles	1
Parents were demanding in their expectations	2
Parents compared children frequently	2
Grew up economically disadvantaged	2
Parents still put many time demands on him	4
Has to work dates around errands/activities he performs for parents or other family members	5

Work/School History

History of good academic performance attributed to hard work	1
Volunteered for a lot of activities at school	1
Seems too involved in work	2
Works too many hours consistently	2
Volunteers to work extra hours	2
People at work depend on him to bail them out	3
Maintained good balance of study, extracurricular activities, and socializing when in school/college	−1
Healthy attitude toward balancing work and social life	−1

(test continues)

Friendships

Often in position of helping friends	2
Breaks dates with you to help friends "in crisis"	
Occasionally	3
Often	4
Constantly	6
Seems to have friends who need or are dependent on him	4

Past Relationships

Remains friends with ex-girlfriends or ex-wife	2
Still helps ex-girlfriends or ex-wife with problems (does not count if done for benefit of his children)	5
Does not seem to know why relationships ended	4
Reveals that relationships often ended by woman, not him	3

Body Language

Open, relaxed body language	1
Makes good eye contact	1
Nods head appropriately when you talk indicating he's paying attention	1

Dress/Hygiene

Dress and hygiene not significant in this profile	—

Behavior

Waits on you too much (opens doors, holds coat, drops off at curb then parks car, etc.)	2
Does little chores around your house/apartment/car	3
Starts big projects around your house/apartment	6
Arranges for things to be done for you by his contacts/friends	3
Unexpectedly buys you things that you "need"	4
When out shopping, will point out and offer to purchase things that you "need"	3
Always pays for dating entertainment	2
Offers you money	3
Gives you money	6

Conversation

Makes many suggestions during conversation	2
Responds to your conversation as if you have asked for help	2
Within first hour of first date	6
By end of first date	4
During future dates	3

(test continues)

Conversation

Tells tales of how he has helped other people	3
Makes offers of help that are	
Reasonable and asked for	−1
Larger than would normally be expected at stage of relationship	3
Clearly inappropriate	6

When Confronted

Apologizes and admits to being wrong	−1
Shows insight into his behavior	−1
Apologizes but	
Notes he was only doing it to help	3
Suggests you are being too sensitive to his genuinely nice offer	5
Suggests you are being ungrateful	6
Does not apologize	
And gets defensive	3
And blames you for not knowing how to graciously accept help	6
And compares you unfavorably with more appreciative friends/girlfriends	8

Your Impression

You feel smothered at times	2
You sense he is almost pressured to help you	3
You sense that he has trouble relaxing or being intimate with you unless he has paved the way with some form of help/suggestion	4
His identity seems tied in to all the help he provides others	4
Total Score	

Score 15 and lower: No reason for concern at this point
Score between 16 and 30: Yellow Flag—There's reason for caution
Score 31 and above: Red Flag—His shiny armor is scrap metal; recycle him

The Knights Are Waiting in Line for Damsels in Distress

If your date falls into the Yellow Flag range, help yourself to some more time with him. He may just be reacting to the initial dating jitters. Trying to help you can't hurt, particularly if it's not too extreme. He may hope that you will be able to see that he is a sincere guy who can be a good partner in a relationship.

The Yellow Flagger will know and respect boundaries. His offers will be small, timely, and based on conversation with you. Accepting his help won't cause that something-is-wrong feeling in your gut. You may have found a genuinely nice guy. Sure, he may want to be liked, but hopefully he'll come by it honestly. Look to see if he accepts a no answer, or if he does things behind your back that you tell him not to do. See if your conversation with him can focus on more than solving your problems. Do you bring them up, or does he? There are plenty of signs to see just how far he is going with this rescue thing. Look closely.

If your date falls in the Red Flag category, watch out. We aren't talking a nice guy with a little bit of insecurity. He has an agenda. He has a style of interacting with women. And he won't change.

The Rescuer has spent years making up for his insecurity by being the ever-helpful, quintessential nice guy. At first, he will offer to help you with everyday problems. He will lend you money if you need it and then not want to be repaid. He will arrange for your car to be fixed, program your VCR, help you get on-line, and arrange for your girlfriend to get theater tickets.

Little by little he will try to make himself indispensable. He will form a relationship based on what he does for you. He wants only strokes and praise in return. He will expect your gratitude, admiration, and loyalty. He will expect you to give in to his decision because he knows best. The problem is that beyond the helpfulness, you won't get to see what is underneath. The Rescuer fears intimacy. He fears that once exposed he will no longer be desirable. He does not see himself as having much to offer and compensates with acts and things. He eases his insecurity by trapping you into dependency. You will find him making decisions without consulting you, "for your own good." Should you protest, he will likely get angry and remind you about all of the great things he has done for you. He will play on your sense of fairness. He will tap into your desire to have someone take care of you. But take care of yourself first. In the stories of *Faust*, the devil is always dressed well, and performs feats of great magic to build desire. When he sweeps you off to hell, he'll have horns and a forked tail. Only fairy tales have a good ending. Reality reverses fairy tales. How many times has your kiss transformed a prince into a frog?

Escape Is More Exciting than Rescue

When you've been rescued to the point that you're in Red Flag distress, it is time for you to leave. Let the Rescuer know that you find yourself being smothered. Tell him that you have appreciated his good intentions, but overall they have created a negative effect on your relationship. State forcefully that the relationship is not going in the direction you would like. Let him know that you are the type of woman who needs the challenge of helping herself. This is how you learn. This is how you grow. This is what you want. You will accept nothing less.

At this point the Rescuer will start to remind you of the things he has done for you. Cut him off. State again that you appreciate his help, but that you are ending the relationship anyway. If you owe him money, get it from someone else and give it back to him. You may have to listen to a few minutes of how you are being ungrateful. Assure him you do not mean to be ungrateful but wish to save you both from ending up in a long-term relationship for the wrong reasons with the wrong type of person.

When you leave, take a close look at yourself and what you may have done to send out the signals that you wanted his help. You should be stronger from the experience, and more careful about affairs of the heart and soul. Your romances need to be a little less of a legend. Get your problems under control before you begin the next relationship. We don't need some new guy trying to slay your dragon.

The Brainwasher

*If This Isn't a Cult, Why Do I Have
to Chant, Shave My Head, and
Sell Roses at the Airport?*

There are a variety of techniques that cults use to indoctrinate new members. They start by trying to find people who are already a little unsettled in their lives. They take them to an unknown place with promises of solving their problems or finding new answers to the question of the meaning of life. The cult then takes these prospects and deprives them of necessary human functions like sleep, sometimes food and drink, sometimes the ability for sanitary elimination. After the initial deprivation period, they begin to indoctrinate them with the cult philosophy, promises of a new and better world, a new cult vocabulary, and a new way to interact. All the while they start removing the deprivation and letting the prospect become part of something bigger and better. Soon the prospect is ready to give them whatever they want. All kinds of cults, governments wanting secrets, and warriors wanting information have successfully perfected these techniques through years of study, trial and error, continual practice, and science combined with espionage. An experienced Brainwasher can take weeks, sometimes months, to completely reduce a person to have as much free will as the nutritional value of a can of Diet Pepsi. The great news for you is that some men have been enlightened by a combination of overly active testosterone glands combined with years of watching *Mission Impossible* so they can condense the entire process of en-cult-erizing a woman into the course of two or three dates. And these Brainwashers are looking for you!

At some point Sue just got tired of dating. She had been out with a number of guys and had gotten pickier and pickier about finding someone with whom she would even take a first date. In her mind it was time to settle down and she was ready to rule out any new guy who was not a serious prospect for a long-term relationship, potentially marriage. Ed owned a well-established computer network installation company and happened to work on the company computers where Sue worked. They were making small talk when the subject of good dating prospects came up. Both single and unattached, they decided to give it a try even though there really wasn't the spark that each of them normally looked for in a person.

"So, Ed the computer man, where are we going to go tonight?"

"Well, Sue the manager, I like to go to this Irish place called McGee's. You've got to pass the Irish jig test. Can't go out with a girl that can't learn to jig."

"That's not fair. I didn't study. I mean, at least you could have told me, so I could play some Irish cloggin' music or maybe some old U2 or something. I guess all the other girls you've dated couldn't drink a good stout, huh?"

"Actually, I do like to take girls I date out for an Irish night. I mean, I'm Irish and you gotta have something in common. Imagine dating someone that doesn't like anything that you like."

"I guess you call that the 'corned beef and cabbage' standard of dating. I have enough trouble finding guys that pass the 'reads beyond the sports page and comics' standard. Actually, usually I'm lucky to find a guy that can read."

"Well, I can read. And I'm going to suggest you order the lamb stew or shepherd's pie—they're a lot better than the corned beef and cabbage. Sounds like you're having a run of some bad luck in the old dating scene. Looking for a little more out of life, are you?"

"Nah, I got a great life. I go home. I sleep. I go to work. Once a month I pay the rent. Oh yeah, I tape my soaps and *Oprah*. A lot of my friends are already married, so I sort of lost my hang-out crew."

"Yeah, a lot of my friends are married too. I'm not real crazy about a lot of the wives though. Only one of them has a wife that I really like. He owns a business and they work it together. That's the way I'm going to have it when I'm married. That's like my dad. He was an accountant, and every tax season for as long as I can remember Mom worked with him. Makes them real close. A real team. That's what I want."

"Not me. My mom went back to school after her kids were grown, got her degree, and went out to work like she always wanted. She has a career now and I'm really proud of her."

"Yeah, but she stayed home and raised you guys and that's the right way. Besides, your dad didn't own his own business, right? I mean, your mom would have wanted to work with your dad if he had his own company."

"Well, I guess so. Dad does work for a bank, and Mom didn't want to work for the same company. Anyway, how'd we get talking about this stuff? Give me a little Irish Jig 101 before we get there."

Years of modern-dance lessons paid off this night for Sue, as the jig was very easy for her to learn. They danced well together. He led.

It's nice to be with a man who knows what he wants in life. They seem more stable and more willing to settle down. But when he starts telling you what you should want, what you should do, when you should eat, and how you should worship the moon, he may be indoctrinating you into a cult of the Red Flag.

The man that has predesigned roles for his girlfriend most often grew up in a male-dominated household, where the father, stepfather, or mother's boyfriend made all the major decisions. The mother's domain was the household, but running it only in the way the man wanted. As a male child, his mother probably pampered him. Most likely the mother continued to do things for him into his teenage years that he should have begun to do for himself, such as laundry, cleaning his room, or making his bed. There is even a good likelihood that the mother continued these "mothering" activities into his young adulthood and maybe even at the time you are dating him. His goal is to brainwash you into serving him like his mother did. If you fall short, you might find some real difficulty between you and his mother. You won't understand why everyone is looking at you funny at the family party until you catch his mother introducing you as "the Bimbo of the Week."

This man has fantasized the entire path of your relationship, long before he ever met you. By experiencing control over his mother, he has grown accustomed to getting his way. This makes the Brainwasher too opinionated, since he has been able to express himself without any sense of accountability while growing up. He will take control over all major decisions, and although he may be willing to leave you in charge of a specific activity, he will complain constantly about the way you handle things. Generally, the things he allows you to control are the ones he would prefer not to handle himself because there is no glory associated with them, because he knows nothing about them and doesn't want to look bad if he makes mistakes, or because they involve too much menial work. This comes from a need to always appear good, like he was to his mother, and to have a person to blame for failures.

Guys with this pattern tend to be selfish. They feign support for your independent activities and your career while you are dating, but if the commitment expands, they start cultivating you into the roles they need you for, such as housekeeping, cooking, business support, or selling flowers at the airport. When you are brainwashed into a cult, they usually pigeonhole certain activities for you. Needless to say, the roles they will put you in are not intended to propel you to new heights of independence but reduce you to subservience. Brainwashers tend to be too self-conscious and feel that it would make them look bad if their girlfriend, fiancée, or wife didn't act in a fashion that was appropriate and of course traditionally female.

As desirably as this man has been painted, how does he survive, find women, and build a relationship? Remember the cult story. They start by finding women who are a little unsettled in their own lives. Perhaps these women are frustrated with the workplace. Perhaps they are unhappy living with their parents and have no other way out. Perhaps they are just tired of being treated badly by constantly dating the more vicious types of Losers. It is the state of perceived deprivation on the part of the women that allows the Brainwasher to sneak into their lives. You are particularly at risk if you are sensing the need for more in life, tend to be accommodating, and have a central agreement with some of the ideals of the traditional lifestyle.

Sue was not so much at risk by belief in the traditional lifestyle. She was enjoying her career and had a particularly good role model in her mother who went back to school. However, Sue was exposed by being an accommodating person and being ready to settle down. She never felt quite right about Ed, even at their first meeting, but didn't believe in her own intuition because it hadn't gotten her very far up to that point. She continued to see Ed, figuring things would click later. They dated for almost nine months, and Ed was talking about making a commitment, as in getting engaged. Sue started listening more closely once this came up as a possibility.

What she started hearing were plans for them to move into a basement apartment in his parents' house while they saved money. What she heard was that Ed's mother was never really sure about Sue and always took her son's side, even in disagreements where Ed was obviously wrong. What she heard was Ed making plans without much discussion or input, except an occasional "This is what we're going to do, so what do you think?" Finally, what she heard was Ed's desire to build a world, a colony, around himself, calling it a family, but with the purpose of serving him. As a nonbeliever in animal sacrifice, Sue decided not to throw her life into the volcano.

Before you are asked to chant, wait for a spaceship following a comet, or drink spiked Kool-Aid, you may want to take the test below after the first few dates you have with a new guy.

IS HE A BRAINWASHER?

*Circle the number and
add up the score*

Family Background

Male-dominated household, father set the rules, mother served	1
Single-parent household where he was in charge	1
Mother pampered long into high school and still does too much for him	2
Never learned to make his bed, never had chores	2
Seems in control of his mother	3
Mother is very critical of girlfriends	3

Work/School History

Problems with a female boss	3
Expresses he could never work with a female boss	3
Problems with female employees who are on an equal level	3
Discusses a lack of teamwork at his job	2
Never likes group projects where he wasn't in charge	2
Takes credit for other people's work	3
History of quitting activities due to "personality conflicts"	4

(test continues)

Friendships

Does not accept feedback from friends well	2
History of a number of friendships breaking up or fizzling	3
Has conflicts over where to go out if friends have a different idea	2
Seems to hold grudges too much	2

Past Relationships

Talks about women in derogatory fashion	1
Says past girlfriends were too controlling	2
Talks about how they were not interesting	2
Talks about past girlfriends being unable to work together with him	3

Body Language

Won't sit with his back to a wall	1
Tends to sit at the head of the table	2
Wants to be the organizer of where people sit	3
If sitting together, you have to mold to his position	1

Dress/Hygiene

Definite opinions about how people should dress	1
Lack of tolerance for unusual or divergent dressing	2
Tends to stick to a grooming schedule	1
Comments that he thinks you are underdressed in comparison to him	3

Behavior

Tries to move relationship along quickly	3
Nonacceptance of others' lifestyles	2
Orders for you at restaurant or makes very strong suggestions	4
Brings you only to places where he knows someone	4
Not a good listener when he disagrees with an opinion	3
Argumentative	3
Tries to give you advice without your asking	3
Makes all date decisions without consulting you	4

Conversation

Expresses opinion too freely	2
Talks a lot about forming a team	4
Talks about how mother helped father	3
Expresses opinions about men and women needing roles in life	4

(test continues)

Conversation

Talks about qualifications to be his girlfriend/wife	5
Paints an overly rosy picture of a future with him	2
Talks about raising a family too early in the dating scheme	3
Does not ask follow-up questions to your statements	2
Conversation includes tales about how he was right and many others were wrong	3

When Confronted

Gets extremely defensive and questions your motives	2
Does not listen or interrupts	3
Tells you he has no intention of settling for less	4

Your Impression

Seems like he is looking for a wife	4
He wants someone to melt into his identity	5
You feel he is inflexible	4
Total Score	

Score 12 and lower: No reason for concern at this point
Score between 13 and 23: Yellow Flag—There's reason for caution
Score 24 and above: Red Flag—Brain is on the spin cycle; go hang it out on the line away from this washer

Dirty Brain, Clean Mind

If a guy earns the Yellow Flag distinction, you've got to look more closely at him and yourself. Do you share some of the same values regarding traditional male and female roles? Are you a little needy at this time because of the sting of bad experiences with vicious dates? Are you feeling somewhat relationship deprived? Do you like mothering guys a little too much? If you answer these questions honestly, they should determine some of your decisions. Don't allow yourself to make decisions based on an unhappy temporary state you find yourself in. Don't make decisions on the basis of some misplaced mothering instincts. Get some professional help, then make a cleaner decision, not a washed-out one.

As you look closely at him, look first at his flexibility level. Is he understanding and supportive of women making their own decisions about balancing the role of family and career, or does he believe there is only one way? Do you look at his family background and see a lot of pampering? Do you both dream together about things or are you expected to share his dream? If you see a Yellow Flag, it is very important to discover what is going on before you get too wrapped up in the relationship. There will be less justification in your mind for leaving once you have a lot invested, so do some work before you invest.

Red Flag score? Either you get yourself deprogrammed or start reading about those Arab guys with forty wives, because you are selling yourself into slavery. Staying with this kind of guy is like being on a roller coaster—the cart moves on a track and is safe, but you have no control over what's coming ahead. We all like roller-coaster rides once in a while, but if we stayed on them constantly we'd start to puke.

Consider that you would slowly start to lose your identity. You would lose your capacity to make choices regarding your own career and how you spend your money. During these moments of "bliss," you will most likely be contending with a mother who is not sure she wants to let go of her baby boy. Chances are she will be nice to you but somewhat critical behind your back because you will not take care of her boy like she does. She'll think you're too selfish. By the way, if his mother is saying this to him, prepare to hear him tell you the same thing. The funny part is that you will be the one deemed as selfish, while your life revolves around accommodating him. This is one of the more riotous rooms of the fun house of dating.

Running Your Brain Through the Dryer

So your man is flexibility-challenged and you need to get away. No problem. This is one of the easiest breakups. He's given you all the material. Just don't let him tell you what you think. He will try to change you by realigning your view. Don't let it happen.

"I think you and I have too-different views for a relationship. We have completely different goals, and frankly I want you to find someone that will be the kind of girl you want. There are a lot of women out there who want life the same way you do. I'm not one of them."

His retort will be to point out your similarities, then tell you how you think. You respond by saying you know how to think, and his talking is convincing you even more that you are right. Any time he talks just point out how his views are good for him, but you're in a different mode in life. The more he talks, the more convinced you are that the two of you are different. He will eventually shut up because he keeps losing ground. Let the two opinions peacefully coexist.

Remaining friends with this kind of guy might be difficult, especially if he has built a whole fantasy world about your life together. Best to stay apart until he, not you, has a steady. If you want to be friends after that, there is a chance it can work.

Women often feel guilty about leaving guys that didn't treat them badly. This one probably wasn't such a bad guy. Rest assured he will soon find a laundry-washing girl who wants 2.3 children and who will man the pooper-scooper behind the family dog. And his mother will hate her too.

The Pleaser

The German Word for Jewelry Is Schmuck, *or All That's Gold Does Not Glitter*

Greek mythology tells us the story of a courtier of King Dionysius named Damocles, who was always too quick to flatter the king and his blessed life. One day Dionysius tired of the flattery and asked Damocles if he desired to replace him as king. Damocles knew responding positively would enter thoughts of rebellion in Dionysius, a negative response would be a lie and face equal consequences, so he said instead he would like only to experience being king for one day. Dionysius told Damocles that he would grant him that wish. The next day Damocles was awoken and led into the king's chamber and given royal treatment. He was dressed in regal robes and anointed as king for a day. As he leaned back against the silken cushion of the throne he gasped in horror as he noticed a giant sword suspended over his head by only a single thread. He asked the king about the presence of such a macabre ornament. Dionysius responded that if Damocles wanted to know the true feeling of being king, he should know that the price for a king's riches was to be fearful at all times that he could be slain. Being king meant living with the sword over your head. Many men live with the sword over their head and can transfer that feeling to you. That's why being in a relationship with these men can be such a royal pain.

It was finally time for a decent, wholesome kind of guy, thought Terry, when she agreed to go out with Dylan. They met at a church retreat for singles. He complained about how bad boys got all the girls, she about how she picked only very self-centered men. Terry was very relaxed this time. She knew Dylan pretty well. They had already shared their emotions in a group counseling session, had already somewhat bonded. He was down to earth, perhaps not as good-looking as she'd like, but it was time to stop worrying about appearances. Besides, he asked her out to dinner and the opera. The opera! This guy was cultured and had class! Terry found the nicest, figure-flattering, medium-length black dress that had just the right amount of glitter on it—refined yet sexy, with a touch of wildness. It was one of the few times she looked in the mirror and saw herself as beautiful, *da morire* ("to die for"). She had become the princess she dreamed about in her preadolescence. It was going to be nice to be treated with elegance for a change.

Dylan showed up in a gorgeous black designed suit, with a colored shirt and a luscious silk tie. He handed her a dozen long-stemmed roses and a card with a lovely poem about their first night together. In the front seat of his sports car awaited a little teddy bear with a note—"I couldn't bear waiting for our date." He swept her away to dinner at an expensive restaurant, where a table, seemingly specially chosen, awaited them.

"I haven't been to the opera in so long. This is quite a treat. Do you go to the opera frequently, Dylan?"

"Not really. I wanted this night to be special for you. I got tenth-row seats right in the middle. Had to sign away rights to my firstborn male child, but it's going to be worth it."

"Well, maybe you'll have a baby girl first, or were you demeaning female children?"

"Ooh, better watch what I say around you. Sorry, I can't believe I am actually on a date with you."

Terry felt a little embarrassed by that statement, but she ignored it. "This is a lovely restaurant. You sure know how to find special places."

"And special people. I always wanted to try this place. I have so many things I'd like to do, places I'd like to go. You know, I can probably get tickets to the Grammys, or the Academy Awards, or the Super Bowl, if I work through my contacts. I'm sort of lucky, I guess, to know a lot of people who can make things happen."

"Wow, that's great. You'll never have any male children to keep. Have you ever gone to any of those things?"

"Once or twice when I was dating someone I really liked. It's hard to find a girl who can handle those kinds of people and look right doing it. Class is hard to come by these days."

"I think I'd put a tux on a male blow-up doll if I had a chance to go to the Academy Awards and didn't have a date."

"Like you would ever have a problem getting a date. I must say, you certainly look stunning tonight. That's a beautiful dress. Did you do one of those 'I-don't-have-anything-to-wear-to-the-opera' things that women do all the time?"

"I guess so. I must have tried on thirty dresses at ten different stores before I found this one. But I like to shop, so I guess it was sort of fun."

"Have you ever been shopping on the Champs Elysées in Paris, or Fifth Avenue in New York? That's where a girl like you should shop. That's where I would like to take a girl like you shopping. Next time I'm in a relationship, I'm going to go to all those places I've always wanted to go, do all the things I've dreamed of doing. That's what life should be about. I want to show someone the world."

"Isn't that strange. I always thought I should be shopping on the Champs Elysées too. I think I was probably Jackie Kennedy or Princess Diana in a past life. You really seem to like the finer things in life."

"What I want is to spend my life enjoying all the quality I can bring to it. I have a feeling we'll be doing some of that together. You are certainly quality."

Terry enjoyed being with Dylan. He was a man with many dreams, took her to the best places on the first three dates, and never let her open any door. Terry didn't have to talk about any of her dreams on these dates, Dylan was kind enough to dream for the both of them.

It would be nice if all men treated women with great respect and made them feel special. But when you start feeling a little nervous, that the pedestal he's put you on makes you feel less armed than the Venus de Milo, you could be sculpting a relationship with a Red Flag.

How do men get to be too nice, too attentive? How do they get to be a Pleaser? As with all relationship difficulties, the roots begin with the parents and develop through the teenage years. The Pleaser usually starts as a young child who is very sensitive to others, a child with a genetic homing device that is locked in on the way people feel. The relationship between his parents is somewhat out of balance. On the healthier side, his father may teach him to revere his mother, which is a good thing, although the father may have gone a little overboard. On the more negative side, his father may be explosive or not present and his mother may be overemotional. The child engenders protective feelings toward the mother early on in life. The young boy learns that his mother is a little more emotionally fragile, and perhaps doesn't understand why that is the case. He is hard on himself because he feels he should understand women, even as a child. Unlike grown men, of course, who completely understand women. Right!

The next important factor is the planting of a strong need to please in the child. This can sometimes be done by a demon-child older sibling who acts up, making the Pleaser feel he has to take up the slack, or by the parents setting the two siblings in competition with each other for parental attention. The Pleaser won by being more sensitive and always doing the right thing, always pleasing. Good child, tough adulthood.

By the teenage years, the Pleaser becomes a little intimidated by women. He knows they are different, doesn't understand them very well, and is tuned in to them as fragile beings. He becomes intimidated by girls and is usually very insecure about attracting women because it is such a hit-or-miss proposition. Frequently, the Pleaser is tuned in to one or more of his negative physical characteristics, like acne or being overweight, and becomes very hard on himself. The Pleaser feels insecure and almost as if he is younger and less valuable than women his age, particularly attractive women. The Pleaser sublimates his frustrations and often accomplishes a lot in high school, college, and even afterward. It is interesting that as hard as the Pleaser is on himself, he is often talented in other areas of life whether it be academics, sports, the arts, or sometimes multiple areas. Regardless of what he accomplishes, he rarely feels he has achieved what he could. If he were female, he'd be living in a beauty salon, changing hairdos every other day. But his inferior gender role does not allow for such an easy solution.

The Pleaser chokes up completely when attracted to a girl and is unable to overcome it. Dating may have started late as a result, and the first dating experience is often bad. Being more sensitive than others causes him to take the early relationship breakups harder and blame himself more. By the time he is an adult he almost has a feeling that an attractive woman is doing him a favor by going out with him, even if he has built himself into a very accomplished and talented adult. His overly nice acts create uneasiness in the woman he's dating, and these potential romances end up reduced to friendships, which of course further feeds his insecurities and feeling of inferiority. They get credited with being "nice guys" and learn the mantra "nice guys finish last."

On the surface, the Pleaser may seem very similar to the

Leech (Red Flag #7) and the Rescuer (Red Flag #13), and, in fact, they do share many characteristics. However, there are differences. The Leech is looking for someone on whom to be dependent; the Pleaser is only looking for someone to love him. The Rescuer looks to control by fostering your dependence, the Pleaser is much more focused on trying to make you feel and be better. He is just a nice guy who tries too hard. He's what you want every man in your life to be—your father, grandfather, brother, best male friend, uncle—everyone except your boyfriend.

Dylan showered Terry with everything he possibly could. He set up romantic evenings, evenings of fun and frolic, evenings full of new experiences. By the third date, he gave her a valuable piece of jewelry that had belonged to his deceased mother. Terry tried to make him more secure. She liked him and enjoyed being treated well but left each date feeling like she didn't know Dylan that well because he was trying too hard. She started feeling a little insecure about herself, always wondering what she could do to control the direction of the relationship. There was also a pathetic quality to the relationship, and Terry hated having to pity the man she wanted to love. It was not an easy relationship by any means.

When Terry asked Dylan if he'd back off a little, he got very upset and reminded her of everything they had done together. He never backed off. Terry always had fun with Dylan, so ending it after four months was very difficult. She would pull away and knew Dylan was getting upset. She knew the inevitable was going to be very hard on Dylan, but after four and a half months, she ended it. She wanted to be friends, which Dylan agreed to in his usual accommodating way, but the friendship faded when Terry got another boyfriend. Terry misses Dylan and thinks about what could have been if he were only a little different.

It is important to be very aware that when you are with a Pleaser they can rip your heart out, because you can love them a lot and know it just isn't right. The test below will help you identify this character before you get too involved.

IS HE A PLEASER?

*Circle the number and
add up the score*

Family Background

As a child he was extremely sensitive	1
Father taught him to revere mother, observe all courtesies of chivalry	2
Felt mother was overemotional, fragile, needed to be protected	3
Father was a little explosive	1
Older brother or sister rebelled very strongly against family	2
Parents put children in competition with one another	2

Work/School History

Intimidated by women in high school	4
Started dating late	1
First sexual experience late	1
Focused on a physical flaw throughout high school	3
Multitalented but never felt accomplished enough	3

Friendships

Popular with friends	1
Friends say he's too nice	2
Always there with a helping hand	1
Likes to entertain at his home	1
Enjoys some domestic tasks like cooking, gardening, etc.	1
Tastes are more refined than friends	1

Past Relationships

Has been the one dumped more often than not	3
Still keeps in touch with past girlfriends	2
Has done a lot for past girlfriends, either helping them or exposing them to a lot of new things	2
Talks mostly positively about past relationships	1
Says past girlfriends couldn't handle a nice guy	4

(test continues)

Body Language

Very open, attentive	1
Is not the first to touch	1
Looks away shyly when you look him in the eye	3

Dress/Hygiene

Dresses less comfortably than other men	2
Tends toward patterns of dress after you tell him what you like	2
Rarely goes a day without a shower and washing hair	1

Behavior

Frequent gifts or things to indicate he is thinking of you	2
Never lets you pay for anything	2
Automatically includes you in his plans	3
Doesn't get angry at you when you do wrong	1
First date is expensive and he foots the bill	4
Sends flowers after first date	3
Insists you drive his car if you say you like it	3
Lets you use house or apartment if he is away before he knows you well	3
Brings you a gift before your date	3
Calls a little too frequently	3
Buys or shares a lottery ticket with you so you can dream together about winning	4
Frequently cancels plans with a friend to go out with you	2
Always asks you before he makes plans	3
Gives you something of sentimental value in the first three dates	5
Tries to be your best friend in the first couple of dates	2

Conversation

Makes a quick judgment and states you are a good match for him	2
Tells you what he can do for you	1
Tries too hard to impress you with his goodness	2
Uses the phrase "nice guys finish last"	4
Tells you he is too nice or too good	4
Never interrupts you when you are speaking	2
Remembers even insignificant things you have said	2
Tries to get you to dream and set goals with him	2
Compliments excessively	1
Talks about other guys wanting only one thing	1

(test continues)

When Confronted

Reminds you of everything he has done for you when you tell him to back off	3
Tries to appear pathetic or hurt to get sympathy	4
Tells you he is trying very hard and will try to improve to meet your standards	3

Your Impression

Shy	2
Very insecure	2
Dependent on you	4
You feel sorry for him	2
You can't be as nice as he is, so you're feeling guilty	3
He is trying to push the relationship where it shouldn't go yet	3
Total Score	

Score 10 and lower: No reason for concern at this point
Score between 11 and 22: Yellow Flag—There's reason for caution
Score 23 and above: Red Flag—He'll nice-guy you to death; go please yourself elsewhere

Killing Me with Niceness Is Still Killing Me

When a man scores in the Yellow Flag category, you have
quite a decision to make. Because Pleasers are so endearing, it
is difficult to leave after you get attached. They truly become
your best friend who will help you in any way they can. The
best way to test whether the relationship has a chance is to
ask him in specific ways to back off a little. Never say, "You're
being too nice," because that won't be understood and will
just raise resentment. Better to ask that he let you pay, that he
just hang out and not plan something so glamorous for every
date, or maybe that he be less complimentary and helpful.
Help him understand how he's put you on a pedestal, and you
want to be more of an equal. Work to help reduce his fear of
rejection. Let him know that he can be free to relax because
you like him. Try to build up his ego so he's comfortable with
you, perhaps focusing on the areas he is most insecure

about—his complexion, baldness, weight, lisp, etc. If he responds positively, and you can work on your own feelings regarding becoming physically attracted to him, you may have found a good, faithful lover and friend.

If a man falls in the Red Flag category, the stakes have changed. Even when a Pleaser is aware that his niceness is overwhelming, he may have gotten into such a habit of treating women well that it is the only way a relationship feels good to him. Backing off is hard. Unfortunately, the pressure his niceness puts on the woman to be nice as well is often a barrier to intimacy. The Pleaser is frequently expecting little in return except love and acceptance. The woman feels obligated to do as much as he is doing. That is the sword of Damocles. The relationship hangs by a thread and when the sword drops the Pleaser asks, "What more could I have done?" This guy needs another couple of good dumpings before he has the chance to change. He needs to figure out that too much niceness is still too much. You never do a Pleaser a favor by hanging around, because only harsh realities will make this guy different. This is one of the few Red Flaggers that it makes sense to check back with later on, since they do tend to make good mates once they've backed off their behaviors a little.

Cutting the Last Threads from This Loser

Make no mistake: This is a sensitive guy, and there is no way for you to break up without hurting him. He will look for the best in you even if you have snakes for hair like Medusa, you have PMS, and your eyeliner is crooked. There is nothing that will lessen the blow. Bringing up that he is too nice will only get you a thoughtful lecture on how women say they want nice guys but are only attracted to scumbags. Being a bitch will only make him concerned that something is wrong, because he knows you are better.

It is important in any breakup, but especially in this one, to maintain your dignity and the softness of your character. Make this about your inability to feel self-assured with a man who is so attentive. In a beautiful scene from the movie *The Accidental Tourist*, a man explains to his wife why he wants a divorce to be with a woman of seemingly lesser stature. He says that it's not that the woman is better—in fact, in most ways his wife was a better person—it's that he feels better with her. This is about you feeling comfortable as his girlfriend, which you don't. Let him know that everything he has taught you and shown you has made you a better person, but it has also made you realize that you are not as relationship-ready as you thought and you need to develop on your own. Remember there is no letting him down easy, so you have to be very strict about not seeing him for a period of time afterward. You need time for self-reflection. It's happened to him before and he has survived. It will happen again until he learns a little about himself and that too much of a good thing is no longer a good thing. He will tell you that he is going to swing the other way and become a jerk like the guys who get all the girls. Rest assured there will be another girl who will break a nail or two on the hidden treasures he has to offer.

The Possessor

*There's No Room for a Control
Freak in the Sideshow of Romance*

When sushi became the new yuppie craze in urban America there began a hedonistic quest for variety among neophyte sushi aficionados. Willing to try anything, they stumbled upon an ancient Japanese flavor that was forbidden in America: *fugu*, or Japanese puffer fish. The problem is the flesh of the *fugu* becomes poisonous unless prepared with the most ethereal care. The sushi chef must be highly experienced, the best chefs leaving enough poison to prickle the diner's lips. Of course, a number of diners must die midmeal to achieve this effect, but the excitement of the challenge is enough to mitigate the risk. We so love in our relationships a little puffer fish of passion, to tingle the lips of our souls and give us the experience of living on the edge. It's like Cinderella defying the stepsisters to attend the prince's ball. The problem is the carriage turns into a pumpkin without warning, the slippers to military marching boots, and the prince is only a monocle short of being a villain in a James Bond film.

* * *

A disclaimer came with Demetria's telling Jill that Dennis had asked for her phone number. Jill met Dennis at Demetria's wedding at the dreaded singles' table where all the people who didn't get invited with a guest sit. They danced once or twice, had a few exchanges of words, and Jill thought nothing of it. Dennis called Demetria after her honeymoon and asked whether she would give him Jill's number. Demetria informed Dennis that as a proper lady she wouldn't give out the number until she asked Jill's permission. So she called Jill, told her of the situation, and warned her that Dennis had been prone to jealousy in his last relationship. They decided that part of that could have been because Dennis's last girlfriend was a big flirt, eventually leaving for a past boyfriend. The numbers were exchanged, a phone call was made, and a date was set. Tennis and a burger afterward.

"I'm glad we got off the court before I had a heart attack. You've got quite a serve—for a girl, that is."

"Don't like losing a game or two to a girl, do you? Men usually like it when I give them a good beating."

"I bet they do, especially in that outfit. Sort of unfair making me look at those legs in that little tennis skirt and trying to concentrate on hitting a ball at the same time. I guess you'll want to change before we go to the restaurant."

"Nah, I'm fine. I don't think there's a dress code at the pub. Besides, the waitresses are wearing less than I am."

"I think you'll get a lot more attention than the waitresses. I took a female friend of mine once to the pub. She was wearing a beach cover-up, having just come from the pool. There was this guy at the bar who wouldn't take his eyes off of her. So I go over to him and tell him to buy a magazine or rent a video instead. Well, he gets these "beer muscles" and comes back in my face. What happened next wasn't very pretty."

"I could put some shorts on if it will make you feel more comfortable. I'm not quite in the damsel-in-distress mood."

"I didn't mean anything by that story. Guys are just that way.

They get turned on easily. I think if girls knew what guys were really like, they would have left us in the caves."

"Ah, if we left you in the caves, you wouldn't have anything to draw on the walls about. We're sort of stuck with you guys."

"So, have you ever dated any of Demetria's friends?"

"Actually, I dated her husband a couple of times. That's how they met. She was going out with one of his friends. We sort of did the old switcheroo."

"Guys will do that—steal away another guy's girl. Who was the guy you ended up dating? Was he at the wedding?"

"No, actually, come to think of it, I didn't see him there. I think he moved to the Midwest, somewhere obscure like North Dakota. I drove him out of the state, probably into desolation, away from all the civilized world. He's probably sitting in some missile silo right now thinking of our one date. Poor guy. But I hear you dated Bella. Pretty girl."

"Yeah, didn't she know it. She always used to wear short little dresses and flirt with every guy in sight. Always said the entourage of guys she kept around her were 'just friends.' Guys don't do the friends thing with a pretty girl. She used to tell me some of her male friends were gay, but I could tell even they were hitting on her. She used to drive me nuts."

"Maybe I'll put some sweats on instead."

And so on, and so on. Jill liked that Dennis noticed her and was concerned for her safety. They had a pretty decent date after she dressed down. There were no single men at the bar.

Most women like to feel that a man is going to be a little protective, and most women like when a man feels he is with someone special. But when the protective shield makes you as crowded as when the airbag inflated in your two-seater, you may be facing a head-on collision with a Red Flag.

With jealousy we see another barometer of male insecurity, although perhaps a more insidious version than most. Jealousy slaughters love while trying to keep it alive. It destroys self-respect, replacing it with loathing and disgust. It torches the very house where affection and caring live, making a relationship homeless, groundless, and without foundation. And it doesn't feel very good, either.

Yet many women like to see a little jealousy in their men, especially younger women. It makes them feel loved, as if the guy really cares. Wanting to see a little jealousy is like looking at a bad car wreck on the side of the highway; we all do it, but we can end up seeing things we really don't want to see. Some amount of jealous feelings are normal. It's the expression of jealousy that carries the bad news. When the expression of jealousy starts to control and confine, you may have found a Possessor.

The insecurity men express through jealousy can come from a number of different places. He could be a spoiled only child and used to getting what he wants. He was spoiled by his mother and can't understand why he is not the center of your universe like he was of hers. The other profile depicts a man who grew up fighting for attention and affection from his mother. It's a matter of extremes one way or another, and the propensity for explosiveness is obvious from their early patterns. They consider another man vying for their "possession" a personal attack.

You become the personal property of the Possessor. Jealousy is an expression of self-love, not love for you. The Possessor feels you, as a woman, are weak and inconsistent. You are naive and capable of betrayal because of your basic moral ineptitude. Men are the stronger creatures that need to keep women in check. The Possessor has determined that if you are to be his girlfriend, fiancée, or wife, he must make decisions that you can't make, particularly when it comes to your relationships with other men. In one of its sickest forms, women who go to psychologists with pathologically jealous men will be told that their therapist has designs on her too.

The fear in jealousy is of being supplanted, replaced. This would cause great humiliation and reveal the Possessor as weak. There is an inner deprivation to the jealous man, a feeling that something is missing. Yet when this inner feeling is strong, he tries to control the outside, not the inside. For example, some of his lecherous views of men come from an inability to deal with his own impulses. He projects these feelings outward. Sometimes other men will be the target, particularly if he feels confident in his physical ability to compete with men. At other times, the women in his life become the target, when he has concern over fighting with men. Aggression is likely either way. Regardless of who is the target, you will suffer the most.

Jill and Dennis actually dated for over a year, even moving in together. At first she sort of liked that he was jealous. She felt protected and cared for in a passionate way. They also had a very passionate sex life, which added to Jill's feeling of being loved. The jealousy monster would emerge now and then, but Jill found that if she was careful about what she wore and said, she could keep it in check most of the time. They did have a few nasty arguments over Jill's going out with her single girlfriends, and Jill finally gave in to meeting them at someone else's house or just lying if her friends wanted to go out to dinner. Jill figured Dennis would "grow out of it." After all, she was not doing anything to foster his jealousy.

When they got engaged, they went to a Catholic church to get information about getting married. He was Catholic, she was Protestant. The young priest gave them information and talked with them a little about their religious differences, the raising of children, etc. When they left, Dennis started their private conversation by accusing the priest of flirting with Jill. This was quite disturbing to Jill. Not wanting to alarm her parents, she went to her aunt and uncle to discuss it, not telling Dennis where she was going. When she got home, Dennis was in an angry rage, accusing her of meeting another man behind her back and not believing she was with her aunt and uncle. Jill spent most of that night in her car and made an appointment with a psychologist the next morning. She had therapy sessions for three days in a row, told her parents what was going on, and by the weekend went with her father and three brothers to move out of the house. She never spoke another word to Dennis.

There is a lot of misery that comes in a jealous relationship that could all be avoided if you catch it early. The following test will help you look for this Red Flag.

IS HE A POSSESSOR?

Circle the number and add up the score

Family Background

Competitive home environment between brothers and sisters	1
Children fought for parents' attention	3
One of both parents were not attentive	1
Criticized a lot by father	2
Spoiled by mother	1
One or both parents were unfaithful in their relationship	1
Father left mother for another woman	3

Work/School History

Talks about flirtation at work	2
Got into a couple of fights in high school	2
Had only one or two girlfriends throughout high school	2
Paints himself as more valuable at work than anyone else	1
Feels peers are incompetent or don't know how to work hard	1
Gets angry about work issues	1
Remembers himself as better in high school than he was	2

Friendships

Places less emphasis on male friendships	1
Talks about how friends can only be trusted to a point	4
Seems to put up barriers between you and his friends by telling you bad things about them	3
Seems to prefer a lack of mixing of gender with friends, parties split up to all guys in one room and all girls in another	2

(test continues)

Past Relationships

Long-term relationships were with low self-esteem women	2
Feels women have cheated on him in the past	4
Previous girlfriends were stalked by other guys and he had to intervene	2
Played the rescuer in other relationships	2
Angry a lot in other relationships	3
Says previous girlfriends were flirts	4
Problem with jealousy before	5

Body Language

Stands between you and other guys at social functions	3
Controls seating arrangements so you are sitting next to women	2
Gets fidgety when you are conversing with a guy	3

Dress/Hygiene

Spends a lot of time in front of the mirror	2
Some obsessiveness about cleaning	1
Dresses one level above others at social functions, then criticizes others	1

Behavior

Listens to your answering machine messages behind your back	5
Gets upset if you mention another guy in conversation	3
Can't accept your having male friends	5
Has argument with a guy looking at you	5
Starts a fight with a guy while protecting you	4
Quick to anger	4

Conversation

Says a lot of guys are looking at you when you don't see it	2
Talks about how women are weaker than men	2
Talks about guys stealing girlfriends or wives	3
Questions you a lot about past relationships	2
Says he does not think a girl should date more than one guy at a time	1
Uses terms like slut or whore in describing women	3
Expresses rescue fantasies where women are helpless	1
States women cannot have male friends	3
Tells story about verbal altercation to protect a girl	2
Tells story about physical altercation to protect a girl	3
Tells story about setting a "guy straight"	2

(test continues)

Conversation	
Talks about how people cheat all the time	1
Talks about liking old-fashioned gender roles where women stay home	2

When Confronted	
Gets angry	2
Demeans you	5
Expresses attitude that all women are naive	3
Cuts down your self-esteem	5

Your Impression	
There is a little depression	3
You feel very protected	2
Overall intensity seems very high	3
He is overly controlling	1
You feel life he is getting possessive	5
	Total Score

Score 10 and lower: No reason for concern at this point, he's about as insecure as you can expect this early in a dating relationship

Score between 11 and 20: Yellow Flag—There's reason for caution

Score 21 and above: Red Flag—He wants a possession; time for a buyout

Let's Do Sushi

The Yellow Flag for jealousy is truly a sign of caution. It's like the lips tingling a little too much after a serving of puffer fish. This is one of those very serious Yellow Flags where you should make some quick decisions and review them very often. Start by asserting yourself, very firmly. "When you ____, you are treating me like a possession. That is not going to cut it, and it stops or we move on." Fill in the blank with "tell me not to go out with my girlfriends" or "tell me what to wear" or "talk about how other men are always hitting on me" or whatever else fits. Tolerate a small discussion afterward that should end with, "I am a grown woman who will make my own decisions. You have to accept that and hold back on telling me what to do." If an argument ensues or he starts telling you how naive you are or how you're just not aware, you're in Red Flag territory. You now must act appropriately or decide to be locked in the tower of his jealousy.

If there is a Red Flag score consider yourself in a movie theater on fire. Go to the nearest exit, move quickly and orderly. Expect that the jealousy problem will get worse and worse and has the strong potential to lead to abuse. Understand that he will make every attempt to separate you from your friends. He will attempt to set up your life so that you will not be able to wander any further than the grocery store without his presence. Then again, single guys shop in grocery stores so he may occasionally follow you.

He will want to know what you have done each day, where you went and to whom you talked. If you leave something out, you will be called names—minimally a liar, most likely names not printable in this book. You will probably be the victim of considerable degradation, and if you do have children with this man, they will learn not to respect you and, of course, women in general. Bite, scratch, and claw to get away from him as quickly as possible.

The Check, Please!

As you have been reading, most breakups aren't pleasant. This one can be downright volatile. Do not attempt this alone, particularly if you've let this relationship go to the point where you have stuff at his place. This may be a time you want to have a couple of male friends and family around.

In the first place, remember he does not have a lot of respect for women. The Possessor will try to bully you into submission, or harass you for revenge. He is less likely to act if there are strong males involved, not necessarily physically strong but mentally strong. One of the biggest problems women make with this kind of guy is they change their phone number because of harassing calls. That fuels the fire, as he knows he's got you on the run. Stand your ground. Handle him by other means. You may need to get the police involved to stop the harassment, or even a lawyer. Has it been impressed upon you that this is serious?

No blame on this one, please. Do not blame yourself. Never blame him. Try to do this in under ten words: "I am leaving, I don't want to date anymore." His first line of defense may be about how much he loves you and how you'll work it out. Your next line should be: "I am leaving, I don't want to date anymore." The conversation may start to turn slightly emotional, and he may try to draw you into a discussion. Your next line should be: "I am leaving, I don't want to date anymore." Anger and bitterness will probably come out next. Want to guess what your next line should be? Be a broken record, and try not to give any more than the one line. If you do talk, you're going to be trashed—your choice.

As far as remembering the good times, feeling sorry, etc., go back to the Japanese *fugu*, but imagine knowing that the dish was prepared wrong. It might taste great for a while, but your demise would be imminent. Within weeks, he will find some other adventurous diner that he can tingle, titillate, and eventually poison. Who wants cold dead raw fish anyway?

Mr. Ego

If He Thinks He's God's Gift, Exchange Him!

The tale is an ancient one of Greek mythology. In a small Greek village, a child named Narcissus was born so gorgeous that none could rival his beauty. As he grew to be a young man, he learned of his beauty from everyone who kept falling in love with him. He never saw himself but knew he must be spectacular. He was as vain as he was handsome, and he rejected the fair, the quick of mind and wit, the homemaker, the worker, any woman who came his way. Then one day he saw a beautiful nymph named Echo while he was hunting in the woods. Echo was cursed by Hera so that she could only repeat what was said to her, never saying anything original. When they met, all Echo could say was exactly what Narcissus said. He thought her so brilliant, he fell in love. But when he went to caress her, he recoiled in horror, disgusted by the touch of something lesser than himself. Echo ran away and Narcissus lay down beside a lake to process the encounter. In the lake, he saw his reflection and found true love at last. So in love with the face in the water, he would not leave to eat. When he would take a drink from the lake, he shattered the image into a thousand pieces, so he would no longer drink. Echo pined away for the love of Narcissus, while Narcissus pined away for the love of himself. Although he never reproduced any offspring, it seems there are many men of today whom Narcissus could call his sons.

Maureen met John at the gym. He was a regular and seemed serious about his workouts. Maureen loved the way he looked! His body was developed but not overdone. You could see definition in all of his muscles, but he did not have that bulky, steroided-out weight lifter look. He seemed to pay careful attention to his body's proportions. As a result, no one set of muscles overshadowed another. What balance! Maureen was impressed with his commitment. He was always in the gym, and she certainly liked the idea of a guy who could stick with a project. Too many of the men she dated did not seem committed to anything, and she always turned out to be one of those "things" escaping their commitment. With the encouragement of her friend and treadmill partner, Maureen went over and talked to him.

"This is so politically incorrect to admit, but I can't seem to get the knack of that machine you just used. Could you spare some time to help a klutz?"

"Actually I have one more set on that machine and then I'm through for the day. Why don't you watch me, and I'll help you after I'm done."

"Of course. I see you're pushing more with your . . ."

"Please let me finish, then I'll show you. . . . Okay, now let's figure out what it is you're trying to do. Do you know what this machine is for in the first place?"

"I think I can figure that out. I know something about this stuff."

"I'm surprised. Most women don't want to work their laterals that much. It makes their abdomens thicker. Makes them look heavier."

"Oh. Actually, maybe I don't want to work on that machine. I'm trying to work these muscles right here."

"You want the washboard. That is something completely different. Abs are my specialty."

"I noticed that."

"Yeah, I've worked hard on mine. I could get you a six-pack in no time at all."

"Now you're talking. Let's get out of the gym and get that six-pack."

"Cute. You want an abs lesson or what?"

"Maybe a little of both—an abs lesson and an 'or what.' "

"You want to sit upright and place the bar firmly against your shoulders like this. See how I execute the movement slowly. See how my abs flex on both the upward and downward movement. It's important to flex on the downward movement, you maximize resistance that way."

"I've seen you here often, you seem so into the health scene."

"It's the only scene to be in. I won't miss my workouts. I've been working out since high school. I went from being a scrawny kid to being proud to look in the mirror."

"Is that why you like the gym, all the mirrors?"

"Actually, the mirrors are real important. You should always look in the mirror when you're working your muscles. It helps you make sure your form is right, and it gives you motivation when you see the muscle pumped. I love the pump." He glances in the mirror as he flexes a little.

"You seem so involved in life. Are you the type of guy who seeks out new adventures all the time, one of those adrenaline junkies?"

"I don't need to seek out adventures, they seek me out. Sort of like you coming over here. I guess I have the look that breeds opportunity. Dream it, believe it, achieve it. That's my motto. You can make anything happen that you want. It all falls in your lap if you work hard at making yourself as good as you can be. Even getting a date with the best-looking girl in the gym."

"My name is Maureen."

"I'm John. Shall we go dancing tonight or pick up a video at my house?"

"I don't do videos on a first date."

Maureen had a great night dancing with John. He was a good dancer but tended not to look at her much while he was "feeling the music." He also looked great on the dance floor. His was so nicely groomed and he had the right amount of jewelry. By the time the night was over she thought she knew John pretty well. He told her a lot about himself, his dreams and how he was making a success out of a sales business that many people fail at. He was such a positive person and one of the more interesting guys she had dated in a long time. She hoped that the next time he would want to know a little about her.

All women want a man who will open up and talk about himself. Self-disclosure not only lets you see what you have in common with him, it helps build the foundations of intimacy. But, when your conversation has as much balance as Charlie Brown executing a triple-toe loop, you're skating on thin ice and ready to fall smack dab in the middle of a Red Flag.

Self-absorption starts with others' absorption. From childhood, Mr. Ego has been the center of attention. He may have good looks, charm, a charismatic personality, or be the best athlete in the school, but it is the constant attention of parents, teachers, and friends that make him believe he can do no wrong. He learns that he is better than anyone else, and his confidence makes others look up to him, which only convinces him more of his superiority. It is usually his mother who takes away any semblance of humility, as she gives him her complete undivided attention and places him above other siblings and usually above her husband, if he has stayed around. The worst part is, she puts the budding Mr. Ego above herself! He is more than happy to take over as he gets older and starts acting disrespectful toward his lowly mother. Fear not, there is some of that maternal feeling left for you and any other woman for that matter, as Mr. Ego is probably the man most likely to believe women are inferior and need to be kept in their place.

All children are born seeing themselves as the center of the universe. Typically, though, we learn that we revolve around a common sun. Because Mr. Ego has been systematically directed to believe he is the sun, he is always looking for others to luxuriate in his glow. Unlike Narcissus in the opening story, Mr. Ego is not a loner who doesn't want social contact. His core personality requires admirers—admirers with unrelenting passion to bask in the warmth of his goodness and beauty. Although this is not intentional, when people start to get a little tired or burned by Mr. Ego's glow, he can get rude and demeaning. He is the lit stove you shouldn't touch, the sharp knife you should keep away from your finger, the ball that you shouldn't play with in the house—all useful items in the right place but bound to hurt you when used incorrectly. Using Mr. Ego as a boyfriend is incorrect.

Women are often initially attracted to Mr. Ego. Typically he has good looks accented by excellent grooming and takes care of himself well. Since so many men have trouble opening up, women initially may think they have found a very confident and sharing man. There is usually a measure of success in his career that further compels women to judge him well. But at some point, these women get sick of a man who doesn't listen to the events of their day. They get tired of a man who wants adoration but doesn't give it. Besides, women don't appreciate Mr. Ego having nicer hair and more jewelry than they do.

Maureen, with the help of friends, tried to analyze the situation. What was she doing wrong? How could she communicate better? Was she being assertive enough? Was she understanding enough? Was she interesting enough? Initially, Maureen did what so many women do. She tried to please him by listening harder. John did like that, but he talked even more about himself, never really including Maureen. She felt like a spectator at her own date. What seemed so full of promise sitting on an ab machine in the gym started giving her stomachaches in her social life. Maureen decided to quit sharing her bathroom with a mirror hog.

The test below can help you determine if the guy you're dating is just a futile exercise or the start of a healthy lifestyle change.

IS HE MR. EGO?

Circle the number and add up the score

Family Background

Grew up as only child	2
Physically pretty infant/child	3
Doted on by parents (most likely mother)	3
Mother continues to consider son as shining star at the center of her life	5
Always center of attention as child	3

Work/School History

Teachers "loved him," teachers' pet	2
Very popular in school	1
Participated in school government, plays, or sports	2
Many pictures in yearbook	1
In "spotlight" position at work	2
Brags a lot about achievements at work	3
Gives himself credit for things at work without attributing anything to other coworkers	3

Friendships

Has large number of acquaintances	3
Does not know much about friends' lives	2
Friends tend to contact him most of time	2
Friendships seem shallow and one-sided	2

(test continues)

Past Relationships

Past relationships seem unimportant to him	3
Past girlfriends seem not to have impacted his life	3
Past girlfriends were "crazy"	2
States that he broke up with all past girlfriends	3

Body Language

Eyes never look at you	1
Looks around constantly (to see who is looking at him)	2
Always has back to wall	1
Flexes muscles and stretches a lot	1

Dress/Hygiene

Dresses sharply most of time	1
Spends a lot of time on hair	2
Constantly adjusts clothes	1
Very style-conscious	2
Gets more services at beauty salon than you do	3

Behavior

Looks at self in mirrors often	3
Is into exercise and health	2
Plans dates around his needs/schedule	2
Dates often include groups of people	2
Easily moves to center of groups of people	2

Conversation

Favorite pronoun is "I"	2
Conversation seems unbalanced in his direction	2
Asks few questions about you	2
Does not ask follow-up questions to your statements	3
Constantly changes subject to himself	3
Interrupts your conversation to redirect it back to him	3
Conversations always lead back to him and his accomplishments	4
Makes comments about other people's possessions, clothes, or actions, relating them back to himself	4
You cannot get a word in edgewise	3
Tells humorous stories that poke fun at himself	−1
Asks you questions about yourself and follows up on your answers, keeping focused on you	−1

(test continues)

When Confronted	
Never admits to being wrong	2
Seems not to understand your point	3
Attacks you or finds fault with you	2
Gets defensive and questions your motives	2
Continues same behavior without regard to your confrontation	2
Apologizes and admits to being partially wrong	−1
Shows insight into his behavior	−1
Your Impression	
Very self-confident	1
Self-absorbed	3
Not a team player	2
Needs to be center of attention	3
Expects you to worship him	4
	Total Score

Score 15 and lower: No reason for concern at this point
Score between 16 and 30: Yellow Flag—There's reason for caution
Score 31 and above: Red Flag—He'll stare at himself in the lake forever; swim away

Many Ripples on the Lake Make a Wave

If your date falls in the Yellow Flag category, cautious optimism is recommended. You may be dealing with something as simple as an only child who was used to being the center of attention but does not still demand this role. The Yellow Flag guy may not spontaneously compliment you or ask you about your day. However, if you start to talk about yourself, he will listen. He will ask follow-up questions, make comments, and offer suggestions. When the topic comes up at a later time, he will remember what you have talked about. He may need a little more encouragement than other men but doesn't demand total adoration. The Yellow Flag guy may be capable of genuine concern for you; he is just not used to inquiring. After a few dates, you'll find that a style of expressing yourself assertively works well with this type. He may even learn from you, and he'll be interested in self-improvement in the intimacy category, not just his looks, achievements, or perceptions of others. The biggest way to tell if he is going to stay below the dreaded Red Flag line is if he tries to develop a team approach with you to the relationship, where you play an important role. If you don't see these ripples of hope, look out for the undertow of his ego.

Mr. Ego scoring in the Red Flag range has already made up his mind about his true love. He invests time and energy into that relationship. He defends his true love against any naysayers. His true love is his first priority. You can't compete with his one true love—himself. Mr. Ego cannot make room for you in his life. Period. He'll let you hang around. He'll talk with you, about himself. He'll let you admire him, wait on him, and love him. But do not expect him to return the favor. He is otherwise occupied.

If Your Man Is Staring into the Lake, It's Time to Go Fishing

First, understand that you can't tell Mr. Ego anything, least of all that he is a narcissist. While it might be tempting to try, you will get nowhere by telling this guy he is not meeting your needs. He just doesn't care. Why would he possibly care what a lesser human being has to say to him? Women who try to get the last licks into this one are bound for frustration. Keep the final conversation short and focused on *his* needs. Tell him that you just can't give him what he needs. Let him know it is best for both of you to move on to explore other relationships. Despite protests, maintain your position. Most of his protests will be his ego not wanting to be dumped. Be calm and strong. Repeat that you cannot meet his needs. Goodbye, he's gone, it's over. Then go out and find a new date without delay and let Mr. Ego sit and starve while admiring his reflection in the lake.

The Isolator

Relationship Roadkill: Keep Your Pet
Close and Your Friends on a Leash

There is an ancient Indian tale about a time long ago when the great spirits decided to depart from the earth. They drew a line in the ground separating themselves from man. The spirits kept the dog on their side of the line, opposite man. The line soon became a crack and the crack widened until it was a chasm. Just before the distance became insurmountable, forever separating the earth from the spirit world, the dog jumped across the chasm and took his place beside man. To this day, the companionship of a dog is still the yardstick by which loyalty is measured. The loyalties of your family members, friends, and even your pet are the security blanket that protects you from a harsher world where you are more anonymous. Any man that tries to put a gap between you and that security is definitely not acting in the right spirit and does not need to be a part of your world.

Patty saw him on her lunch break. It was a warm summer day, and she was eating her lunch in the park. He was sitting on a bench across from her, feeding peanuts to the squirrels.

He seemed absorbed in his task. Perhaps a deep thinker type. Patty decided to take a risk.

"It's nice to see a person who cares about animals."

"Oh, I'm not really in love with squirrels, they're just rats with a fur coat and a good press agent. I think it's fun to watch them scamper for the food, to see which one will be the first to get the prize. Sort of a metaphor for what we are like in the face of our needs as humans."

"Gee, I have never seen anyone build such a philosophy around park animals. Sometimes a squirrel is just a squirrel."

"How very Freudian of you. My name is Peter. I didn't think I was going to get such a humbling on my lunch break today. Thank you."

"You're welcome. My name is Jean. You know, I come here often and haven't seen you here before."

"I just started a new job. And kind of a new life, I guess. I'm between relationships, and still getting my head together from the breakup."

"I think I know how you feel. I spend more time between relationships than in them. If I didn't have my friends, I don't think I'd be able to keep my sanity."

They met for lunch in the park a few more times. Peter would actually show up fifteen minutes early just to make sure he didn't miss his unofficial date. He talked about how their meeting was the best part of his day. Impressed with what seemed a dedication to her, Patty finally took the risk to invite Peter over for a small three-couple dinner party. Peter reluctantly accepted.

When he showed up at the door there was an immediate dislike between Peter and Patty's dog, Frisky. Instead of trying to make friends, Peter egged the little sheltie on until Patty had to intervene. Dinner was a little uncomfortable as Peter didn't seem to hit it off with her friends. He kept correcting one of the guys, and kept talking about topics that didn't seem to interest anyone else. After everyone left, Peter and Patty had a little time together.

"I'm not much for dogs, Patty. I never grew up with pets."

"Yeah, I've never seen Frisky act that way. That's the first time I've ever had to put him outside during a dinner party."

"I'm sure it didn't hurt him. Dogs should be outside anyway."

"Not Frisky. He's the greatest little friend a girl could ever have in this world."

"He seems very protective of you. I'm sure he would never be happy if you got close to a man. So have these guys been your friends a long time?"

"Yeah, Marge and I went to high school together, and I've known Debbie since one of my first jobs."

"I didn't get a real feel for them. I was amazed at the way Rich seemed to be a know-it-all. I was also surprised the whole group of them was so far behind on world events. I guess not everyone reads the newspaper."

"I don't put my head in the newspaper that much. I don't really care what is going on in some foreign country when I live day-by-day here."

"I didn't mean anything by it. I guess I just didn't have much in common with your friends. I didn't think of them as your type. You seem so much smarter than them, more in touch with what is important in the world."

"You didn't like my friends?"

"I didn't get to know them well enough to form an opinion."

"I guess I threw you into a strange situation by inviting you over for dinner. I mean, we hardly know each other. I probably wouldn't be comfortable with your friends at this point, either."

"Things like this happen. I would suspect it's hard for them to be themselves around someone new. The important thing is that I do like hanging around with you. Maybe you and I should go out, just the two of us, for a little while before we start adding new people into the mix."

"You mean you, me, and Frisky."

"Oh yeah, I certainly think a smelly dog that's not sure whether he wants to bite me or piss on me would add a lot to the equation."

"He'll grow on you."

"So does athlete's foot."

"I guess it's a good sign that you haven't amputated your foot for that yet. I guess you can get used to anything."

They seemed very capable of clever banter when they were alone. Patty liked Peter's quick mind and liked his sarcastic, cynical view of the world. They settled into a good evening that night after her friends left the "dinner party from hell." They watched a little TV, talked a lot, and made out a little before Peter departed. Frisky spent the evening outside barking as loudly as he could.

There are times when we all would like an isolated romantic paradise of our own, but when that dream world starts to feel like a summer camp nightmare movie, you may be slashing your way to a Red Flag.

The goal of the Isolator is to control his insecurity in any way that he can. Insecurity is part of the human condition that we all own at some point in our lives, many people throughout their lives. Family and friends help us not to be alone, and that makes us feel we always have someone to depend on. We become more secure by their inclusion in our lives. The Isolator is trying to set up a way to guarantee that he will not be alone, so he hides the two of you away. For some reason in his past, he lost trust in the steadiness of family, in the loyalty of friendship. It was probably through a series of events in which he felt betrayed by friends, felt his parents were not protecting him from the harshness of the world, and/or concluded that the people he was depending on were undependable. His only avenue of regaining security is to try to make a small world that is an island apart from the rest of humanity. In the Isolator's relationships, he tries to accomplish this feat of separation.

The Isolator will start by making you the center of his world and pressure you to do the same. Little by little the Isolator will try to carve out all of your time. He will attempt to see you alone and keep you busy so that you have trouble seeing other people in your life. When he is included in plans with your friends, he will find fault, or not have a good time and blame them for his lack of enjoyment. He may even become critical or rude to family and friends right in front of them. He will try to catch them in a subject they know little about and start an argument, because he thinks he will appear in the right. One of the techniques of the Isolator is to make an argument appear as if he is defending your honor. How could he be wrong if he is coming to your defense? His goal is to slowly remove you from other relationships so that he is the only one in your life, and friends and family become more like acquaintances.

If the Isolator can take away all outside influences and distractions, he feels safe and in control. Fear of rejection, comparison, and criticism are minimized when outside influences are curtailed. If he can minimize the threat, he can maximize his control. The type of control the Isolator is looking for is not to control the woman's behavior. It is not simply to get what he wants or do things his way. He may be very accommodating when it comes to choosing places to dine or movies to see. What he wants is emotional control. The Isolator is not necessarily jealous in the traditional sense. It is not other men he fears; it is any other relationship. He even resents pets. He is truly creating an island, just you and him, with no threats of danger, deception, or any outside influence coming between you. One flaw: the island is deserted and you are a castaway. One tires of bananas and coconuts very quickly. Time to send an S.O.S., set off a flare, or just use a Zen thought: be the boat.

Patty really liked Peter and wanted it to work, but he was like two people. Great when it was just the two of them, but a real bear when she wanted to include her friends or family. When she tried to talk about them, Peter became distant and almost angry. He either did not talk with her about her friends or had negative things to say. He always tried to steer the conversation back to the two of them. It seemed Peter was only happy when he had her all to himself. As for her friends, for the first time in her life she heard complaints about someone she was dating. They told her point-blank that they had trouble being with Peter. They did not seem to understand what she saw in him. When she tried to describe the intense deep thinker or the connection she thought they were developing, she would catch them looking at one another and rolling their eyes. When she called friends about getting together, their first question became "Will Peter be there?" Even her mother complained that Peter seemed odd, and her mother never commented on the men she was dating. Something was wrong.

Patty was starting to feel suffocated. She realized that she had started to do something she always thought poorly of in other women. She was ignoring her friends for the sake of a man. She was neglecting her family. It was great that Peter thought she was so special, but there was a high price to pay for his attention. The rescue ship came when her father overheard him criticizing the family during a Memorial Day barbecue. Dad threw him out of the house and gave his daughter the Loser talk. Patty's dad was a smart man. After a day with her cousins and a few of her friends who showed up that night, Patty was over Peter before the grill got cold.

The test below can help you decide if the man you're dating is looking to build a brave new world together or settle a desert island.

IS HE AN ISOLATOR?

	Circle the number and add up the score
Family Background	
Grew up an only child	1
Parents died when young	1

(test continues)

Family Background

Parents divorced or separated before he moved out on his own	2
Father or mother was an alcoholic	2
Father uninvolved with children	2
Raised by single parent, grandparents, other family member, or in foster care	4
Does not have close relationship with family	3

Work/School History

Changed schools a lot when young	2
Notes teenage years were difficult	2
Expresses dislike for his teachers/professors	2
Did not participate in extracurricular activities	1
Felt excluded by classmates	3
Works in very secure job, possibly civil service	2
Owns his own business	2

Friendships

Has few close friends (one or two)	1
Rarely talks about friends	2
Has very few acquaintances	1
Does not want his friends to have other friends	2

Past Relationships

Talks about how special past relationships were	2
Talks about intensity of past relationships	2
Women were usually ones to break up with him	2
States women were not ready for what he had to offer	3

Body Language

Very open body language when just the two of you	1
Makes good eye contact with you	1
Nods head or tilts head to show he's listening when with you	1
Becomes fidgety and tense when you are with others	2
Body language closed and standoffish when around your friends/family	3

Dress/Hygiene

Will start to dress in ways he believes you will like	2
Will style hair or facial hair to your preferences	1
Will find out what fragrances you like and use them	1

(test continues)

Behavior

Tries to talk with you when you are on the phone	2
Walks between you when you are conversing with friend or family member	3
Very focused on you	1
Makes dates very romantic	1
Dates include only the two of you	1
Does not get along with your friends/family	3
Aloof and withdrawn around friends/family	3
Is outright rude to friends/family	4
Your friends/family start to avoid you when they know he will be around	4
You start to separate time between friends/family and him	4
You start to neglect friends/family because of him	5

Conversation

Talks about how special it feels to be with you	2
Talks about how others intrude on that special feeling	3
Does not ask about your friends/family	2
Does not converse well about his friends/family	2
Points out faults in your friends/family	3
Suggests you see less of particular friends/family	5

When Confronted

Apologizes profusely but blames behavior on his deep feelings for you	2
Blames others for getting between you two	5
Attacks you for not understanding what he is trying to do	3
States you cannot appreciate the special relationship he is trying to develop	4
Continues same behavior without regard to your confrontation	2
Apologizes and admits to being partially wrong	−1
Shows insight into behavior	−1

Your Impression

Deep thinker type	1
A loner	2
Insecure	1
Total Score	

Score 15 and lower: No reason for concern at this point
Score between 16 and 30: Yellow Flag—There's reason for caution
Score 31 and above: Red Flag—This man wants you alone on an island; maroon him

Two Is Company, Three Doesn't Have to Be a Crowd

If your date scores in the Yellow Flag range, it does not necessarily mean he's adding a tower for you in his castle. He may be someone who is most comfortable with a small circle of close friends. He may like to invest a greater amount of energy per person than a wide circle of people would allow. He may enjoy the added intimacy that a smaller circle of established friends allows. While he may be a little uncomfortable around your friends, he will make the effort. With time, he will find a place both for them and with them. If he is not used to making new friends, you may observe that he can be awkward, or perhaps nervous. The Yellow Flag guy will not be rude or obnoxious. He will not be cruel to your pets. He will not be overly critical. You need to keep some distance from this guy and not let him isolate you while you are evaluating him further. Make special attempts to include friends, family, and even your cat or dog and see if he gets better with familiarity. If you start to see signs of improvement after a short while, you might be okay to move further. If your inclusion effort leads to rudeness, cruelty, or severe resistance, it's time to retest.

The Isolator who scores in the Red Flag range has an agenda that won't suit your needs. His desire for intimacy and friendship is overshadowed by his need for safety. Safety is defined as eliminating all competition for your affection, not just male rivals. You may like him for the person he is when the two of you are alone, but you should never reject the rest of your world for any man. Little by little he cuts out the parts of your life that have given you support and security, love and warmth, knowledge and purpose. This is not love but an experiment in isolation gone astray. Let down your hair, climb down from the tower, and go find a real prince.

No Man Is an Island, Time to Swim for Shore

The Isolator wants a hold on you. Don't let him have it. In no uncertain terms, tell him that you will not make the sacrifice necessary to maintain this relationship. Make it clear that you have always made your friends and family a priority, and you are determined not to change that now. Acknowledge that you two may be good together, but tell him your world extends beyond the boundaries he needs for a relationship. This is a time when you need to be firm and clear.

Expect him to focus on the positive times you have shared. He will offer to compromise, but no compromise really makes sense. Why would you even consider compromising the value of your friends and family? Are you going to get rid of your dog for a man? If you give in to his offers, the only thing that will happen is you will have a reprieve from the criticism, even though you know he will want to say something negative about anybody in your life. He will wait until he feels you are very entwined, perhaps even engaged, then he will turn back into the person he was and control you through isolation. This is not a temporary pattern. The men who change do it with continuous effort, alone. In a psychologist's office, this pattern is seen a lot in marriages, and the women come in shaking from the damage done to their lives. Perhaps the saddest thing is when these women look back to their first dates and realize that there were signs all along forecasting what their life would be like. They didn't pay attention to the Red Flags. There is someone out there who can expand the connections in your life. There is someone out there who is not looking to build a moat around your castle. Go to the islands for a honeymoon, not as the basis of a relationship. Beach this shark, now.

The Loner

*The Lone Wolf Is Nothing
but a Big, Hurtin' Puppy*

How does one become neurotic? There have been some interesting studies done by social psychologists to try to answer that question. Much of this work has been done with monkeys. The experiments took baby chimps and separated them from all social contact. They were provided with sustenance and shelter, nothing more. What happened? They grew up to be nervous and erratic, easily frightened, unable to socialize—a real mess! They could not form the bonds required to mate. In fact, they did not know how to perform the mating act itself. Female monkeys artificially impregnated did not know how to care for their young. Male monkeys could not find their place in the group and were outcast. Like monkeys, man is a social creature. Our development and adjustment is dependent on social contact, social bonds, and social learning. Without healthy relationships during childhood, a person can never be complete, his mental stability is uncertain, he becomes a Loner. If you've found a guy like this, before long you will start swinging from the trees. Better evaluate the relationship before he makes an ape out of you.

* * *

Melissa had read about meeting a man at the grocery store in magazines, but she didn't think it could really happen. She remembered some of the article: He would have a confused look on his face, his cart would be filled with a combination of junk food, TV dinners, and beer, he would seem to be in a hurry. Randy had all these signs and he was cute. The first time she saw him, she smiled. He looked her way, then moved to another aisle. Oh well. But there was a next time. A few next times. Each time, Melissa got bolder until one day she struck up a conversation about the relative merits of buying frozen fried chicken over the deli section fried chicken. After an exchange of names and some introductory personal revelations (they were both single), Melissa dropped a mild hint about her fried chicken and picnics with her ex-boyfriend. It was tenuous for a moment, but Randy finally asked her out. He knocked on Melissa's door dressed in the same clothes he wore at the grocery store five hours earlier.

"Hi, Melissa, are you ready?"

"Hi, Randy. Come on in first, I'm one shade of lipstick short of perfection. Would you like something to drink?"

"Just water, thank you."

"Are you sure? I've got wine, a little daiquiri mix in the blender, vodka and orange juice."

"Water would be fine. Actually, I'm not really thirsty. I could drink whatever you're having."

"Oh, so you want a frozen strawberry daiquiri. I just happen to have one ready."

"Good. I've never actually had one of those."

"You've never had a strawberry daiquiri?"

"It's even worse than that, I've never had any frozen drink."

"Really! Are you that guy they found in the glacier or something?"

"Well, I only lived at college for a semester. I couldn't see partying away my mom's money. It was so hard to come by, so I commuted. Never was much of a drinker after college. Wow, this is really good! Tastes like fresh strawberries!"

"Yeah, that's the strawberry part of the strawberry daiquiri. What about dating? You never went out with anyone who liked fruit drinks?"

"Actually, Melissa, I don't have a lot of long dating experience. I never seem to get past the third date. I'm not a real aggressive kind of guy. In fact, I'm surprised I asked you out. I haven't been on a date in over a year and a half."

"A shy one, huh? I can handle that for a change. Most of the guys I date are anything but shy. The last couple of guys I dated could have written a book on losers. They had them all covered."

"This is really a good drink."

"So, Randy, what do you do for a living?"

"I work in a research firm."

"A scientist?"

"No, it's a library research firm. Companies hire us to find all the information we can on a certain topic. I go into the computer and into libraries to find out about the most bizarre things."

"Sounds interesting. You must learn a lot."

"Yeah, but it's a little lonely. I don't work with anyone. I live with my mom, so I end up pretty much a loner."

"Where's your dad, if you don't mind my asking?"

"Dad passed away when I was young, at least that's what I was told. My grandparents raised me until I was eleven or twelve, then they died. Mom was working all the time to save enough money for me to go to college. I was pretty much on my own. I'd cook for her and stuff, then she stopped being able to work, and now I work."

"Well, you're not alone tonight. So, Randy, where do you want to go?"

"I was so caught up in seeing you, I didn't actually plan anything. I'm sorry. I thought we'd just make a decision once we got together. Unless you have any ideas."

Melissa thought for a while. "I've got some melon liqueur and some honeydew. How about a melon daiquiri next?"

It was a pleasant night staying in and talking. Melissa wasn't used to a man being so honest and sincere. They ordered a pizza and learned more about each other that night than many couples do after two years—at least about all the pain they'd been through.

It's nice to have a relationship with someone who treats you like you're the only one in his life. However, man is by nature a pack animal. We collect together in groups and form bonds. By socializing, we learn from one another how to be social animals. If the guy you're dating seems to have lost his pack, this relationship could be a dog, and you're barking up the tree of a Red Flag!

There are two distinct patterns of the Loner. The first is the guy who has learned to turn his emotions inward. He will be like Randy, who seems on first meeting like a hurt puppy, too damaged to face the world. He never makes any connections because he doesn't take risks and doesn't know how to make friends, so he ends up alone. The second type of Loner has turned his emotions outward and is rebelling against the world. He too is a hurt puppy, but his reclusiveness looks like anger from the outside. He pushes people away from interacting with him, thus he ends up just as alone. Although they look almost completely opposite, the path that got them there is basically the same.

The roots of the Loner always go back to some form of deprivation during childhood. Through no fault of his own, he failed to get something during his formative years. He may have come from a family that did not know how to show or give emotion. Cold reason and logic may have ruled the day in his household. No hugging, no kissing or physical contact, no expressions of affection. Each person had a job to do and was expected to do it. The emotional side of life was either silly or a sign of weakness. An attempt on the part of this child to show or get affection from his parents was rejected. He learned not to try. He never learned the full depths of emotion or the communication skills needed to express them.

Another scenario is the single parent—either a mother or father having to do double duty. The stress of running a household and bringing in an income solo cuts down on the time one has for a child. The result may be a boy who never gets an opportunity to develop a strong enough bond with his parent. Time limitations don't permit learning by example. The interactions between the boy and parent are of poor quality and too short duration. Social skills never develop. If the child is not exposed to other children with whom he can develop friendships, the situation is made worse.

There are other routes to social and emotional deprivation. The death of a parent, mental illness of a parent, poverty, and abuse are but a few. Not all people are as severely affected by these tragedies. Certainly, many people from tragic backgrounds grow into healthy adults. Usually, there is some intervention by community members, extended family, or other loving and caring adults that help the child develop emotionally. If he can get the warmth, regardless of the source, he has a better chance of not being a Loner.

Whatever the cause of the early deprivation, the Loner will give off certain telltale signs. He will tend to be socially clumsy. He will become confused when confronted with social situations. His behavior may seem silly or immature at times. He may seem cold and unemotional. He may appear insensitive or even unaware of your emotions. The Loner often does not see that his behavior has an effect on others around him. His social skills are fixed at a low level. His capacity to interact emotionally is diminished. The bottom line is he lacks the necessary skills to form and maintain healthy relationships of any kind.

Many Loners project a "little lost boy" type of innocence. This helplessness can press the buttons of maternal instinct. Without realizing it, you can fall into the role of nurturer and caregiver. He's the child you eventually want. This instinctive feeling can be misinterpreted as attraction, or even love.

The Loner can also seem romantic. His social clumsiness

seems cute. His cluelessness seems innocent. He always has time for you and talks only of the two of you. It seems that you can have a world all to yourselves. By the time you realize your darling is defective, you're hooked. And pulling out the hook will hurt.

Melissa went on a few dates with Randy. She thought him a bit odd, but he seemed so harmless. She always had to plan the date. Conversations were restricted and repetitive. The one time she took him out with her friends, he sat away from everyone with a painted-on smile and nodded once in a while. Melissa didn't know whether to be embarrassed or heartbroken for him.

Randy was not a bad guy; in fact, he was really sweet in many ways. She didn't like that she felt more like his mother than his girlfriend. She had gone out with Losers before, and they were easy to break up with. Her heart went out to Randy; he seemed to need someone to take care of him. Melissa was smart enough to remember that she had to take care of herself. With some difficulty, she broke it off with Randy. She really meant it when she told him that she wished him luck.

The test below can help decide if your date is pulling your heartstrings or your apron strings.

IS HE A LONER?

Circle the number and add up the score

Family Background

Grew up an only child	1
Parents died when young	3
Parents divorced or separated before he moved on his own	2
Father or mother was an alcoholic	2
Father uninvolved with children	2
Raised by single parent, grandparents, other family member, or in foster care	3
Does not have close relationship with family	3

(test continues)

Work/School History

Changed schools a lot when young	3
Notes teenage years were difficult	2
Expresses dislike for his teachers/professors	1
Did not participate in extracurricular activities	1
Felt excluded by classmates	2
Seems too involved in work	2
Works at an isolated job	3

Friendships

Has:	
No friends	5
Few friends	3
One close special friend	−1
Socializes infrequently	4
Avoids contact with people	6

Past Relationships

Has had limited experience with relationships	4
Has limited experience dating	3
Past relationships have been of short duration	3
Women ended the relationships	2
Not sure why relationships ended, states they just did not want to see him anymore	4

Body Language

Eyes dart	1
Looks down when talking to you	2
Body gets tight when you touch him	3
Covers mouth or parts of face a lot with hands	3
Eyes seem to wander during conversations or when spending a long time together	2

Dress/Hygiene

Mode of dress is just a little bit off	2
At times has rumpled look	2
Dress is inappropriate for place you are going	2
Does not seem to know how to dress for different events	2
Wardrobe is sparse, old, with most clothing in same style	2

(test continues)

Behavior

Does not know how to plan dates	3
Lets you make all decisions regarding entertainment	2
Clumsy in social situations (i.e., how much of a tip to leave, ordering at restaurant)	3
Withdrawn and nervous around your friends or family	3
Friends and family have concerns about him that they "cannot put finger on"	3

Conversation

Takes a long time to respond to your questions	2
Asks awkward or inappropriate questions	2
Conversation is one-sided with you doing much of the talking	2
Has trouble making conversation	3
Does not talk about friends	2
Avoids topic of friends when asked	2
Makes statements indicating he likes to be alone	3
Does not seem to know how to give a compliment	2
Does not seem to know how to take a compliment	2
Embarrassed or upset when you make a suggestion	2
Often apologizes for things that do not require an apology	2

When Confronted

Stammers, does not know what to say	3
Seems confused, does not understand your point	2
Withdraws from conversation	2
Cries	4

Your Impression

Deep thinker type	1
A loner	2
Insecure	2
Social skills are off, almost immature	2
Nervous or hesitant when out in public	2
Seems confused when you suggest things to do or places to go	2
Total Score	

Score 15 and lower: No reason for concern at this point
Score between 16 and 30: Yellow Flag—There's reason for caution
Score 31 and above: Red Flag—Solitaire's his favorite game; go play hearts elsewhere

After All He's Been Through

So, what about the man in the Yellow Flag category? What you could be seeing is shyness made worse by normal early relationship jitters. He may be the reserved type with a few close friends. His style, though healthy, may be slightly reclusive. He may be capable of deep, intimate relationships, of connecting with you and sharing. Maybe crowds, loud nights out, new experiences, and playing mayor to a group of people are not his thing. Your ability to connect with him will depend on how compatible a match you are. That's what dating is all about.

The Yellow Flagger may also be someone who is socially inexperienced. He may even have that touch of innocence. A childhood that was sheltered, rather than deprived, might constitute his background. Many women find this type of man attractive. Since he was loved as a child, he can love as an adult. His lack of experience can result in a bit of wonder appearing on his face as he explores the world with you. This type will be eager to learn. If he shares the feelings he is having, whether they are embarrassment, curiosity, excitement, or humor, you know that he has what it takes to connect. You might have the opportunity to see someone grow, and grow with him.

The man who falls in the Red Flag category is a different story. He lacks more than just skills. He is innocent only by default. The mechanism for social discourse is not developed in this man. It is not that he hasn't learned how to connect, share, and be intimate, it is that he can't. The wounds developed early on have healed over, leaving a scar that is covering a void. Unlike the man who falls in the Yellow Flag range, the one in the Red Flag range will not be able to learn. He won't express a wide range of emotions, only frustration or perhaps fear. His innocence will eventually expose itself, turning into avoidance of intimacy. Understand that this man may be incapable of learning to connect and feel; you may pity him, but that is not the foundation for a long-term relationship. Be prepared to leave.

Breaking Up Is Hard to Do

Ending this relationship, even in the early phases, can stir up strong emotions. You may find yourself in an extreme state, pitying this man and feeling responsible for him. This may turn into anxiety, anger, or even suppressed fear. Breaking up with the Loner is unique in that you frequently can be more concerned about his emotions than your own.

The breakup should be as gentle as possible. Emphasize that the two of you are different. Note that you have enjoyed his company and always felt good around him, but you realize that the relationship is not going to develop. Let him know that he had qualities that made you think long and hard before coming to this decision. But make it clear that you have come to a final decision.

Remember that the Loner is not socially adept. The message must be clear. Beating around the bush will confuse him, and he may interpret a statement such as "we need to back off a little" literally and expect to see you twice a week rather than three times.

Avoid the temptation to help him by naming his faults. He will not understand and this will probably hurt him more. Instead, suggest that he really needs to try to date a number of women. Assure him that even though it did not work out with you, as a woman you believe that he has admirable qualities that make him desirable. Encourage him to call other women he may have met while you were dating. Experience through trial and error is the Loner's best hope for becoming a pack animal.

The Bug-Eyed Boy

He Only Has Eyes for You, or Does
He Have Only *Eyes for You?*

There was an interesting social psychological study years ago that showed women became more attracted to men who were already with an attractive female. Being able to get a date with an attractive female made men more desirable to other women. The effect was not the same for women with attractive men. Unfortunate as it may be, studies have shown that physical "prettiness" is a factor in how much attention a baby will get from its parents, what grades a child gets in school, achievement scores (probably from the attention), success in job interviews, how one adjusts to work, promotions, higher wages, finding mates, and who's in control during a romantic relationship. There are even studies showing that prisoners fare better after cosmetic surgery than after counseling and psychotherapy. Aristotle probably said it as well as anyone: "Beauty is a far better recommendation than any letter of introduction."

One of the major factors in attraction is novelty. Whatever is new is more likely to hold our attention than something we have seen awhile. So, given two women of equal beauty, the newest will be more attractive to the average man, unless there is some learning process that intervenes. However, if you are within the first three dates with a new guy, your newness should not have worn off. After that, your character should make you more beautiful. If the man you are with is looking around this early, you can guess that he either has problems maintaining his attention for one person for very long, he has not figured out it is good manners to pay attention only to you, or he has a hunk of salad in his eye and he hopes that by moving his eyes around a lot it will come out.

Carolyn met Jim on the Nautilus machine where she works out. She was sure he was looking at her for a while, so finally she went over and asked a question about a new piece of equipment. It turns out she knew more about working out than he did. They struck up a conversation, she smiled in the right places, and he asked her to go to the juice bar. Carolyn knew he was going to pop the date question because he couldn't take his eyes off her Spandexed body. They went from there to a movie later that evening, and went on a second date for dinner at a Chinese restaurant a couple of days later. The Chinese restaurant was the first time they were together in a lit public place and Carolyn noticed early in the date that Jim tended to "check out" just about every attractive woman that entered the place. When he did focus on her, half the time his eyes were on the revealed part of her chest, and this was not a particularly cleavage-oriented outfit. A few umbrella drinks later, Carolyn thought she'd hint about his looking around.

"So what's the deal here? If you'd rather be with one of those other women walking by, go for it!"

"Carolyn, where'd that come from?"

"Well, you seem to be very interested in looking at every woman walking by, so don't let me stop you from going over and talking to one of them."

"Wow, I'm sorry if I offended you. I guess I sort of do that naturally. I think most guys look around a lot. I didn't even realize I was doing it. You're the best-looking woman in the place."

"Well, in that case, I guess there are an unusually high number of pretty women in here."

"You know, I just love the way women look. I love their shapes, their smiles. I'm one of those guys that is mesmerized by beauty. I mean, look at you, you just blow me away." Jim's eyes go down to her breast area again.

"So what is your favorite part of a woman?" Carolyn asks knowingly.

Jim chuckles a little and stumbles before he answers. "Well, really, I think it is just the essence of them, at any age. Look at those kids over there, they can't be more than thirteen or fourteen years old and I can see the beauty in them. The older woman over in the corner, she's beautiful too. I guess I should have been a fashion designer or something."

"Yeah, I noticed how you commented on their clothing."

"Touché, but you don't know what I'm thinking. I'm not as perverted as you think."

"So you're telling me you don't look at those men's magazines, or go on-line and pick up pictures of naked women."

"Carolyn, every guy does that and if some guy tells you he doesn't, then he's lying. I mean, the *Sports Illustrated* Swimsuit Issue is the best-selling issue of the magazine not because women buy it and not because of basketball season."

"Yeah, but those women usually have clothes on."

"Well, it wouldn't matter because men buy magazines that have women in them regardless of what they're wearing. How'd we get talking about this? Right now I'm with the most beautiful girl around and I'm not interested in anyone else."

"I guess that's quite a compliment from a man who seems to have observed every woman around."

Jim stopped looking around for the rest of this date and Carolyn was satisfied. They ended up seeing each other again.

*   *   *

A sense of keen observation and awareness of surroundings is an important characteristic for anyone. A sense of beauty and art is a sign of culture and appreciation of the world. But when the only thing your date sees is the curves, wiggles, bumps, and grinds of the ladies walking by, you may be staring into the face of a Red Flag.

The tendency for men to look around is innate and must be programmed out, or at least fought against for the purpose of manners. The Bug-Eyed Boy who does not accept undertaking this battle has a problem that could be coming from various origins. Regardless of origin, the underlying attitude is the same: a perceived lack of sexual fulfillment giving birth to sexual frustration. Understanding the origins will lead you to understanding the development of the problem and hint at the solution.

One type of Bug-Eyed Boy is a man who has a background of being very shy around women, living alone, and perhaps working in a job that requires a suppression of his ability to be himself with women. He may tend to fantasize a lot to make up for his lack of real contact, and carries home images of women with him to aid him in his fantasy life. This may sound a little perverted, or sadder than anything, but it is more normal than you might think. It would seem that a normal sex life would snap him out of this pattern, but habits run deeper and require concerted efforts to change. The extent of the pattern, and how alone he feels in his life, will determine how long it will take him to change. Remember, changing a habit takes time and is not smooth. There will be a lot of setbacks.

Another type of Bug-Eyed Boy may be the sexually active man who exhibits many of the patterns of the Sex Guzzler (Red Flag #10), but perhaps is not as emotionally bereft. He may really wish to have an emotional connection with women but lacks the capacity for intimacy or has not made a good connection yet. He may feel he always has to be out on the make because his patterns in the past have proven that there will be a quick turnover and he needs to find the next prospect. This often happens with the transplanted person who comes from another state or country and doesn't quite know where he fits in yet.

The third type of Bug-Eyed Boy is the unsatisfied customer. He is always looking for a woman better than the one he is with at the time. He wants to find the best-looking woman that will go out with him. He is always going to test the limits. Unfortunately, this makes any woman that goes out with him the new baseline. Once you accept the date, he starts looking to go up a level or two. His fantasies are often focused on the unobtainable—the playmate, movie star, or supermodel whom he is very unlikely to meet or date. Until he reaches the pinnacle, he will be looking for someone new.

None of these three types is very desirable. They will pass their sexual angst on to you in one form of frustration or another. Trying to be with one of these guys, hoping he'll change, is like buying a dress two sizes too small, hoping you'll lose the fourteen pounds you need to fit in it. Maybe you've done this, but it wasn't fun, and the dress probably didn't get very much use.

Carolyn gave her Bug-Eyed Boy a good shot at changing, even after she found a stockpile of explicit magazines and videos in his apartment, and an Internet favorites list that would make a porn star blush. Carolyn told Jim whenever he went over the line, and Jim would make a temporary effort to change. She figured if she kept reminding him he would develop new habits. She also figured if she kept him sexually happy he wouldn't need to look further. Carolyn knew she was better-than-average-looking, and had a pretty decent body. She kept telling him, "Why look at hamburger, when you've got filet mignon?" Carolyn was witty, cute, understanding, and sexy. Jim still scanned the room like a copy machine whenever they went out. Carolyn found someone who was happy with filet mignon.

If a guy you're with has an ocular problem, score him on our eye chart below.

IS HE A BUG-EYED BOY?

*Circle the number and
add up the score*

Family Background

Was not active with clubs or lessons as a kid	1
Parents left him to entertain himself a lot	3
Brother or sister got a lot of the attention, even if it was negative	1

Work/School History

Job suppresses his ability to be himself around women (boss, profession, etc.)	2
Job is very male-oriented	1
Works with a lot of young women in subservient roles	3
Didn't date much in high school or later	3

Friendships

Friends do or did spend a lot of time cruising for chicks	3
Female friends tend to be less attractive than the women he dates	2
Talks about how beautiful one of his friend's wives is, admiring his luck	2

Past Relationships

Dated mostly very attractive women	2
Talks about their looks first before he tells anything else about them	3
Relationships fizzled rather than bad breakups	1
Lot of very short-term relationships	1
Still says he would go out with one or more of them if he could	2
Will not talk about sex life in past relationships	1

Body Language

Eyes dart around the room	3
Turns body toward an attractive girl if she is sitting close to you	4
Drops things on the floor a lot to bend over and pick them up	2
Always sits with back to a wall	1
Looks at body part, not face when he is talking to you or other women	2

(test continues)

Body Language

Eyes keep dropping to chest of woman he is talking to	3
You touch him before he touches you	1

Dress/Hygiene

Spends a lot of time in front of the mirror	1
Always asks your opinion on what he is wearing	2
Uses too much cologne	3

Behavior

Always looks at women when with you	5
Does not maintain focus well for a long period of time	2
Collects graphic "men's" magazines	3
Frequents striptease clubs	3
Has a collection of hard-core videos or rents them frequently	4
Has a fetish of some kind	5
Evidence of Internet sex site (in his favorites section)	3
Seems to have a very active fantasy life	4
Evidence of frequent Internet chat site use	3
Points out pretty girls to you	4

Conversation

Talks about beauty a lot	2
Asks questions about other girls you know	2
Talks excessively about how pretty someone is	3
Rationalizes by saying he is "just a lover of beauty"	3
Talks about one part of your body or friends' bodies	4
Identifies himself as a "leg man," "breast man," etc.	2

When Confronted

Denies that he was looking around	3
Gives excuse or rationalization	2
Says "all men look at women all the time"	2
Continues to look around after confrontation	
On same date	5
On next date	3
No decrease in score after you retest a couple of dates after confrontation	5
Apologizes, says he has a problem and will try to change	−5

(test continues)

Your Impression	
He is sexually frustrated	3
He is a little kinky or perverted	3
He is shy	2
He is a little sad	3
	Total Score

Score 14 and lower: No reason for concern at this point, he's a guy and he will look, expect this early in a dating relationship

Score between 15 and 25: Yellow Flag—There's reason for caution

Score 26 and above: Red Flag—He's looking around too much; time for you to start looking for a new guy

Visine Won't Cure the Myopic Relationship

If you've got a man who is scoring in the Yellow Flag range on this test, fear not, you have a chance for redemption, as this is one of the best "wait and see" profiles in this book. If you like other parts about him, give him some feedback to let him know what he is doing and tell him that you think it is a bad habit that you would be willing to help him change. If he is the type that reacts well to feedback, let him know when he is doing the "eye thing" with a gentle manner, a good sense of humor, and a smile. Try to make him feel comfortable and let him know he could have the best relationship going if he changes this bad habit. Then, observe and retest to see if he makes efforts to change. Don't worry about it being too early in the relationship to give him feedback. This is an area where the first date is not too early, because a wandering eye is just plain bad manners and he may not even be aware of the extent to which he is doing it. If you don't see any effort, the time has come to position him at the Red Flag level.

If you've found yourself with a Red Flag Bug-Eyed Boy get prepared for a very frustrating experience while you convince yourself that this is a fatal flaw. If he is the shy type and his habit won't change, you're in for an experience of never feeling really close to him, because his fantasy life will be more satisfying than your sex life. The guzzler Bug-Eyed Boy will be flirting and fantasizing about the next woman he will date because he can't make a connection. The unsatisfied customer will be looking around to see if he can find bigger and better. You will know that there is not the full commitment to making your relationship work, and it will be from there that the seed of frustration will find ample ground and fertilizer to grow into a major bed of weeds.

Myopia is the inability to see long distances clearly. If you find yourself in a long-term relationship with a Bug-Eyed Boy, you will learn that it is a myopic adventure. You will see your self-esteem disappear like Halloween candy during a third-grade recess. You will begin to question your looks constantly, always comparing yourself to the women he is looking at. You will start to become acutely aware of any signs of aging, and spend greater time in front of the mirror or at the shopping mall than ever. You will become obsessed with needing more appropriate sexual attention, and may find yourself engaging in activities you never thought you would. Want to stay? Is it time for a total brain makeover? Don't let it happen to you. You've got too much going for you.

Exterminating the Bug-Eye

This is a Red Flagger that you will be told to break up with slowly. It is better for you to fade out of his life than to make this a quick breakup. As you start to withdraw, he will slowly revert back to his fantasy life. This will make it easier for him to withstand the breakup and thus easier on you.

Tell him you're too busy or you have other plans when you become sure you want to do the big dump. Let him think that you are still somewhat interested, but the timing is wrong. As he continues to call, be very nice but somewhat preoccupied. He will push, and as he pushes, use the excuse that you just don't have what it takes to build any kind of relationship with him right now. If you end up going out, you can start pointing out girls for him to look at, letting him know it is now okay for him to revert to the same behavior as before. In essence, you don't care anymore. After a couple of weeks, lower the boom and tell him that the two of you are simply on different paths and he has to move on to find a woman that can give him what he needs. Talk along the lines that two people can both be good people but just not make it together. If you want to remain friends, you can do that, but remember, as long as you are in touch, you will probably always star in his fantasies. This may be uncomfortable for you and may not be best for him. It's probably better for him that he stay home with a stale beer, monster trucks, and a *Big 'Uns* magazine than fantasize with a wallet-size photograph of you.

The Quiet Man

Anatomically Correct,
Personality Challenged

We all did it as children—we stared into the sky and de-fined shapes in puffy marshmallow clouds. Accounts of rock formations outlining man's symbolic representations of life or gods predate written history and are part of most all cultures' folklore. It is intrinsically human to provide form and substance to the chance occurrences of nature. In the 1920s, a psychiatrist named Hermann Rorschach decided to take advantage of this human tendency by devising a test that would look into people's subconscious thoughts and ideas. He took a series of totally ambiguous inkblots and asked people what they saw, asked them to give the blot form and substance. Soft-textured blots might tell a psychiatrist about the patient's mother. A more harsh and bold blot would reveal feelings about a father or authority figure. Rorschach called his smears of ink "projective tests," as he theorized a person would "project" their inner being to provide a framework for the nondescript. Psychiatrists used these tests for years and some still do. There has been research to suggest, however, that the psychiatrist looking to discover a description of a patient's inner feelings with an inkblot is often getting something else. Interpretation of the inkblots will oftentimes represent the inner feelings of the therapist more than the feelings of the patient. Inkblot analysis requires the professional to make assumptions, often projecting their own personality that is falsely attributed to the patient. Psychiatrists end up analyzing themselves. Many men are little more than anthropomorphic inkblots to whom you give shape and form through your own interpretations and analysis. They sit quietly by and let you make assumptions based on the way they don't respond, rather than how they do respond. You end up in a relationship and eventually find out you have a guy that is as emotionally substantial as a cloud, as communicative as a rock, and has as much personality as spilled ink.

One of Nancy's married friends gave her a video dating membership. She thought the whole idea was a little bizarre, but knew it was already paid for, so she went and recorded her video. Someone named Roger expressed an interest in her video about a week later and Nancy went to the office to look at his video.

Roger was average-looking—a jeans and flannel shirt type. His message was short and simple. He talked slowly and softly, but had enough power in his voice to make himself heard. Nancy did not like men who whispered because she thought they seemed sneaky. She thought loud, talkative men always seemed to be self-centered and not willing to give you a chance in the conversation. She was Goldilocks of the three bears, thinking that Roger's voice was "just right." When Nancy called, the conversation was short and simple, like his message. They would meet on Friday for a little picnic in the park. Roger would bring a bottle of wine, Nancy the cheese.

"Roger?"

"Hi, you're Nancy?"

"Yes. You know you look just like your video. That was a

pretty good idea to wear the exact same clothes. You're really thinking ahead."

"Clothes? Oh yeah. It makes it easier for you to recognize me, I guess."

"It is nice to meet you. I brought some really good cheeses from the Cheese and Stuff store, and a few crackers and some sausages. What kind of wine will we be drinking?"

"I think it's French. Here, take a look."

"Ah, a Bordeaux. I really like wines from that region of France. Do you have a favorite kind of wine?"

"Don't really know that much about wine. I like red wines."

"So, Roger, have you been doing the dating routine for a long time? This is my first video date. Have you had much luck with this process?"

"No, not really."

"I guess that's a dumb question or you wouldn't still be trying new dates. My friend gave this video dating thing to me as a present for my birthday. I really think all she wanted to do was hear the stories of what happens to me when I go out on the dates."

There was a pause for Roger to speak, but he didn't offer anything.

"Have you been using this service long?"

"For a while. A couple of dates."

"And . . . ?"

"You sure did get a lot of good cheeses. I've never seen most of these."

"Well, I spent a summer in France and got to learn about cheeses. I enjoy the really smelly ones. Making cheese is a whole different art in France. People really appreciate variety, much more so than here in America. You seem a little shy. Are you a shy type, Roger?"

"I think I'm a better listener than a talker."

"Oh, the strong, silent, listener type. Tell me about yourself."

"Let's see. I'm a mechanic . . . airplane mechanic. I work at the airport on the big planes. And uh, what else . . ."

"You must get to travel a lot."

"I travel a little. I get reduced rates. That's nice. You travel. Sounds like it at least."

"I love to travel. A guy in the airlines is right up my alley. I wish I had enough money to do nothing but travel."

"Where have you been?"

"I went all over Europe when I went to France. Actually not all over, but a lot of places. I've been to about half of the United States and four of the Canadian provinces. I've gone to the Caribbean a couple of times. And you?"

"I went to Alaska last year. That was pretty cool. Tell me more about yourself."

Nancy and Roger sat there and ate cheese for a couple of hours. Roger asked a lot of questions, seemed really interested in Nancy. He wasn't much on offering spontaneous thoughts, but he was very open, answering questions honestly but simply. Nancy liked to talk a lot, so she didn't mind having a guy who was a good listener. She figured he was the pensive, introspective type, and must really like the outdoors or he wouldn't have gone to Alaska. She also figured he was not a sophisticated guy, he didn't seem to know much about wine or cheese. He was probably just really down to earth, by choice. She guessed he wasn't very close to his family because he didn't talk much about them. He was a simple man, so his home must be pretty simple. Nancy definitely could use a little simplicity in her life, so she took the impetus to call him for another date.

There is a certain charm to the man who seems to be quietly introspective and thinks before he talks. He seems more assured than a person who says whatever is on his mind. Many people could benefit from learning when to be quiet. However, when that quiet becomes a deafening void, and your ears are experiencing sensory deprivation, you may be hearing the scream of a Red Flag.

It's difficult to pinpoint why a man becomes painfully quiet. Sometimes it is because he really doesn't have verbal intelligence and he's never worked at developing verbal skills. Like all abilities, the ability to generate conversation is a combination of inherent propensities from birth, and the development from that time to the present. He may be particularly weak in that area, not endowed from birth. Because it is a weakness, he may shy away from practicing his verbal skills, thus if he doesn't use it, he loses it. The Quiet Man may be quiet because he is just not generating anything to say. Meanwhile, you're sitting there trying to hold a conversation with a human form with the personality of Silly Putty.

Communication is the foundation of any lasting relationship. While not as much fun as lustful attraction, it is the key to an enduring connection and partnership. Communication is what really creates intimacy. With intimacy comes vulnerability, and the willingness to be vulnerable leads to trust. Without trust, vulnerability is uncomfortable. The Quiet Man has trouble with intimacy. By avoiding communication, he never develops intimacy and stops the entire intimacy-trust cycle. It may stop the pattern that relationships strive toward, but it also decreases the feeling of discomfort that happens in the intimacy-trust process. He is already uncomfortable, so decreasing intimacy makes sense to him.

Why is he uncomfortable? It may be that his childhood relationships with his parents were shallow, mechanical, or worse. We learn intimacy and trust as children. If we are deprived of this at a young age, we will not know how to deal with trust as an adult. If our attempts to connect with our parents are met with rejection or punishment, we will learn the wisdom of withdrawing and keeping our mouth shut. The harsher the childhood, the greater this tendency. Pity the poor child who is constantly told he is dumb, whose accomplishments are ignored or ridiculed, and whose need for affection is spurned. He learns to live without love and intimacy, and to keep quiet. This pattern becomes ingrained and gives birth to the Quiet Man.

When a man with this background becomes involved in a relationship in which communication and intimacy are both called for and desirable, he becomes frightened. He is not aware of his anxiety, just that something does not feel right. The safe thing to do: keep quiet. It is the pattern from the past that has always worked. He becomes blind to the fact that his silence is a road back to the childhood he wanted to escape.

Why are some women attracted to a Quiet Man? Often it is a reaction to the frustration they are having with dating in general. They are not finding what they want, despite trying to do all the right things. They have an image and possibly a fantasy of Mr. Right, and they are losing patience with all the wrong guys they have been dating. A Quiet Man allows a woman's fantasy to intrude into reality. Looking for a break, she can paint her image onto the blank slate that sits before her sipping coffee. She is able to interpret his silence to suit her needs. His silence deprives her of the feedback of knowing she is on the wrong track. What's more, the Quiet Man often goes along easily with suggestions. This can offer a feeling of being in control and can let her design the Prince Charming of her dreams. A nice break from what she has been experiencing, he can become the Stepford boyfriend, mechanically programmed to do what she wants.

Nancy went out with Roger a few more times. She analyzed all the things unsaid during their first encounter and their second date. The conversation went wherever she directed it, but she did not seem to be learning more about Roger. By the end of the third date, Nancy was starting to see Roger as a little too quiet for her. Carrying on conversations with no help became tedious. With no feedback or opinions from Roger, it was also boring. Roger seemed fine with this. He liked Nancy. At least, she guessed he liked her. Nancy realized that she had found a deep thinker. She had found a persistent person of uncompromising values. She had found a goal-oriented person. Only that person was not Roger. *She* was that person! She liked her own company better than trying to project herself onto Roger. She broke up with Roger and met someone very quickly after she came to the realization that being alone wasn't so bad. Roger didn't say a word.

If you want something to listen to, take the following test and listen to its results.

IS HE A QUIET MAN?

Circle the number and add up the score

Family Background

Grew up as only child	1
Parents died when young	4
Parents divorced or separated before he moved on his own	2
Father or mother was an alcoholic	2
Father uninvolved with children	2
Raised by single parent, grandparents, other family member, or in foster care	4
Does not have close relationship with family	3
History of verbal abuse in family	3
Disturbed relations with siblings	2
Parents frequently compared children	2

Work/School History

Never finished high school	4
Started but didn't finish college	3
Works with hands, has a blue-collar job	2

Friendships

Has few friends, all male	2
Sees friends infrequently	2
Social activity with friends always involves some physical activity, does not just hang out or go to dinner	3

(test continues)

Past Relationships

Few past relationships	2
Unsure of what went wrong in relationship	2
Women broke up with him	3
No real breakup, just seemed to fade away	2

Body Language

Eyes dart	1
Looks down when talking with you	2
Body gets tight when you touch him	3
Covers mouth or parts of face a lot with hands	2
Eyes seem to wander during conversations or when spending a long time together	2
Becomes fidgety and tense when you are with others or in public	3

Dress/Hygiene

Hygiene is not what it should be	3
Does not use aftershave/cologne	1
Limited wardrobe	2
Mode of dress is a little bit off	2
Dress clothing is old and out of style	1
If dressed up, clothing does not match	1
If dressed up, constantly adjusting clothes	1
Looks uncomfortable in clothes other than his usual outfits	1

Behavior

Rarely compliments you	2
Lets you plan dates	1
Dates he plans usually involve doing something that allows for minimal conversation (i.e., movies)	3
Clumsy in social situations (i.e., how much of a tip to leave, ordering at a restaurant)	3
On dinner dates, the focus is on eating	3
Withdrawn or nervous around your friends/family	2
Friends/family have concerns about him they "cannot put finger on"	2

Conversation

Does not or rarely initiates conversation	3
Has trouble maintaining conversation	3
Does not ask expected follow-up questions to your statements	2
Rarely talks about friends	2

(test continues)

Conversation

Talks in short sentences and sentence fragments	3
Will respond at times with grunts or "uh-huh" or one-word answers	4
When answering your questions, he:	
Takes a long time to respond	2
Gives little information	2
Shows little emotion in answers	2
Few topics of conversation seem to interest him	3

When Confronted

Stammers, does not know what to say	3
Seems confused, does not understand your point	3
Withdraws from conversation	2
Continues same behavior without regard to your confrontation	2

Your Impression

Not that bright	2
Mechanically adept but not good with words	2
Just "not there" at times	2
Just "doesn't get it" at times	2
Total Score	

Score 15 and lower: No reason for concern at this point
Score between 16 and 30: Yellow Flag—There's reason for caution
Score 31 and above: Red Flag—He'll never talk; tell him to take a walk

Listening to the Sounds of Silence

If your date falls into the Yellow Flag category it does not immediately spell good-bye. He might be shy. He might be cautious after a bad experience in a recent relationship. In fact, it might be that he is quite taken with you and does not want to say anything stupid to ruin his chances. If the above things are true, his behavior will change over the course of a few dates. Keep your eyes open. You can expect him to talk more and reveal more. Try finding something in this man that stirs up his passions. It could be a hobby, a member of his family, the guy that cut him off when he was driving over to your date, anything that arouses a strong feeling or thought base. Try to get him to talk about this area in depth, maybe explain things to you, just to see if he has the capacity to rise above his quiet approach to life. If it is still like pulling teeth, it's time to extract the relationship from your life.

If he falls in the Red Flag range, watch yourself as much as you watch him. It can be tempting to see what you want rather than what is there. If he falls into this category, be advised that he is not going to change by anything you do. Years of avoiding the pain of relationships will prevent him from developing and enjoying a good relationship. He will quietly lead you into a world of silence, broken only by your pleas for more. The Quiet Man's only chance is to take a clear look at himself and get some help learning to hold conversation. This takes insight, self-acknowledgment, and humility. None of these will come from the outside; thus, you are powerless.

Breaking the Sound Barrier

It is not hard to break up with the Quiet Man. After all, you can count on him not to say much about it. Focus on the fact that you two seem to be different. You may point out his quietness as one of the differences but do not fault him for it. It is his way, and it is his decision to change it, not yours. If he should ask what he can do to better please you, tell him nothing. He has done nothing wrong, he just is not your type. Follow up this sentence with some reassurance that he is not bad but different from you. Don't approach the idea of becoming friends. He is likely to hang on to this as a possibility that the relationship can continue, making for difficult times later on. Cut your ties completely and move on. It is hard to leave the Quiet Man because he is truly one of the more pitiful types of Losers. He doesn't do anything really wrong, he just seems to do nothing. You will not be able to get him out of this mode. If you want to do nothing, better to take a vacation at a beach resort or a cruise. Work on a tan, not on a man.

The Boozer

The Party Animal Does Not *Make a Good Pet*

There are no alcoholic rats, at least not in the wild. If you give a rat the choice between water and wine, beer, or liquor, it chooses water. If you give it only booze, it doesn't drink. Unlike many other mammals who like the taste of beer, the rat would rather thirst. This spuriously provoked a group of scientists to create the affliction of alcoholism in rats. They took the sober little vermin, made a hole in their brains, and started to inject different chemicals into key areas of the rats' brains. After a number of trials, they found that the right chemical through the right hole, in the right part of the brain, and the rat became a regular lounge lizard. The rat will actually like being a drunk! With a hole in its head and something wrong with its brain, you can create an alcoholic rat. As humans, we generally like the taste and effect of alcohol even without surgical alteration. In moderation, it is an addition to our lives that can help us loosen up, feel good, or just add to our taste sensations. If you find that a new guy you are dating is using alcohol more frequently or intensely than might be appropriate in a new relationship, he may turn out to be an altered rat, and you'd have to have a hole in your head to continue dating him.

Kathy was tired of the bar scene. It was chaotic, noisy, and most men seemed to want just one thing. She decided to take a risk and try the personals. She had heard some horror stories, but she had also heard some success stories. She read them carefully and one struck her by its title: "Getting nowhere with the bar scene." She called the number and left a message. Her message was one of mutual understanding. She too "was tired of the bar scene and was ready to settle down to the business of getting to know someone for real."

A phone call from Ben went splendidly. He was witty with a certain shy charm. His voice was a melodic baritone. If he looked as good as he sounded, she would really be in heaven. If not, so what? It was time to focus on the person, yet she could hope. They arranged to meet at a local pub-restaurant. Coffee and talk, and if things went well they could stay for dinner. That was the plan.

"You're just like I pictured you, only prettier."

"Why, thank you. It's nice to be with a man who knows the right things to say. So you're tired of the bar scene."

"Absolutely. You meet women there, but it always seems like such a game. You can't just sit, talk, and get to know someone."

"I couldn't agree more."

"Would either of you care for something from the bar?" the waitress asked.

"A vodka and seven on the rocks would be nice. And you, Kathy?"

"Well, I was thinking more of coffee."

"It's Friday. Why waste a good weekend night with coffee?"

"How about a glass of white wine, please. So, tell me about yourself. What've you been up to since we talked?"

"Well, my team won our darts match last night so we'll be representing Doc's at the regional bar Olympics. I'm pretty excited about it this time. Our bar volleyball team almost made it too, but we lost by one or two bad serves. I think we started partying a little too early and lost focus."

"Sounds like you have a pretty active social life down at this bar. I thought you were tired of the bar scene?"

"What made you think that? Oh yeah, the ad. What I meant was I don't meet anyone in the bar scene."

"Did you stop at the bar on the way here? Seems like you already had a drink or two."

"Nah, that was a couple of hours ago. I'm not a big drinker. I don't even keep beer in the house. I used to party all the time in college but I've slowed up since."

"I like to have a drink every once in a while. I love wine with dinner. I'm more for those fruit drinks after the beach or pool."

"Well, here come our drinks, let's toast. To a beautiful blind surprise. . . ."

"Cheers. So, Ben, what's work like for you?"

"I work with a bunch of uptight pencil pushers. No one really knows how to have a good time."

"What, is everybody married or something?"

"No, they are just really straitlaced. With the kind of work we do, you'd think people would be able to take themselves less seriously. They're always on your case. Always want you to stay late. They think that work is supposed to be your life."

"My work is just the opposite. Everybody is very close and there's a lot of social time. In fact, they go out to happy hour every Friday."

"We could join them if you'd like. I love happy hour."

"No, thanks, it's nice of you to offer. It's good to be face-to-face with just one person for a change."

"I need to have that kind of group at work. Nobody at my office knows how to party. I'm probably going to leave after I've been there a year."

"A year. What did you do . . . ?"

"Waitress . . . Waitress! Would you like another drink, Kathy?"

"No, I think I'll take a second sip before I order another."

The small talk continued, drifting naturally to work, interests, and general attitudes about people. They had agreed to up their coffee encounter to an early dinner. They placed their orders, with Ben almost as an afterthought telling the waitress he could use another drink. During dinner, Ben had another. He talked and listened, was funny and serious, the drinks didn't really seem to be affecting him. Overall, the evening went as well as Kathy could have hoped, except for the nagging concern about the amount Ben had to drink. As long as it didn't affect him, why worry?

In moderation alcohol can help one relax, open up, and have a good time. Certainly not all people who drink are problem drinkers. In fact, most are not. However, if the recipe for a date starts to be two parts alcohol, one part juiced, you're about to be shaken, not stirred, by a Red Flag.

Why do people drink too much? The answers are limitless. To forget or remember. To celebrate or commiserate. They had a rough day or a great day. Happy hour, dinner hour, fun hour, time to go to sleep. When the drinking is done by a Boozer, the reasons are unimportant. The alcoholic does not need a reason, except to explain his behavior away to you. Alcoholism is a disease. It is a disease that a person often does not know he has and will deny if you tell him he does. When not drinking, a Boozer can be charming, witty, and intelligent. In fact, when not drinking, a Boozer is a regular person. What sets them apart is their drinking. They are not able to stop. They won't stop when told. They won't stop for you. Make no mistake, alcohol is all-consuming to the alcoholic. It has been said that the bottle is an alcoholic's mistress. No matter how much an alcoholic screws up his life, he will always make time for his mistress. You can't compete.

Unfortunately, many women underestimate the power of

alcohol. They minimize its effects or importance in a man's life. They may assume he's "just going through a party stage." They may see it as "cultural" like a St. Patty's Day blast. Worst of all, they may see the situation as changing once they are on the scene. It won't happen. Al-Anon, a self-help group for people involved with alcoholics, teaches a concept called the "three Cs": you didn't *c*ause it; you can't *c*ontrol it; you can't *c*ure it. Your only hope is to stay away from it.

Kathy stuck with Ben for a while. They had some nice times and some good talks. But on occasion, Ben would call and Kathy would notice he was drunk. He became belligerent when she tried to get him off the phone. The next day he did not seem to remember the conversation. Of the few dates they went on, there was always booze available. Kathy suggested seeing a play at a local community playhouse. She was surprised at Ben's reply: "Why not go somewhere where we can relax and have a drink? I always feel cooped-up in theaters." The more comfortable Ben got with Kathy, the more he drank in front of her. She tried talking to him about his drinking, but Ben either made a joke of it or got angry. She did not feel she knew him well enough to push the issue.

On their last date at a local restaurant, Ben drank so much that his speech slurred. The conversation went from witty to stupid and worse: Ben started to repeat the stupidity. His statements about his blossoming feelings for Kathy evoked strong feelings of nausea in her. Kathy finally had enough when in the parking lot she told Ben that she wanted to drive. He got angry and told her not to question his abilities. He knew what he was doing. She argued a little about him being unsafe, tried to get the keys, then he got verbally abusive and physically threatening. He was going to drive and that was it. If she did not want him driving, she could take a cab. She did. She never looked out the back window of that cab!

The test below can help you decide if your date is likely to get the two of you in a pickle.

IS HE A BOOZER?

*Circle the number and
add up the score*

Family Background

Father or mother was an alcoholic	3
Both parents alcoholic	4
Other relatives have history of alcoholism	3
Drinking is part of family culture	4

Work/School History

Real party guy in high school or college	3
Organized parties in college	2
History of disciplinary problems in high school or college	2
History of being disciplined on job (late, absenteeism, missed deadlines, careless work)	3
Fired from job in last five years	3
Fired more than once from a job	4
Frequently changes jobs	3
Has trouble holding a job	3

Friendships

Friends are primarily male	2
Lots of "buddies" he sees socially, few close friends	2
Much of social life conducted in bars/clubs	2
Friends are all heavy drinkers	3

Past Relationships

Met past girlfriends in bar scene	2
Past girlfriends described as partyers	2
Drinking was a problem in a past relationship	4
States past girlfriend had a drinking problem	3

Body Language

Can be fidgety and restless	1
Attention seems to wander	1
Hands shake at times	3
Seems to be in pain, as if he has a headache	2

(test continues)

Dress/Hygiene

At times hygiene is not what it should be	2
At times has rumpled look that contrasts with his regular appearance	3
At times looks hungover (hair out of place, bloodshot eyes, ruddy complexion)	3

Behavior

Late for date	2
Drinks prior to date, alcohol on breath	3
Shows up for date drunk	6
Chews gum, uses mints, uses breath spray a lot	3
Has more than two drinks on first date	2
Gets drunk	
On first date	8
On second date	6
Gets drunk often in your presence	10
Has been drinking when he calls you	8
Has poor memory for things the day after he has been drinking	8
Avoids going places where alcohol is not served	6

Conversation

Speech is slurred at times	5
Talks about a lot of parties in past	3
Conversational style changes when drinking (becomes louder, quieter, talks faster, etc.)	3
Repeats statements or stories	4
Conversation does not make sense	3
Makes strange leaps in conversation	4

When Confronted

Never admits to being wrong	2
Blames others a lot	2
Compares himself to others	2
Attacks you or finds fault with you	3
Gets defensive and questions your motives	2
Denies having a drinking problem	3
Makes excuses for drinking (i.e., under stress, party time)	4

(test continues)

Your Impression	
He drinks too much	2
Acts slightly off as if he has been drinking	2
You get impression he keeps some of his drinking from you	2
Total Score	

Score 15 and lower: No reason for concern at this point
Score between 16 and 30: Yellow Flag—There's reason for caution
Score 31 and above: Red Flag—He's far too much of a Boozer; say good-bye to this Loser

Check the Vintage Before Buying the Wine

Drinking and relationships can make a very explosive mix, especially when in excess. Be careful no matter what score your date receives. If your date scores in the Yellow Flag range he might be a practiced social drinker. He may use alcohol often but responsibly. So you don't necessarily have to be alarmed if he seems to know the difference between a pinot noir and a cabernet, or an ale and a lager. If he has too much information from firsthand experience, or those two drinks turn into two times five, his drinking will not age well in your life.

If your date scores in the Red Flag range, he might have a serious alcohol problem. In this case your course of action is simple. Find someone else. Avoid the mistake of the many women who have been down that path. Trying to change him won't work. He won't grow out of it. He won't stop when he is married and away from his friends. He won't quit when the kids arrive. He will continue to drink. He will get worse.

Professionals who work with alcoholics suggest that there is seldom change until the person reaches rock bottom. As long as you are with him, he will be kept off the bottom and will remain the same, unless of course he can bring you down to the bottom with him. A great way to occupy a number of years of your life, if you happen to like misery or are applying for sainthood. Treatment of alcohol problems is at first a daily event, then progresses to a few times each week. Most professionals suggest that in the first year of getting off alcohol, the person have no significant new relationships. Men are told to rely on the three Ms: meetings, meditation, and masturbation. Meetings are the self-help meetings of Alcoholics Anonymous or appointments with a professional; meditation is to get him to relax and know himself better; and masturbation because he should not have a woman around. Take the hint and get away.

If You Get No Kick from Champagne

The Boozer is a destructive Loser. This is easy to see when he is drunk but not so apparent when he is sober. Don't be confused. Leaving is the only thing to do.

Do not try to get him to see that he has a drinking problem. Don't try to change him. Don't bargain with him: "I'll stay if you stop drinking" or "I'll stay if you get help." Don't fall for his lines that somehow you are responsible for his drinking: "I get nervous around you" or "I wanted so much for this relationship to work I just needed a little extra help." You're setting yourself up for a lot of heartache when your energy could best be spent finding someone who deserves your heart.

Tell the Boozer that you have enjoyed the dates, but you find that the connection you seek is not happening. To the inevitable question "Why?" simply state again that you do not see the relationship happening, and that you don't want to lead him on. When asked to try "just a few more times," respond simply with "No, it would not be the right thing to do."

If you have been dating a long time, it may take a while to get your life back together again. Boozers tend to take you hostage. Never question your decision to end the relationship. Remember, with every cocktail he mixed, it wasn't just his drink that was on the rocks.

The Wanderer

Let a Man Find Himself Before You Plant Your Flag

Imagine hailing a taxicab in a major city, jumping into the back-seat, and when the driver asks where you want to go you answer, "I don't know, just take me somewhere!" How would you feel as the taxi driver rings his fare clock and starts to drive? Chances are you would be financially diminished, see a number of things you didn't particularly want to see, and end up in a place not of your choosing. Lest you think this is some Zen koan designed to put you in the mind of the present, living life with spontaneity, this book is certainly not recommending that you attempt such an imprudent act. Yet many women jump into the backseat of a relationship with guys who don't know where they are going, always take the long route to get somewhere, and have the "relationship drain" meter running the whole time. Many men are willing to let you join them on this taxi ride from hell, guaranteed to create more aggravation lines in your face than an equatorial sun shining through a pair of fishnet stockings.

Sheila went against all her strongest instincts and self-imposed rules and joined a phone-dating service. After a year of being alone, Sheila figured out that Mr. Right was probably not going to miraculously knock on her door while she was painting her toenails. She would leave a message on a machine and men who joined the same service could call in and leave her a voice mail, telling her about themselves. Sheila would then make the final decision on whom she would call back. Doug sounded really sweet in his message, and modest, maybe even a little shy. Sheila mustered up the nerve and called him back, her first attempt at phone-dating contact. He was just as sweet in a live conversation, so they set up a blind meeting at a local bookstore where they could have coffee and listen to some quiet guitar music. He was decent-looking, and she could tell he was looking past her physical imperfections as well.

"Classical guitar just brings me to a whole different place, a different world." Doug had a dreamy sound about him. "I really wish I had continued to play guitar when I was younger."

"You were a guitar player?"

"Yeah, among other instruments. I played drums for a while, trumpet, a little piano. Guess I should have stayed with just one instrument and gotten good, but I just wanted to learn everything. Did you play an instrument?"

"Oh yeah, I was a mean Autoharp player in third-grade music appreciation class. You've heard of a tin ear. I have an aluminum ear. Sort of flimsier than tin, cheaper, and less tonal."

"When I was on the West Coast, I used to go to this little coffee place that had the best classical music I've ever heard."

"When were you on the West Coast? Were you like a surfer dude or something?"

"Nah, I was backpacking for a year around the country. Living with people I met in college. Just sort of trying to find myself, figure out where I wanted to live."

"Sort of a 'road surfer,' huh? Follow the waves of the highway. What college?"

"Actually a few of them. I went to three or four, quite a few majors. I guess school wasn't my bag. I write well, so I left school and went on the road trying to sell some of my poetry and a few short stories about my travels. I just got word that one of my stories about a thing that happened to me in France is going to be published in this big literary magazine. I think that's going to open a lot of doors for me. A lot of people in the business read those things. I think I'm going to work on my writing career."

"I always wanted to do the backpacking through Europe thing, but college loans put me right in the work world. So tell me, do those magazines pay by the word or by the article?"

"Well, this is such a major honor. They don't really pay, but the opportunity is huge."

"So how do you make a living?"

"I work a few jobs here and there. Haven't really caught on to anything yet that's stuck. I have a couple of screenplay ideas out there, a couple of books in my head. I'm going to hit it big before long. I just have to sit back and wait. How do they say it? 'Opportunity knocks!' I left my last job because I was promised an opportunity to write a few of those teenage adventure novels, but it sort of fell through. I have a lot of people who believe in me, like my grandparents and friends, so I can always get by. I have my whole life to work if I don't get a hit on any of my projects, so I'm not too worried about it. Never struggled too hard, never will. Sit back and wait and the whole world will come to you. How about you?"

"Seems like when I sit back the only thing that comes to me is bills."

Sheila found Doug's boyish charm endearing. He had such a carefree attitude about life, such a positive view of the world—exactly what she was missing in her life as an accountant. They had a very enjoyable evening of coffee and music. Sheila woke up in her apartment the next day and went to work. Doug woke up with a big smile and turned on his parents' stereo.

* * *

Responsibility sucks. We would all like to be able to spend the day relaxing and taking advantage of opportunities. But when the entrances to opportunities have no exit, you may be knocking on the door of a Red Flag.

So, how does a man acquire more flounder than a fish market? As always, it probably started with the early patterns he developed as a child and adolescent. The Wanderer probably grew up with the luxury of being able to begin and end activities when he chose. This may sound well and good, but the unfortunate part is that he was never forced to complete anything. Life as a youth was all exploration, without a sense of completion. Many of us begin our piano (guitar, drum, tuba, etc.) lessons full of enthusiasm, only to encounter a parent nagging us to practice when we act like children and want to shift our sources of pleasure. Many of us start to play a sport or take dance lessons, then want to quit the team or troupe when we are not overnight superstars, yet our parents force us to finish a season or at least until one set of lessons *is* complete. This builds our character and persistence. The Wanderer was not forced to complete things. Guess what that means for commitment? You'd have better luck finding a man watching the jewelry special on the Home Shopping Network during the Super Bowl!

Another couple of patterns to look for in a Wanderer's past are the tendency of one parent to be a little flighty and the other to be extreme. For example, the mother could be down to earth and the father a fanciful dreamer. Or, the father an absentee high achiever and the mother a flower child. Most negative characteristics that develop in people develop not because of the direction of the parents' traits, but the extremity of the traits. When two parents are so out of balance that one represents almost a pure type and the other represents the pure opposite, expect some Red Flag stuff to be the result. Guess what that means for a relationship? You'd have better luck finding a macho man at a quilting club while the Miss Nude Spring Break pageant is going on a block away!

Throughout elementary and high school the Wanderer was able to get by on his good looks, charm, or sometimes talents, without ever really working hard. As he progresses in life, god-given talents start to find limits and hard work becomes a necessity to keep up. He is not used to hard work and starts to falter. As when growing up, falter means quit or change direction. He overfocuses on his social life rather than any sense of achievement. As a college-age person, the Wanderer was not forced to be accountable for his decisions. Changing majors or colleges, low grades, etc., will force good parents to make a kid go to a lesser college, pay for his own education, or work for a while before continuing. Not so for the Wanderer. No accountability, no negative consequences. As long as he presents his parents with a loosely cohesive dream, the parents will pay and pay, never letting the Wanderer have the inconvenience of changing maladaptive patterns. He learns to use whatever and whoever they need to get by and becomes the ultimate minimalist. Guess what that means for commitment?

Now you get him. By this time, the Wanderer has convinced himself that spontaneity is an overriding important characteristic of any human being. Again, direction may not be the problem as much as the extremity of his view of spontaneity. He doesn't set limits to keep his spontaneity-drive from being extreme. This guy is convinced that life will come to him. He is convinced that a direction will magically appear and he will find "what he is meant to do" without any effort on his own. If he finds a barrier, he will not work through it, but rather see it as a sign that he wasn't meant for the task at hand. He will never understand the pleasure of working and accomplishing something for himself and tasks become just things he has to get out of the way. Most women can look at this kind of guy and say they would never hire him; yet some of these same women would date him. If that's your choice, better let him pay for the cab.

Shelia and Doug dated for quite a while. She believed in

him. She figured with her support and drive and his talents, she would get him on his feet in no time. She begged off his job-free status to her friends by saying he was "the artistic type." Sheila and Doug had a great relationship with a lot of fun, but for some reason it didn't seem to be leading anywhere. What a shock!

Shelia set Doug up with a job in a friend's company. She told the boss he was an honest guy that learned quickly and wrote well. What she didn't tell the boss was Doug wasn't much for doing things other people's way, and didn't particularly like to keep other people's time schedules. Doug worked at the company twice as long as her friend wanted him, to spare Shelia's feelings, but business wisdom needed to take its course. Her friend's words about Doug made Shelia realize she was running up the meter and had to jump out. The Loser-cab was moving when she jumped, so she got a little scuffed up. Doug lost the fare.

The Wanderer is one who requires early detection before you get wrapped up, especially if you are highly ambitious and need to be a little more spontaneous. Use the test below for early warning signs.

IS HE A WANDERER?

*Circle the number and
add up the score*

Family Background

Grew up an only child	1
Father uninvolved with children due to business	2
Raised by grandparents	3
Grew up overindulged by parents/grandparents	3
One parent described as off, eccentric, or disturbed	3
Parents described as understanding or laid-back	2
Not disciplined as child	3

(test continues)

Work/School History

Started but never finished many activities as child (music, sports, drama, religious instruction, etc.)	3
Switched frequently to different things within an activity (changed instruments, went from sport to sport, joined different clubs)	3
Started but has not finished college	2
Switched schools or majors a lot in college	2
Lived in many places, never really settled down	3
Has trouble holding down job	3
Switches jobs very frequently because	
Fired	4
Can't find one he likes	5
New opportunities keep showing up	5
Moves a lot	4
Already has plan for leaving job when he takes a new job	4
Has borrowed money from or is supported by	
Parents	3
Grandparents	3
Other relatives	4
Friends	5
Government programs	6

Friendships

States he has lots of friends but never sees them	3
Friends scattered in different places	3
Describes friends as having unique or offbeat characteristics	4
Contacts friends when he needs something	3
Relaxes about accepting help from friends	3

Past Relationships

Talks positively about past relationships	1
Relationships ended by woman	2
Relationships ended by his moving to different location	3

Body Language

Open and relaxed body language	1
Attention wanders with prolonged conversation or time together	2
Eyes look up to the right a lot	1
Gets dreamy, unfocused look when talking about his plans	2

(test continues)

Dress/Hygiene

Appears younger in both looks and dress than stated age	
3 to 5 years	3
5 to 10 years	4
10 to 15 years	5
Underdressed for date	2
Hygiene inconsistent but good majority of time	2
Tries hard to look like individual through his dress	3
Mode of dress is a little bit off	2

Behavior

Late for date	1
Does not plan dates	2
Often makes spontaneous plans, which he states is his preference	2
Changes plans a lot at the last minute	3
Many dates are at unusual offbeat places	2
Many dates involve little money	2

Conversation

Talks about minor successes as if they were building blocks to major careers	3
Tells you of his get rich/famous schemes	2
Talks about having to risk it all to get ahead	2
Tells you he has no worries about making it as soon as he finds a niche in life or is discovered	3
Uses phrases such as: finding self, experimenting with different lifestyles, finding his dream, understanding life	3
Has a lot of "just missed" stories	2
Complains about barriers that have kept him from making it	2

When Confronted

Apologizes and admits to being partially wrong	−1
Shows insight into behavior	−1
Gets defensive and questions your motives	2
States you are jealous of his talents/lifestyle	2
Does not defend himself except by repeating idea that you don't understand	2
Compares you to other people who did not understand him	2
Gets angry and states he will not let you ruin his dreams	2
Continues behavior without regard to your confrontation	2

(test continues)

Your Impression

Has big unrealistic dreams	2
Does not handle frustration well	2
Hard worker only when mood/interest strike him	2
Short but intense attention span	2
Total Score	

Score 15 and lower: No reason for concern at this point
Score between 16 and 30: Yellow Flag—There's reason for caution
Score 31 and above: Red Flag—He'll never find his way; time for you to get lost

Isn't This the Long Way Around, Cabbie?

If you scored the guy in the Yellow Flag category, beware. There is a very thin line between the Yellow and Red Flags on this profile. If the person is just floundering, but is still in the Yellow Flag category, don't get too close until you see some progress. Don't buy the "love me for who I am" crap until you are sure he is something, instead of wanting to be something. A job doesn't define a man, but his behavior does. Don't just buy into a man's dream. If he's not actively out there, trying to be productive every day (not every other day, but every day), you've got a Red one, so get your token out for the next trip and let this ride go empty.

Red Flag category! You're on the ride to nowhere. Stick with it and what you will find is a number of just misses, broken efforts, and barriers that have kept your relationship from being any more than it was on the first couple of dates. On the worst side (and there is worse), when a man has been nonproductive and moves from young adulthood toward his middle years, there is a strangeness that emerges. The strangeness is hard to explain, but his ability to relate to people in the working world gets diminished. His idealism and lack of contact with current thoughts and ideas makes others look at what he says as a little weird, and people discharge the Wanderer's opinion as not worthwhile. The wives of the Wanderer tend toward depression and feelings of being trapped. They shoulder the entire responsibility of the family and for some reason find it hard to leave. A lot of these women end up overinvesting their self-worth in their children or having affairs, and many end up in therapy. Funny how the lack of the man's direction seems to make the woman's direction pretty clear. Affairs and therapy most every time.

Next Time Take the Subway!

You will not feel good about this breakup, so "Just do it!" "You know, I'm the kind of woman who needs a guy with a little more direction in life. I'm sort of into the making-life-happen thing, and I don't want to get a lot older waiting for something that may never materialize. So, I think it's better if we go the friends route, and not get romantic." If he's really got it for you, maybe he'll go out and start being productive. Remain phone friends until both of you are dating others. If after another relationship or two, he has a job for a while, seems into achieving, and has changed some of the "going nowhere" behaviors, you can slowly go out again and retest him. Usually wandering is a long-term pattern so make sure that he has been changed for a lengthy period of time. Remember, if you think you want to get back together, look at his behavior, not just what he says. Usually, the bigger he talks the less he is actually doing. You could say, this is one taxi ride where the driver needs to leave some distance between cars, proceed slowly, and not blow his own horn.

The Burdened Beast

Limit Baggage to Two at the Check-in Counter and One Small Carry-on

The gondola is the symbol of Venice, Italy, one of the most beautiful cities in the world. Nowadays it is a plain, black, thin wooden boat with simple adornments, but that was not always the case. In medieval Venice gondoliers decorated their boats with gold ornaments and beautiful linens in an attempt to lure customers and outdo one another. At first, it dressed up the canals of Venice, but after a while the competition became so severe that the boats were overdone. Some were so adorned with gold and jewels that they began to get very heavy and took much more effort to move. The canal became more crowded as the boats got larger and more elaborate. The traffic also started moving much slower as the overburdened boats got weighed down. The pretentiousness of these gondoliers started to wear on the merchants and citizens of Venice, and especially on the doge, the Venetian leader. Finally in 1582, the doge decided to proclaim a law that all gondolas had to meet a uniform standard of simplicity, thus giving birth to the modern-day modest gondola. Men have a way of weighing themselves down with adornments that often detour them on the road to relationships.

That's why trying to get into a relationship with many men can seem like standing still in water, or chartering a sinking ship.

Mary met Andy through a personal ad she placed in a local newspaper. She said the right things to attract guys. "Thirty-one-year-old single damsel looking for knight in shining armor to ride into the sunset with." Corny but it worked. She and Andy set up a date for a cup of designer coffee. He was very attractive, honest, sincere, and had a good job. A great beginning for any blind date.

"So, how long have you been doing the personals, Andy?"

"Actually, yours was the first I ever applied to. I guess it's not apply, but whatever it is, yours is the first."

"My brilliant short literary form got you, huh?"

"No, actually I think it was the way you spelled damsel: d-a-m-s-l-e! I thought it was cute."

"Gee, I don't mean to disappoint you, but that was probably a typo by the paper. Do you think dumb is cute?"

"Let's see. How do I get out of this one? Actually, I thought you were just very bright and nonjudgmental, that the misspelling was a ploy of brilliance and that's what I needed for my first date back in the singles scene."

"I like the nonjudgmental part. Sort of keeps me from saying anything else. You're not as dumb as you . . . uh . . . as the other guys that responded."

"Good save!"

"Why whatever do you mean, Mr. Andy?" They laugh. "So what do you mean first date back in the singles scene?"

"Well, I'm in the process of a divorce. My ex is dragging it out. I can't believe this sometimes; she cheated, she wanted to leave, but I'm the one who has to suffer."

"Exes can be a tough thing, I guess. Never had one myself, but I was with a guy for six years. It was like we were married."

"I hope it wasn't as difficult a situation as mine. I mean, I must be the only man that was abused by a woman. I was abused by my father growing up, but this lunatic I married starts beating me in the middle of our honeymoon. I know she was stressed out from the wedding, but give me a break."

"Wow, sounds like a tough life. You don't sound like you're through with it yet."

"I could be. Except she gets drunk and calls me in the middle of the night all the time. I don't mind the abusive day calls, but the middle of the night is really bad."

"Why don't you call the police?"

"Ah, it'll pass. I don't want her to get into trouble. I don't know why it's always me that has to put up with the crap, but I guess that's my lot in life."

"You can learn from anything."

"Not too much to learn when you're the victim. So let's leave this topic and consider maybe taking this show to dinner after the coffee. My treat."

"Sure, how about the Mexican place on Line Road? Heard it's very good, but I've never been there."

"Um, it's really good, but I sort of have a bad memory or two there. If you want Mexican, let's go across town to Seville. They have those singers and everything and some of the best margaritas you have ever tasted."

"I could do a margarita. I already had the coffee. Does that count to sober me up afterward?"

"Not quite, but they sell coffee there too. Wow, when you said sober that gave me a flashback to a woman I was once engaged to who used to get blitzed all the time, abuse me to the limit, and then she'd say, 'Don't worry, coffee will sober me up.' "

"Well, I promise not to get blitzed on a couple of margaritas. Besides, I just get silly and sleepy when I drink too much. You're safe with me. I guess we both have a little damsel in distress in us."

"You know, you sure are making this dating thing easy."

"Well, it won't be that easy forever. I just haven't gotten my free meal yet." Mary laughs at herself. "How hard did you expect it to be?"

"I don't know. I guess with all the criticism I've taken, I just get down on myself. I also figured women may not be as nice to me because of the limp I have and the scar over my eye."

Mary looked closely and still didn't see either malady. "The limp and the scar? I didn't quite notice, but now that you mention it, I'm sure a margarita will make it more tolerable if I start to become aware."

The rest of the date went pretty well, although the topic of past relationships did enter into the conversation a few times. Mary was an understanding girl and liked the other parts of this guy. Besides, she was getting toward the end of the personal ad list and had been exposed to some really strange acts. Andy looked so much better in comparison.

We all have a history that involves traumas. It is an expected part of the pilgrimage through life. Relationship trauma is one of the worst. But when you are starting a trip with a guy carrying too much baggage from journeys past, pack warm, because he is taking you to a cold place where they fly a Red Flag.

Baggage is not simply a matter of the past events that have happened in a person's life but a compilation of attitudes and personality. Everyone suffers trauma, perhaps many traumas, by dating age. As far as relationships are concerned, we have all experienced bad situations with that guy or girl where the timing was wrong. We have all experienced a time when we were more in love than our partner was and ended up being tossed around emotionally. Most of us let it go, but the Burdened Beast never does. He holds on to past trauma, thinks about it constantly, and lets it be a guiding force in his life. He is more than willing to bring you along with him. A kindly offer. Putting pepperoni on your face and shoving your head in a pizza oven may be slightly more desirable.

Some people believe that outside events control their lives. Others believe they control their lives by their own thoughts and actions. No one is exempt from bad events, but we are given the freedom to react. When a man is constantly concerned with his past, then he is not exercising this freedom. Believing you are controlled by what happens to you instead of how you react to it, tends to be an attitude and thought process that remains pretty consistent in a person throughout his life. The development of this attitude is ingrained in a person's early upbringing. Usually one or both parents are the type that always had excuses for why things weren't going the way they liked. Often a Burdened Beast's parents feel they would be more successful if they had just caught a break, and they present the view to their children that life should be fair. This gets taken in and establishes what is called in psychology as "external locus of control," meaning a view that what happens outside controls a person's life. The opposite, an "internal locus of control," suggests that you have the power to control your own life. Either attitude can be healthy at low and moderate levels, but when taken to extremes both attitudes are unhealthy.

The Burdened Beast exudes a basic viewpoint that if life was more "calm," or more "fair," or he wasn't "singled out" as much, he'd be in a much better position. In essence, he believes that there is some kind of problem-free perfection that exists for some people but not for him. The reality is that life is a matter of problem solving, and reacting to bad events as well as good. What is missing in the Burdened Beast's conception is the acceptance that life is not smooth and that everyone takes some knocks. He doesn't accept the bad events in his life as normal, thus ends up making himself into a martyr for having to put up with so many bad things. Through all his wailing and complaining he does manage to get some pity, but it is short-lived, as people generally want to be around happy folks. And he is certainly not happy.

A Burdened Beast makes a bad partner because he doesn't let a relationship have normal disagreements. Instead he holds on to problems and arguments and tries to make you feel that you are the cause of pain. After an argument, he may say, "You showed your true colors," and make you spend your time trying to get him to forgive you. A Burdened Beast always has a built-in excuse for stopping or not doing things because he has an unlimited resource of terrible past events that can free him from living up to responsibility, or from facing something that has the potential to be unpleasant or stressful. He will tend to be moody, given to the whims of a good day or a bad day that is determined by what happens in the outside world. His moods will control you and make you feel like you are always walking on eggshells. You will end up canceling a lot of social functions because of his moods. The Burdened Beast will be very judgmental when you make a mistake or when he perceives you've made a mistake. He will accuse you of being insensitive if you do something that stirs up his past or creates a problem for him. He is not a happy person. Your major defense to this is either to leave and give him something else to ruminate about or join his misery and become a Burdened Beast yourself. Misery does love company. The two of you can wail away at the rest of the world, complain about how unfair life is, and rummage through catalogs and moan about all the things you would buy if life had given you a break. Sound appealing? Get your credit cards out now.

Mary really felt a need to be patient with Andy as he went through his divorce. They stayed together for close to a year while he went through court and everything else that goes with a divorce. They decided to live together so they could be a more supportive unit. Mary felt needed as she listened and offered soft advice. After the divorce, Andy wouldn't let go of it. He kept talking about it, keeping it alive. Finally Mary confronted him with her need to move on. Andy accused her of being insensitive and "just like his ex-wife."

The light bulb that went on in Mary's head at that time could have lit a sports stadium. She was told constantly that she couldn't be trusted, that she was just like everyone else in his life. At first, she wanted to prove that she was different, so she tried to stick it out. In the following weeks when Andy kept bringing up how insensitive Mary had been, it hit Mary in the stomach like she'd just had her navel pierced with a rusty corkscrew. Mary took the day off from work, got a new hairdo, and rented a U-Haul. If you turn off the lights in your room right now and listen very closely for the littlest sound, you can probably hear Andy still telling the story of the psycho-woman who moved out on him with no notice and no reason.

Before you find yourself at the rent-a-truck place, you may wish to give the guy you're dating the following test.

IS HE A BURDENED BEAST?

Circle the number and add up the score

Family Background

Grew up an only child	1
Parents died when young	3
Parents divorced or separated before he moved on his own	3
Father or mother was an alcoholic	2
Father uninvolved with children	2
Raised by single parent, grandparents, other family members, or in foster care	3
Does not have close relationship with family	2
History of verbal abuse in family	3
History of physical abuse in family	4
Disturbed relations with siblings	3
Parents frequently compared children	2
Parents were complainers and never content with their lives	4

Work/School History

Sheltered childhood	2
Missed a lot of typical activities due to illness/phobias	3
Parents thought of him as a frail child	3
Finished education as average student	1
Works in secure job setting such as civil service or a large company	2
Seems too involved in work	2

(test continues)

Friendships

Mostly female friends	2
Talks with friends on phone a lot	1
Emotionally dependent on these friends	2
Activities with friends are either venting his feelings or seeking advice	3

Past Relationships

Talks extremely negatively about past girlfriend/spouse	2
Exaggerates reasons for breakup	2
Describes past girlfriend/spouse as "crazy"	2
Still fighting with ex	3
Stalked or harassed by ex	3

Body Language

Timid and closed body language	2
Eyes dart	1
Looks down when he talks	1
Eyes never look at you	1
Body gets tight when you touch him	2

Dress/Hygiene

Overdressed for first date	1
Looks uncomfortable with the outfit he is wearing	1
Looks for you to approve of his attire	2

Behavior

Dates have limits due to bad past experiences (restaurant has bad memories for him)	3
Moodiness affects dates (cancels date, changes location of date)	3
Has specific rituals that he must attend to	3
Has rules for you (mode of dress, avoid certain phrases, avoid certain music or scents), so you won't remind him of past incident	4

Conversation

Talks a lot about pain or difficulties of his past	2
Talks a lot about previous relationships	2
Paints himself as a victim	3
Calls you by name of past lover	3
Talks about the limits on a relationship with you because of his need to avoid being hurt as he was in past	3

(test continues)

Conversation

Talk about past dominates conversation	2
Talks about physical or mental insecurities a lot	2
Talks about past trauma having limited his success	2
Responds to your conversation with memories of past issues, problems, or relationships	2

When Confronted

Apologizes profusely but without sincerity	2
Becomes timid and quiet	2
Makes sudden transition from listening to you to becoming angry	2
Compares you to other women in his life, noting you are just like them	3
Compares you to his mother	3
Gets defensive and questions your motives	2
Brings up all the little things you have done "he never mentioned before"	3

Your Impression

Seems to live in past	2
Does not appear to have learned from past relationships	2
Looking for magical, safe place to live his life	1
Memory for bad events is too good	3
Total Score	

Score 15 and lower: No reason for concern at this point
Score between 16 and 30: Yellow Flag—There's reason for caution
Score 31 and above: Red Flag—Too much baggage; pack him away

There's No Life Jacket on a Sinking Gondola

So you've got a Yellow Flag? We have definitely become a society that whines a lot, so it's going to be hard on the first three dates to figure out if you've got a guy that has hit a bad time, or if you've got the full-blown all-the-world's-at-fault Burdened Beast. You may have to put a little time into this one. Don't get close yet, and let him know that you're a little leery of getting too close because of everything he's carrying with him. Once you give this clear message, if he's not a Burdened Beast he will soften his attitude a little and try to keep his problems separate. You have to resist the urge to get him to talk about his past problems, mistaking that for some kind of caring and sensitive sharing. You are not with him early on in a relationship to help him through his problems. The best help you can provide is to get him out having fun. If he's not able to drop it after you've given him the key to stop bringing it up, guess what? You've got yourself a Burdened Beast. Let him gather all the baggage he wants and wait for the next boat.

If you have the Burdened Beast, resist the temptation to get drawn into his problems. Resist the temptation for him to see you as a loving, caring person before you dump him. (Many women won't dump a guy until he is completely smitten.) He will be making his list of earthquakes, hurricanes, plane crashes, fires, and you, as the worst tragedies of the world. It is never going to be fair to him, and change is not imminent when "his problems clear up." He wants to drag you by the hand into the world of misery, and you want to wake up with a smile on your face, so it's time to go. You will be his new person to complain about, but fear not, even you will be replaced as life will continue to offer more fuel for his misery-fire. Remember the gondola stopped being able to move when it got weighed down. You're not weighed down, so move faster than he does down a different canal.

Abandon Ship at the First Sign of the Iceberg

Yes, getting rid of a Burdened Beast is easy, but you must be willing to move quickly and not look back at the sinking ship. This is one that you might want to do on the phone, perhaps preceded by a short letter. It will be easier for him to villainize you if you don't do it in person, and it will give him an easier escape to call his friends and complain about you. Remember you will become part of his plague of bad luck, so accept that role. When women hear he is telling stories about them to friends, they try to explain or make contact with him again to set things right. Resist this temptation. You are not the cause of his misery. You are not causing this ship to go down, and you deserve the first spot in the life raft to get away.

Send a quick note first (letter, e-mail, fax, message on machine when you know he's not home) that includes the sentence, "When we talk tonight I think we have to reconsider dating right now. I will call at seven P.M." He may avoid you by not being home. He will talk to his friends about the impending breakup, which is good preparation for him and makes your job easier. At the beginning of the conversation (no niceties first), tell him you don't want to date him right now until he gets his problems cleared up or lets go of his baggage. Tell him you know he needs to do that without being in a relationship and being with you would just stop him from dealing with what he needs to work on. If he tells you that you're wrong, tell him you have a clear opinion on this and you are not changing your mind. A few Burdened Beasts will say they know you are right and ask if they can get together later with you when things have worked out. That is rare. If that is his answer, he might be friend material. Usually, however, the response will be a variant of your being wrong, overanalyzing, etc. Let him say his piece and say good-bye.

Immediately after you hang up either make a date with someone else, get on the phone and call a male friend that you always have fun with, or call a couple to hang out with where the guy is a lot of fun. You need to be in some fun normal male company that night or at least the next day. It will set you straight by comparison.

And fear not, misery does find company just like double-chocolate hot-fudge banana splits find hips, thighs, and buttocks. His burden had become yours, and you don't need to carry the extra weight. Breaking up with a Burdened Beast is like losing fifty pounds of cellulite off your brain. Consider this chapter the same as a mental stair climber, treadmill, exercise bike, step class, ten videos with a variety of workout music, and thousands of hours of smelly sacrifice and effort. Consider this breakup the first move to developing Brains of Steel!

The Barbarian

Mouthwash Can't Cure a Big Mouth

The bullfrog is not a menacing creature. No teeth, no claws, no poison sacks. Unless you're a small bug, there is nothing to fear from a bullfrog. Unfortunately for the bullfrog, he happens to be a tasty creature to many other animals. Generally, if confronted by a predator, he hops away very quickly. Yet, if cornered, the bullfrog has a trick up its little green sleeve. He swallows air. Lots of air. As he swallows air, he starts to puff up and get big. The predator sees his tasty little dinner blowing up and becoming tremendous. An Incredible Hulk frog carries a whole different dinner versus risk value. It is time to look for a dinner that isn't doing major steroids. The attacker flees, never realizing that it was frightened away by an illusion, a lot of hot air. Men can be bullfrogs: full of hot air designed to scare off anyone that threatens them, or to demean people they want to control. If you choose to share a lily pad in his pond, bring some wart cream because you will not keep his company without major outgrowths making your skin crawl.

Christina was nervous but still excited by the prospect of a blind date. Her friend had set her up with Alex. She had told

Christina that Alex seemed to be a real go-getter, and was making a name for himself at the office. Christina liked ambitious men who knew what they wanted. She had been having a run of bad luck with wimpy, boring dates and thought a more aggressive guy was just the change she needed. The date was set.

Alex was prompt. The doorbell rang exactly at seven. She was pleased when she opened the door. He was tall, solid, neatly groomed, with gorgeous light brown hair. His clothes were meticulous. Dark, pin-striped suit, white shirt, and a tie that pulled the whole outfit together. He looked at Christina with a big smile, pulled a single rose from behind his back, handed it to her, and said, "Hi, Christina, I'm Alex. You really are just as pretty as Sarah said you were." Christina was taken. He was direct, strong, and got right to the point. This had potential! The maître d' at the restaurant they went to knew Alex when he walked in the door. They were polite but not enthusiastic about seeing him. She ordered a chicken dish in a mustard-cream sauce, he ordered a steak.

"Your doorman looks like he's wearing Coke bottles. Oh well, the little people have little use for good looks."

"Actually, he's a very nice guy with a big family that he is supporting on the doorman job and working nights as a security guard at a factory. I never look down on a man who works hard for his family."

"I wasn't looking down on him. I just thought he had unusually thick, unattractive glasses. I think—"

Christina cut him off. "I hear you're a real up-and-comer at the office."

"You just have to know where to walk, and who to walk on. It's not very hard to get ahead in my office. There're a bunch of dweebs there that don't have a clue."

"Really? Maybe I should work there. I'd fit right in."

"Nah, you'd be a superstar. Sarah tells me that you are a cloth buyer for a men's outerwear company. What is that?"

"I buy cloth. After the designers figure out how they want a garment to look, I have to find out where to get the cloth for manufacturing. So I call overseas a lot, work on the computer to find the best cloth at the best price. I end up working with a lot of the Pacific Rim countries."

"Really? Can you understand those slanty-eyed guys?"

"Sometimes it's hard, but it's not a language-based business. We work more with numbers. You know, I'm really not into stereotypes and prejudice. I find it offensive."

"I hope you don't think I'm being prejudiced. I don't mean anything by what I'm saying. I have some friends who are Chinese and Korean. Just the way I grew up, I guess."

The waitress comes to the table with their meal.

"Honey, I really like to have my water glass kept filled, and don't leave before I check whether my steak is medium-rare the way I like it." He makes a cut. "Okay, he got it right this time. Now, please get me some water."

"So, do you eat here often?"

"Actually, I do. I like being at a place I can train the staff to treat me the way I want to be treated."

"Better be careful, there are some people who don't take to training."

"Everyone wants training. There are just some you have to be more positive and sneakier about training. Women have to be trained much more positively."

"Funny, I always thought we were the ones doing the training. We let you think you're in control, sometimes. Men are like dogs, you've got to keep the choke collar on them to train them right. Could you fetch me that salt, please?"

As they talked, the funny bad feeling that Christina felt started to fade. She focused on her date's wittiness. Maybe he was just nervous. Maybe he was trying to impress her. He was a good joke-teller, but some of his humor was quite off-color—those jokes that you laugh at but feel a little bad about laughing because you know they are tasteless. She did notice he cursed a lot when he was telling jokes. Yet, there was some-

thing endearing about him, something very honest and open.
He let her know exactly where she stood and he was very
manly, even if a little rough around the edges.

Everyone wants a partner who is assertive and a whirlwind
of confidence. But when the air starts to resemble a funnel
cloud in a Kansas cornfield, you may be twisting your way to a
Red Flag.

Why are some men rude and crude? Somewhere in his past
the Barbarian has been bruised and frightened. He has come
to see himself as defenseless, and this frightens him. Over the
years, he develops a style that makes him feel stronger, a style
of rude arrogance that puts a barrier between him and would-
be attackers. The Barbarian believes that the only way to make
himself better is to make others look bad. So he steps on the
weak to feel superior. Sometimes this takes the form of put-
downs and insults of people around him, mostly people in
menial roles. Sometimes it takes the form of tough-man talk.
Frequent use of expletives or using the F-word as a universal
adjective, exclamation, verb, and noun, makes a young boy
feel manly. Unfortunately, the Barbarian's inner child never
got his mouth washed out with soap.

The dirty jokes? All men tell dirty jokes from time to time. It
can be a form of male bonding. It can be funny. It can be
naughty in just the right way to build intimacy. The Barbarian
has the tendency to tell the dirty joke in the wrong place at
the wrong time. He does not know the boundaries of appro-
priateness. In his ever-expanding galaxy of rudeness, those
who don't laugh or those who find him offensive are prudish
or unable to have fun. If confronted, he will question your
ability to make this kind of judgment, saying you have your
head in the clouds. The world is his sky and he decides where
to place the stars. This is truly the black hole of dating.

Somehow, many women initially find this behavior attractive.
This is especially true when it occurs infrequently in a man who

otherwise appears strong and confident, a no-nonsense man. These women describe the Barbarian as a "man's man." It pushes their neediness buttons of protector, caretaker, and provider. Only too late do they learn that it is a facade. By the time they see the insecurity underneath, they have suffered a multitude of insults, put-downs, and psychological bruises.

Christina did not leave Alex soon enough. The bad luck (bad choices?) she had prior to Alex made her want to stick it out, give him a chance. What she got was grief. If she tried to tell Alex something was bothering her, he became defensive and deflected the conversation with insults, arrogance, or rudeness. In fact, the pattern was: If things did not go his way, frightened him, or inconvenienced him, he lashed out. The insults that Alex loosely distributed to strangers weren't nearly as biting and harsh as those he directed at Christina.

Christina invited Alex to accompany her to the company Christmas party. She was not sure whether it was a good idea or not, but she wanted to have a date. Alex was good at first when he was talking to the men, but when her boss came over and introduced herself, Alex started taking in "bullfrog air." He made a few demeaning comments about the catering crew, a negative comment about Christina, a couple of statements about how hard it is to run an office full of idiots, and told an antifeminist joke that had a couple of people walking away. Her boss was a strong woman who watched Christina turning the colors of the many fruit-flavored daiquiris in the room. The boss said to Christina right in front of Alex, "I've dated a few losers in my time too. Shall I have security remove him from the party?" Christina responded quickly, knowing her boss liked decisiveness. "Please do! But shouldn't we throw our drinks on him first?" Alex hopped away in a rush, and Christina never heard from him again. The next blind date Christina went on was set up by her boss to celebrate Christina's promotion.

The following test can be used as a guide to help identify the Barbarian.

IS HE A BARBARIAN?

*Circle the number and
add up the score*

Family Background

Parents divorced or separated before he moved out on his own	1
Father, mother, or both alcoholic	2
History of verbal abuse in family	2
Physically abused as child	3
Mother abused by father	4
Mother was peacemaker and pacifier	3
Parents (usually father) frequently compared children	2
Parents (usually father) opinionated and or prejudiced	3
One or both parents loud and aggressive	2

Work/School History

History of disciplinary problems in high school	2
History of disciplinary problems in college	3
Brags a lot about achievements at work	2
Has reputation of being back-stabber at work	3
Claims you have to be willing to step on people at work to get ahead	3
Describes coworkers negatively (e.g., incompetent, lazy)	3

Friendships

Few if any female friends	1
Friends' girlfriends/wives do not like him	5
Has male friends but not many	1
Talks about friction between himself and his friends	2
Criticizes his friends	2
Does not like girlfriends/wives of his male friends	3
Has reasonable number of male and female friends	−1
Is friends with male friends' girlfriends/wives	−1

Past Relationships

Talks extremely negatively about past girlfriends	1
Exaggerates reasons for breakups	1
Describes past girlfriends/spouse as "crazy"	2
Verbally abusive in past relationship	3
Remains friendly with past girlfriends/wives	−1

(test continues)

Body Language

Closed and aggressive	2
Squinty eyes that penetrate sharply	2
Invades personal space before you do	1
Touches you early in conversation before you do	1
Emotion is evident in facial expressions	1

Dress/Hygiene

Excellent hygiene	1
Well-groomed	1
Good, diverse wardrobe with clothes for all occasions	1
Dresses appropriately but sharply	1

Behavior

Teases any person other than you during dates	2
And seems to enjoy it	2
And does so in a cruel manner	2
Makes rude remarks to any person other than you during date	2
And seems to enjoy it	2
Teases you during a date	2
And seems to enjoy it	3
And does so in a cruel manner	5
Makes many judgmental observations about people (clothing, looks, race, speech, handicaps, etc.)	4
Will start "fight" with waiters, waitresses, or clerks when frustrated	4

Conversation

Tells off-color jokes to people he does not know well enough	2
Tells off-color jokes to shock or bully	4
Makes rude or nasty comments when frustrated	4
Responds to personal questions with sarcasm or biting remark	4
Responds to suggestions as if you had attacked him	3
Arguing predictably leads to nasty personal attacks toward you	4
When talking with service personnel uses rude titles such as dear, sweety, honey, bub	3
Mumbles expletives under breath	2
Curses a lot	2
Uses the F-word as an overall adjective	2

(test continues)

When Confronted

Never admits to being wrong	2
Blames others a lot	2
Gets defensive and questions your motives	2
Gets angry and attacks you or finds fault with you	2
Becomes abusive, curses	5
Continues same behavior without regard to your confrontation	2
Apologizes and admits to being partially wrong	−1
Shows insight into his behavior	−1

Your Impression

The macho type	1
Strong	1
Rough around the edges	1
Seems to want to project a tough image	2
Comes across as confident, but you suspect not so underneath	2
	Total Score

Score 15 and lower: No reason for concern at this point
Score between 16 and 30: Yellow Flag—There's reason for caution
Score 31 and above: Red Flag—Rude, crude, lewd; later, dude

Look Before You Leap

If your date scores in the Yellow Flag range, it is not necessarily time to jump into the pond for cover. There is a normal amount of nervousness on a first date, and he may just be overcompensating. You'll know if, after a few dates, his behavior becomes more acceptable. Best that you give him hints when you don't appreciate his rudeness toward others and particularly his statements of prejudice. "I don't like those kinds of confrontations" or "I get uncomfortable when you . . ." If he is listening, he will realize he is not impressing you and may decide you're more important than his expressing an opinion.

A Yellow Flag may also signal that you have found a man with a more stereotypical macho style. He may deal with stressful situations more coarsely than you are accustomed. In an effort to bond, he might use off-color humor but becomes aware of boundaries when you point them out. You might be able to have a fine relationship with him, even if you can't bring him to the art gallery opening or the weekly tea at the ladies' society club.

If your date scores in the Red Flag range, be careful. You are not looking at a temporary state that will mellow with time. You are looking at a lifestyle. This man has built a wall around himself to keep intimacy out. He doesn't look at life as "us and them," it's "him and them." There's no room for you. The closer you get, the more likely you'll be the target of the slings and arrows you've seen him hurl at others. If you want to avoid the inevitable wounds, don't stick around. Leaving will be your outrageous fortune.

If Frogs' Legs Taste Like Chicken, Order Chicken

Once you have made your decision and you need to tell the Barbarian to plunder elsewhere, do it in an assertive, no-nonsense manner. Be clear why you are ending the relationship. Tell him that you do not like the way he treats others or you. But make sure not to argue with him when he tells you that you are too sensitive. Just state again that you do not like what you see, and you have decided to trust your own opinion, not his. Be firm in noting that you have made up your mind. Let him know your decision is based on his behavior, his behavior alone, and not open for discussion. The Barbarian will have to get in some last licks. You can expect some put-downs and snide remarks. That's why doors open and phones hang up. Do not be goaded into a fight. It is pointless. You are not trying to get him to change. After you make clear that you don't like and will not be part of his behavior, the Barbarian will actually be bruised enough to leave you alone. Once he knows you see past his hot air, he will feel defenseless. Fear not, you will not need to look over your shoulder, afraid that he too is enrolling in the Three Steps to Intimacy adult-education class when you sign up.

Red Flag Situations

I Had a Handle on Life but It Broke

The twenty-five Red Flags you have read about in this book have focused on the behavior of the men who come into your life, however briefly, and who have the potential to mince your emotions, grate your sense of balance, and dice your self-esteem. What if life's cookbook already has you emotionally minced, grated, and diced? Sometimes the problems life presents, or the problems you have created, put you in a mode where you are functioning in a Red Flag Zone, a place where your defenses are shattered, your intellect is compromised, and the "Loser detection device" in your brain has been disabled. In the Red Flag Zone, you must forget the "him" and focus on the "me." What is going on in your life is most important. You must understand why you are vulnerable and how that is going to affect your judgment. You must learn how to meet your needs without depending on the wonderful pleasantries that come from having a new relationship. And you especially must learn the stealth moves a man can make in these situations to safely pass through the alarm of your Red Flag radar.

In the American Indian folklore of the Algonquian tribes, it is the vulnerability of women that connects them to men in the first place. Their legends talk of men and women living separately, with men being stronger and better hunters but living rather barbaric lives. Although weaker in hunting, women bathed more frequently and surrounded themselves with nicer things like tanned hides. It was the desire for women to be better protected and men to act more civilized that brought them together. Certain vulnerabilities are not bad, in fact, just as in the Indian legend, they may lead to preparedness for connection. There are times, however, when vulnerabilities created by unusual circumstances set the foundation for a relationship that is weak, one-sided, and potentially usury. The most common situations in which vulnerability affects relationships are: vulnerability by loss, vulnerability by addition, vulnerability by boredom or the need for novelty, vulnerability by emotional state, vulnerability by deadline, and vulnerability by deprivation. We'll leave vulnerability by wearing untanned hides to the Indian legend.

Vulnerability by Loss

Sandra and Tom had only dated a couple of times when Sandra's mom died suddenly of a heart attack. Sandra was emotionally devastated. Although she had not developed strong feelings for Tom, he was extremely supportive during the wake and funeral, even taking time off to help with arrangements and seeing to it that people were as comfortable as they could' be given the circumstances. Of the three sisters in the family, Sandra was the only one that was unmarried. She was also the closest in proximity and emotionally to her mother. Much of the work and decisions of this part of life fell on Sandra, and her sisters were concerned with her feelings since she was involved with their mother most before her death. As much as the family bonded through this period, Sandra felt the most intensely alone. She was very thankful Tom had come into her life a few weeks prior.

Sandra's vulnerability did not allow a normal relationship to develop. The relationship footing that resulted was based on Tom being an understanding, socially appropriate man in a situation that Sandra will only face once in her life—the death of her mother. Many people think that the best time to judge a partner is under adverse circumstances, but this is specious reasoning. In the first place, the adversity being faced was not Tom's adversity but Sandra's. It tells you little about how Tom faces his own adversity. Second, adversity empowers some people's desire to take charge and be controlling, others' desire to be protective, others' to display a sense of nurturing, etc. What comes out may be the positive manifestations of exactly some of the Red Flag problems we discussed. Third, adversity brings forth different needs in you, thus not allowing you to make decisions based on realistic appraisal of your day-to-day desires, but rather your needs in a loss situation. Unless you stay in a constant state of loss, you could be in trouble. Finally, even your body chemistry changes during loss with the release of different hormones and neurotransmitters that make you more susceptible to wanting the attention you get in a relationship. It is a whole mind-body conspiracy that takes over for a period of time, enticing you to forget the Red Flags. Unfortunately in the above situation, the loss that is felt will carry for a long time, making this a Red Flag situation for quite a while.

The other bad news is if the roles of Sandra and Tom were reversed, you'd have an equally deceptive Red Flag situation. His loss creates attachment needs in him and perhaps openness to intimacy that may disappear after his mourning period. Your mothering instincts may be very strong and you can easily misinterpret them for other feelings, creating intimacy where there isn't any. He may need a family, and yours

comforts him with open arms. You may push your relationship readiness because you like the attachment or even perhaps because an inheritance makes your dreams more real
than you imagined. Strangely enough, a different set of internal chemicals, similar to what is released when a woman gives
birth, is discharged in this circumstance to make you want to
connect to a man with a loss. This is not good news. Regardless of what could be happening, there are too many powerful
circumstances that make loss situations the wrong time to be
forming permanent bonds with a man.

Other loss situations include relationship breakups, job
loss, loss of a friend, relocation of residence, disasters that
cost you property, death of a pet, even graduating from college when you lose a goal or a lifestyle. These are good times
to strengthen existing same-sex friendships, and keep relationships with men platonic, minimally increasing emotional
investment. Loss situations are a time for you to recover, not
cover your feelings by bouncing into something new. Use the
initial excess energy loss creates by doing something productive. Walk on a treadmill instead of finding a guy who later will
walk on you.

Vulnerability by Addition

"I just got the job I always wanted, just got the apartment I
wanted, just got the car of my dreams, what do you mean I'm
vulnerable?" So drones the woman who walks into every
therapist's office complaining that just when things were going perfectly she hooked up with a Loser. We often consider
vulnerability as only a product of negative conditions, but
there are times we are vulnerable when things may actually be
going well.

When we add things to our lives we become vulnerable because our focus gets shifted. If we have a new job, we may

tend to overlook some parts of our social lives that we normally would pay more attention to. If things are going well for us, we have a tendency to expect other things to go well also. In essence, when we are having good additions to our lives, we say we're "on a roll" and we look to continue the roll. What could be better if we are having a string of good luck than to meet that soulmate/lover/friend that we always dreamed of meeting? Enter a man who looks the part, acts a little like the part at first, and *wham!* we can fantasize the rest because the rest of our dreams are coming true, why not have it all? The faster the speed the more dramatic the crash and burn. And the speed here can be supersonic.

Some additions in life can begin to overwhelm us. The woman who owns her own business and gets a huge new contract may fantasize about what it would be like to have someone to share the responsibility. The woman who has a child without a father may see the future of being a sole caretaker as much less pleasant than having a partner who isn't quite what she originally wanted. The woman with a new home may be extra vulnerable to a man who enjoys decorating or fixing what is broken. If being a couple wasn't easy at first, we'd have a lot fewer couples in this world. There is some inconvenience in not having a partner, and added work and responsibility add to the vulnerability, which in turn can produce a weakening of the guard against a Red Flag. Turning the tables, wouldn't it be nice if you were in a man's life just to play a role? Sounds like Red Flags 2, 3, 4, 5 . . . !

Finally, there are some additions that are decidedly negative and create vulnerability. Finding out that you have a chronic illness or diabetes or that someone close to you is terminally ill are actually additions in your life and create great vulnerability. When we get very emotional news that is in addition to our daily life, we like to have someone intimate with whom we can share. Our desire for this intimacy can make us ignore glaring characteristics in another person that may be

quite undesirable. As with all additions, it is best to focus ourselves in vulnerable times on structuring our own current
emotional lives instead of adding a new person to share our
burdens or joys. Getting into a relationship now is like adding
new fat to cover up the ugly old fat. It makes sense at the
dessert cart, but not when you're trying on the new season's
line of swimsuits.

Vulnerability by Boredom

It was probably a cruel joke that made humans creatures of
habit and at the same time bored by repetition. Sometimes
life becomes so predictable you want to do something bizarre
and detrimental just to see if you can shock everyone out of
set patterns. Bill Murray played a character in the movie
Groundhog Day who kept waking and reliving the same day
over and over. His first reaction when he kept waking up at
the same time on the same day was to rebel and try to make
things go awry. He reacted by punching the guy who tried to
sell him insurance, or manipulating the woman whom he
liked in the movie. After a while, he gave up his pursuit of trying to change the day and worked on developing himself. We
seem to react in the same sequence when our life gets too
repetitive—first to shake things up, second to self-develop. It
is in that shake-up stage that we become particularly vulnerable to a Red Flag.

Brett would go to work each day from 8:30 until 5 or 5:30.
She'd spend Monday, Tuesday, and Thursday in the gym after
work. Wednesday was laundry and house cleaning night. Friday was happy hour night. Saturday was failed date night.
Sunday was traditionally the recoupment day that she'd get
bored halfway through, and she would call her friends looking
for something to do. She had set shows on TV that she'd
watch or tape if for some reason her day deviated from the

norm. She awoke at the same time, went to bed most work nights at the same time. She started to think something was wrong with her because she seemed to be going to bed on weeknights earlier and earlier. She was feeling old as she sunk into a routine that was quite comfortable but rather unsatisfying. She had found the "quiet desperation" she read about but never understood. She didn't understand even now, but she felt it. She had been the architect of the life she designed, but was acutely aware of an absence, not just of another person but of unpredictability. Like an open wound, she awaited a salve of novelty to heal her, so romance could sweep her away somewhere, anywhere, different. It would matter not if that novelty was the bearer of a crimson banner because she was in the Red Flag zone. She found a Loser so bizarre a tabloid newspaper would have turned him down as unbelievable. She did get some good stories to tell for the rest of her life, once she cleaned the animal blood and nailed voodoo gris-gris off her door.

One very scary way people add something novel in their life is to transcend large boundaries they had set for themselves and find someone who has huge differences. They start to look for men many years older or younger. They look for men who have completely different lifestyles and values. They look for men who are foreign, just because they are foreign. They get these men and don't apply the same principles of date selection, because how can their old standards possibly apply to this new situation? Bad news!! Boredom should never lead to complete abandonment of your life, only small changes at a time. You will be destined to use his differences that you find so compelling now, as the reason your partner is a Loser later on. Although often times he is a Loser long before you started.

When you find yourself bored beyond belief, the obvious thing to look for is some kind of change in your life. That is a healthy response. The change however needs to be self-generated as opposed to waiting for someone to come in and turn you around. If you're bored, you are *vulnerable* in the Red Flag zone, waiting to be damaged by a man who fits our top twenty-five. Where you're bored, start the actions you need to change your life first. Come to enjoy your life, then add a new person to your new life. Do not look to him to "be your new life."

Vulnerability by Emotional State

This category is often a by-product of loss, addition, and boredom, but there are some times when emotional states occur for other reasons, so briefly you should be aware of this Red Flag zone. Evolution of society made humans emotional creatures, since we were able to focus on our internal states as a luxury of not always having to hunt for food. If we had to hunt for food all the time, we wouldn't have time to think about emotions. This is nature's way. This explains why so often when you find yourself very involved in an activity you can forget even the most charged emotions. "If I can just keep busy, I'll forget about it," is the phrase we all hear when someone is facing a bad situation. Part of the treatment for a person who is emotionally charged is to get them involved in something that will make them focus outside themselves. Anxiety is extremely sensitive to outside focus, making techniques like relaxation and hypnosis effective, as the person concentrates on something else. The problem begins when that something else is a male, because we leave ourselves exposed and vulnerable.

Very afraid of an operation, Vicki quickly made a lover of P.J., an old friend. At a chance meeting at a potluck dinner, Vicki somehow saw something different in P.J. this time. He was sensitive and caring. He worried with her about the upcoming surgery. She knew his history of being a scoundrel with women, always cheating, disrespecting them after the novelty of a new relationship waned, but Vicki didn't care. He was there when she needed him and a strong bond was formed. Vicki's lack of self-protection in this Red Flag situation created disaster for Vicki later on. P.J. was again a scoundrel and Vicki ended up losing an old friend and a lover at the same time. She figured out with the psychologist she saw afterward that she probably knew the outcome but was "emotionally loan-sharking," knowing she'd pay big in the end for something she needed at the time.

For you to avoid emotional lone-sharking be aware that if you are in a situation where there is extreme emotionality, you are in a Red Flag zone, and it is not the time for a new relationship. This includes anxiety, fear, depression, mania, desperation, and just about any extreme emotion. Seek professional help and focus on the more stable relationships in your life, whether they are with friends or family. Look for proven stable people to help you, and get yourself together before you move on. Fish stink after a few days. Stay away from the jaws of emotional loan-sharking.

Vulnerability by Deadline

Women call it the "biological clock," an internal timepiece that lets women know that little time is left for having children. There is a card game called "old maid," where players pair up cards, hoping not to be left with the one card without a pair—the old maid. In the early part of the twentieth century, if you were single and in your midtwenties you were already an old maid. By the later part of the century, the clock came into play when you turned thirty. As we enter the twenty-first century it seems there is an older standard for the old maid. Regardless of how society turns the acceptability clock backward, individually we all put deadlines on ourselves as to when we would like to be connected, married, hitched to that one man for life. The deadline that we place in our mind can put us in the Red Flag zone.

Social deadlines are put in our minds in a number of ways. Comments our parents made when we were growing up started the standard for when we felt we should be attached. Comments like "Gee, there must be something wrong with Aunt Helen, because she can't stay in a relationship" or "She'd better hurry up and find someone; time is running out" bring us to a point where we begin planning our lives even as young children. Of course, most of us start with a view that certain ages are much older than they seem particularly as we get closer to that age. As a six-year-old, we figure we'll be married when we're eighteen. As a sixteen-year-old, it becomes twenty-five. As an adult we have less ability to put the deadline off into the distant future and find ourselves closer and closer to D day. As that deadline approaches we begin to pressure ourselves, maybe even go back to those original statements made by our parents. "Gee, if I'm not married or even close, maybe there is something wrong with me" or "If I don't find somebody soon, I probably never will." Or "I've got less than half an hour to decide whether I ever want to have kids." We become open and vulnerable when we start thinking like this and are likely to drop our guard to a guy we might otherwise have ruled out. We justify it by saying we're less picky and feel being picky was a bad thing. Regardless of how picky you are, you still must screen out the Red Flags!

This vulnerability needs to be overcome by taking an active part in changing the number of social contacts you make and working harder at meeting a lot of new people. Taking risks to meet new people needs to be separated from taking risks with men who are sending the "beware signal." It's a numbers game and you have to produce a lot of contacts before you can hope to find a man who fits with you. *Guerrilla Dating Tactics* by Sharyn Wolf is a wonderful book for learning how to create numbers. Keeping a steady flow of men will loosen your desperation and make it easier for you to resist. Be less vulnerable, be careful, then hook up.

Vulnerability by Deprivation

This final type of vulnerability is probably the scariest, and the one of which there is least to be discussed. You haven't had a date in months, maybe a year or longer. The closest you've gotten to sex is channel surfing past an R-rated movie on cable TV. And you're tired of being alone. Chat room sex isn't stopping the Tom Cruise dreams. You're starting to think you're getting weird because you are in your own company too much. Why not be open to anyone at this point? Major Red Flag zone!

Opening your life does not mean letting someone in who is carrying the wrong flag. It's time to muster all the creativity of yourself and your friends and your family and your acquaintances and the guy who sells you coffee in the morning, and your hairdresser and . . . The goal is to produce numbers of opportunities so you can pick out the quality dates. Never be desperate that the guy you're dating this moment may be the last you'll ever find to go out with you. Desperate measures lead to desperate consequences. Solve this type of problem slowly, not all at once. Most chance meetings occur by someone's design. Get every creative person you know involved in finding you dates.

The Red Flag zones or situations that create undue vulnerability are areas where you have to be very careful building new relationships. Be cautious and go slowly, more slowly than before. It is truly an area where you must do exactly the opposite of what you feel you want—the quick fix. So you thought you had a handle on life, but the handle broke. Let the glue set on the new handle before you try to open the door.

The *Good* News

*Beyond Wimps, Jerks,
and Serial Killers*

So far we have talked about men who will lie, entrap, snare, ignore, smooth talk, lust, defile, offend, embarrass, show-off, cheat, control, cling, isolate, piss-off, ingratiate, impress, neglect, possess, criticize, clam up, pontificate, misrepresent, aimlessly wander, and be unable to overcome their past. We've looked at situations that make you a sitting duck, without a clue and culturally conflicted. We've told you when to stay and be cautious, when to leave and how to leave. Twenty-seven chapters of what, where, how, and who to avoid that seems to include most everyone you know or possibly ever met. And, if that didn't leave you thoroughly depressed, you probably have gone through most of your past relationships and learned about all the mistakes you've made, which always increases a person's self-esteem. If we haven't completely made you regress to searching through your suitcase for your old Barbie and Ken dolls so you can create a real relationship, you are probably asking "What's left?" Before all this red makes you blue, rest assured, there is another whole short chapter left to learn the good news.

This book is based on getting you to eliminate men who might have otherwise created problems for you in a relationship. The good news is that we have outlined types of men and the kinds of problems that you could have with these types. If you've read this far, you will recognize that most people you know, including yourself, probably fall partially into some of the categories. We all cannot escape being a combination of Yellow Flags. Now that you know the potential problems of these types, you are on the way to being able to change and thus avoid them. This book can be shared with men and actually makes a wonderful exercise for getting to know each other and yourself. As psychologists, we have found that the use of the insights in this book can improve relationships even of married couples. It is interesting to see how a long-term partner views where you fit. Whereas up to this point we have suggested using this book to avoid the wrong intimacies, it can also be used to nourish the right intimacies! We do not suggest, however, that you copy the tests and hand them out to single men at the sports arena before a professional basketball game, and plug the data into your laptop to see if there are any men at the game that fit the profile you want. Although this may work, the copying cost can kill you. It would be much more efficient to use the large screens by the scoreboard.

There are five very simple, basic "good news" principles in this book that would be useful for you to adapt in your dating process.

1. All men are Losers at some time in their lives. We can all remember a person from high school that just blossomed when we met them a few years later. Sometimes it is just a process of maturing. Usually, it is a matter of fine-tuning from the trials and errors of life in general and dating in particular. Dating is a right-person-right-time thing. Just because a guy is not relationship ready, or perhaps you are

not ready, doesn't make either of you a bad person, just
a not-ready person. It might simply be a matter of assessing
someone and deciding a relationship needs to wait for a different time. Unfortunately, the opposite of the first statement of this paragraph is not true: "All men are *not* Losers
at some time in their life." As we have pointed out in this
book, some men, and some types will always be Losers.
Now you have been given a way to efficiently weed out the
"never-will-bes" and to take a closer look at the "wrong-
timers." That's good news.

  2. Do not get attached too early. Evaluation requires patience and distance. In order to make the appropriate
evaluation of the guy sitting across from you or bringing
you flowers, you have to have some distance. Getting attached quickly means you are trying to make something
work, rather than evaluating if it can work. When you move
a relationship too fast there is a constant evolution of new
roles on each date. If the relationship is evolving into something new with each date, you will not be able to see what
a man will be like on a consistent basis until it stops evolving. Stay at the first stage long enough to see some consis-
tency. If the guy is just someone you're keeping around for
sport, do not get emotionally attached at all. The more you
like someone, the more important it is to keep the distance
for the evaluation. The good news is you now can tell when
the signs are there for you to move ahead.

  3. Do not look for potential. Women have a tendency
when they are looking to buy a house to see how they can
dress it up and redecorate it. They look at walls they
could take down, kitchens they can rip out, fixtures they
could change. They see the "potential." This is wonderful
when house shopping, but a real problem when looking for
a relationship. Ripping out a bathroom and installing cabi-
nets is easy compared to hanging even the smallest picture
on the walls of a man's personality. Date the person in front

of you at the time. Evaluate the person in front of you at the time, because that is the guy you are going to get. People change much better while out of a relationship than in one. When they are in a relationship they tend to maintain the status quo. If you like a guy except for some really important areas, let him make the changes you want before you date him. The good news is you can now have a measure of when he is ready.

4. Assess yourself first. Yes, even *you* can be a Loser at some points in your life. Are you ready for the sacrifices a relationship will cause you to make right now? Are you wanting the pleasures of being attached without the pain of acceptance of another's faults? Are you a little too needy right now, which might create poor decision making? Many women wanting a relationship are willing to undersell themselves. They pick men that fit their momentary low self-esteem level and date beneath them. Then they are frustrated when their relationship is not what they want but are afraid to leave and be alone. Be very comfortable being single before you get into a relationship, and be demanding when you are looking. Women civilized men through the process of their ability to say no. The choosier you are the better you help the male gender to be civilized. The good news is you now have a way to filter out the uncivilized.

5. Finally, if you get involved with someone wrong, move on quickly. Dating is a numbers game. Of the millions of men out there for you to date, who are of the right age and single, why would you think you have to stick with someone wrong in the first twenty or thirty guys that take you to dinner? Dating is just plainly a numbers game. The more you create numbers the better chance you have of finding a great match. Getting a large number of dates taps into your creativity and ability to build a social network. It's not a matter of looks or personality, although these help. Research suggests that in the best relationships, the ones that lasted the longest and were reported the happiest, women were attracted to a man's personality before his looks. They dated the men because they liked who they were, not for an initial physical attraction. You have to try most men on for a date or two before you even have an idea how your personalities will interact. The key is to weed through these millions of men rather quickly. The good news is you now have a weeding process called Red Flags.